John Bach McMaster

With the Fathers

Studies in the history of the United States

John Bach McMaster

With the Fathers
Studies in the history of the United States

ISBN/EAN: 9783744748070

Printed in Europe, USA, Canada, Australia, Japan

Cover: Foto ©ninafisch / pixelio.de

More available books at **www.hansebooks.com**

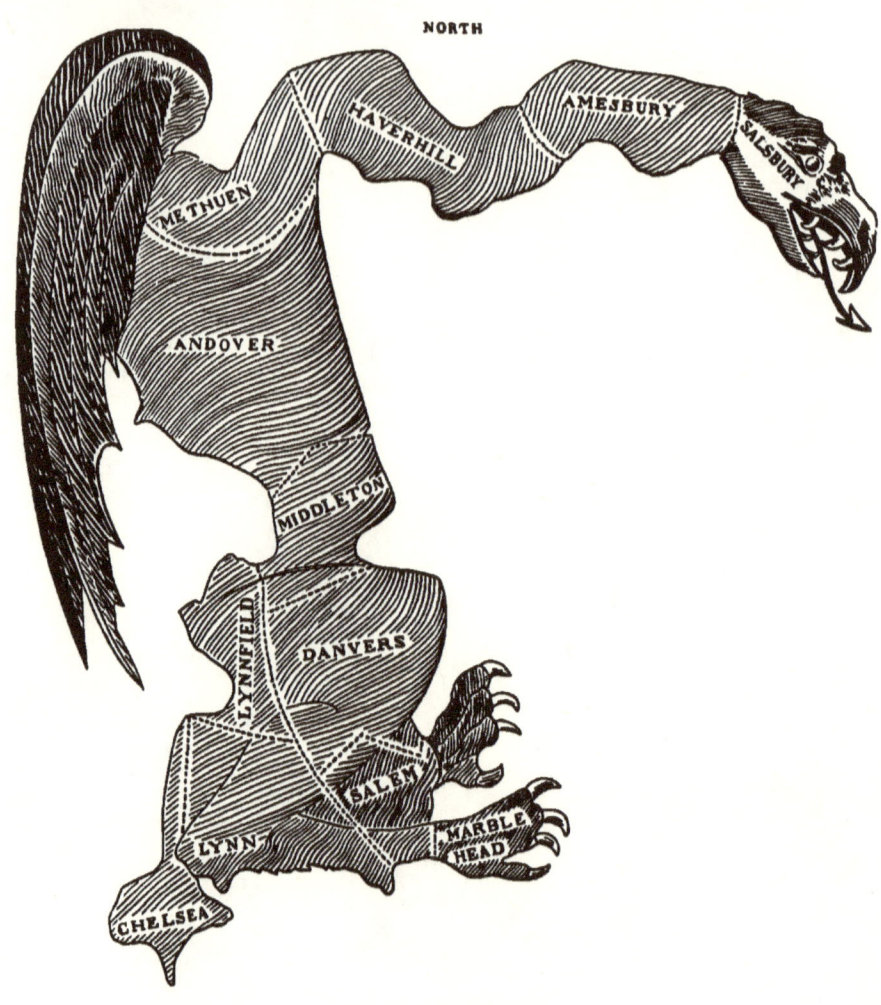

THE "GERRYMANDER."

From original handbill, 1813.

WITH THE FATHERS

STUDIES IN THE HISTORY OF
THE UNITED STATES

BY

JOHN BACH McMASTER

PROFESSOR OF AMERICAN HISTORY IN THE UNIVERSITY OF PENNSYLVANIA
AUTHOR OF A HISTORY OF THE PEOPLE OF THE UNITED STATES

NEW YORK
D. APPLETON AND COMPANY
1896

Copyright, 1896,
By D. APPLETON AND COMPANY.

TO

GERTRUDE STEVENSON McMASTER.

PREFACE.

OF the essays collected in this little volume, "The Political Depravity of the Fathers" and "Franklin in France" were written for the Atlantic Monthly; "The Framers and the Framing of the Constitution" and "A Century of Constitutional Interpretation" were contributed to the Century Magazine; "Washington's Inauguration" to Harper's Magazine; "The Third-Term Tradition," "The Riotous Career of the Know-Nothings," "A Century's Struggle for Silver," and "Is Sound Finance Possible under Popular Government?" to the Forum. My thanks are due, therefore, to Messrs. Harper & Brothers, and to the editors of the Atlantic Monthly, the Century Magazine, and the Forum for their permission to reprint these essays.

The gist of "The Monroe Doctrine" was contributed to the New York Times. "How the British left New York" was first published in the New York Press. To both of these journals an acknowledgment of my indebtedness is made.

JOHN BACH MCMASTER.

UNIVERSITY OF PENNSYLVANIA,
   March, 1896.

CONTENTS.

	PAGE
THE MONROE DOCTRINE	1
THE THIRD-TERM TRADITION	55
THE POLITICAL DEPRAVITY OF THE FATHERS	71
THE RIOTOUS CAREER OF THE KNOW-NOTHINGS	87
THE FRAMERS AND THE FRAMING OF THE CONSTITUTION	107
WASHINGTON'S INAUGURATION	150
A CENTURY OF CONSTITUTIONAL INTERPRETATION	182
A CENTURY'S STRUGGLE FOR SILVER	222
IS SOUND FINANCE POSSIBLE UNDER POPULAR GOVERNMENT?	237
FRANKLIN IN FRANCE	253
HOW THE BRITISH LEFT NEW YORK	271
THE STRUGGLE FOR TERRITORY	281
FOUR CENTURIES OF PROGRESS	313

THE MONROE DOCTRINE.

IN the course of the discussion of the Monroe Doctrine provoked by the recent letter of Lord Salisbury and the message of President Cleveland, there have been developed three views now very current among our countrymen. Some agree with the statements of the noble lord in his letter, and, without giving much thought to the matter, declare that the doctrine perished with the occasion that called it forth. Some admit that it still exists, but incline to the belief that it should not apply to a territorial project that does not involve colonization or the erection of a monarchy where a republic once stood. Others have no hesitation in declaring that what goes on in Venezuela is of no consequence to us, and that the matter at stake is not of enough importance to make it worth while to risk a war.

As the crisis is certainly a serious one, an examination of these views is not untimely. The hour has come for the people of the United States to decide once for all whether there is or is not a Monroe Doctrine. If there is, it should be stated as clearly and precisely as possible. If there is not, then it becomes us to say so frankly and at once.

The doctrine was originally announced by James Monroe in a message to Congress on December second,

1823, and was made necessary by certain things done by Russia and the Holy Allies. Russia still exists. But who the Holy Allies were, and what they did that so alarmed Monroe, requires a little explanation.

As all the world knows, the defeat of the French at Waterloo was followed by a second abdication of Napoleon, by a second restoration of Louis XVIII to the throne of France, and by a gathering of the allied kings or their ministers at Paris in the autumn of 1815. Their renewed triumph over the Man of Destiny was, to the mind of one of them, another signal instance of the workings of Providence, another manifestation of the truth that God in his own good time will raise up those who put their trust in him, and will confound the policy of the wicked. So deeply did this truth impress Alexander, Emperor of Russia, that he then and there determined to rule henceforth, and, if possible, persuade his fellow-monarchs to rule in strict accordance with the principles of the Christian religion. To accomplish this end the more easily, he persuaded Frederick William, King of Prussia, and Francis, Emperor of Austria, to join with him in a league which he called the Holy Alliance, and to sign a treaty which is commonly supposed to have bound the allies to pull down constitutional government and stamp out liberal ideas. It did nothing of the sort. It was, in truth, a meaningless pledge, framed in a moment of religious excitement, and well described in its own words, which assert "that the present act has no other aim than to manifest to the world their unchangeable determination to adopt no other rule of conduct, either in the government of their respective countries or in their political relations with other governments, than the precepts of that holy religion—the precepts of justice, charity, and peace."

Considering themselves members of one great Christian family whose real and only sovereign was Almighty God, they would look on themselves "as delegates of Providence" sent "to govern so many branches of the same family," and would make the Word of God and the teachings of Jesus Christ their guides in "establishing human institutions and remedying their imperfections."

That the King, the Emperor, and the Czar had any hidden motive in forming this far-famed Holy Alliance; that they said one thing and meant another; that their intention was less to rule in accordance with the maxims of Christ than to set up and maintain absolute governments; that when they signed that league they knew they were forming a bond of union against the spread of liberal ideas, and even then contemplated a system of meddling in the affairs of other nations—there is no evidence whatever. Indeed, if we may believe the stories that have come down to us, Alexander and Frederick William were the only sovereigns who looked on the alliance as anything else than a bit of religious enthusiasm. When Francis of Austria was asked to sign, he answered, we are told, that if the paper related to matters religious he must show it to his confessor; if to matters political, to his minister. This minister was Prince Metternich, who described the paper in three words when he said, " It is verbiage ! "

The alliance having been formed, the next step was to invite all the Christian powers of Europe except the Pope to join it. England—whose representative at the congress of the allies, Lord Castlereagh, wrote home that the Emperor was not quite sound in his mind—excused herself. The kings of France, Spain, Naples, and Sardinia, however, signed gladly, and the era of Christian politics was supposed to have opened.

That this little society of Christian monarchs should have any interest for us of to-day is due solely to the fact that their treaty contains the words "Holy Alliance," that the signers have ever since been called the Holy Allies, and that to their league have wrongfully been attributed results which sprang from the quadruple treaty signed two months later by Russia, Prussia, Austria, and Great Britain; a new alliance which bound the four powers to do four things—exclude Napoleon forever from power; maintain the Government they had just set up in France; resist with all their might any attack on the army of occupation; and meet in 1818 to consult concerning their common interests, and to take such measures as should then seem to be best fitted to serve the peace and happiness of Europe.

Unhappily, before 1818 came, a great change took place in the political ideas of Europe. The old families were once again safely seated on their old thrones. The old nobility, the old courtiers, were home from their wanderings eager for proscription and confiscation. A reaction set in. Liberalism was checked. Absolutism came again into fashion, and before five years had come and gone the Holy Allies were hard at work pulling down and stamping out popular government wherever and whenever it appeared in Europe.

The centre of this reactionary movement was Austria, then ruled by Metternich, the very personification of resistance to progress, a man who described his policy as not to go backward, not to go forward, but to keep things just as they were. To do this in Austria was easy. To do it in countries which had been stirred and awakened by the French Revolution was not so easy. But Metternich went bravely to work and began with Naples. In 1813 Great Britain had forced Ferdinand, King of Sicily, to grant a constitution to Sicily and to promise one to Naples; but no sooner had the allies restored him to the throne so long occupied by Murat than Metternich persuaded him to sign a treaty pledging him to keep his kingdom just as it had been, and to bring in none of the product of liberal ideas. Ferdinand kept his agreement, and constitutional government in Sicily and Naples perished.

In Spain the reaction was a popular one. Scarcely had Ferdinand VII crossed the Pyrenees in 1814 and entered his native land than a wild, savage, unreasoning outburst of loyalty swept the country. The courtiers, the churchmen, the military leaders—every one who gathered about the restored king—urged him to destroy the present and bring back the past; to pull down the Constitution and set up the old monarchy as it was when Napoleon drove him from his throne seven years before. He needed little urging, and on May eleventh, 1814, the work of destruction began. First, he sent forth a manifesto from Valencia which destroyed the Constitution of 1812 and declared every decree of the Cortes null and void. Next, he restored the censorship of the press. Then, growing bold, he arrested thirty of the most distinguished of the Liberal leaders; and at this point the people began to lend a hand. Excited and aroused by the priests, mobs appeared all over the country. The writings of Liberalists were burned in the market places. The tablets erected to commemorate the Constitution were pulled down. Men whose sole crime was a firm belief in constitutional government were flung into prison. Great Britain protested and urged the king to stop; but priests, confessors, and palace favorites ruled him, and the work went steadily on. May twenty-third he re-established the monasteries and gave them their old lands; June twenty-fourth he exempted the clergy from taxation; July twenty-first he once more put in operation the most diabolical of all the inventions of man—the Spanish Inquisition.

That France must sooner or later have experienced a like reaction was inevitable. Signs of the coming storm were already apparent when, on March first, 1815, Napoleon landed with his guards in the bay of Juan, and the Hundred Days commenced. When they had ended, when the news of Waterloo spread over France, the storm broke with fury. A Royalist mob at Marseilles sacked the quarters of the Mamelukes, drove out the garrison, and murdered the citizens. Nîmes was pillaged. Avignon disgraced herself by the foul murder of Marshal Brune, and Toulouse by the assassination and savage mutilation of General Ramel. When the Chamber of Deputies, chosen in the midst of this excitement, assembled, there was a new proscription, a new emigration, a new reign of terror. Labedoyère was executed. Ney was shot. Royalist committees, in imitation of the Jacobin clubs, sprang up in every department, overawed the officials, and forced them to drive thousands of Liberalists from the army, from the navy, from the courts of law, and from the schools and colleges.

In Germany, in 1815, it seemed as if Liberalism

would win. At the very moment when Ferdinand of Spain was about to issue his manifesto establishing the monasteries, Frederick William (May twenty-second, 1815) sent forth his promise that Germany should have a constitution and representative assembly, and that the work of framing the Constitution should begin in September. But delays arose, and two years sped by before even the first step was taken. Then it was too late. The middle classes cared not. The nobility were eager for a restoration of their old privileges. The sole defenders of a Constitution were the professors in the universities, the students, and the journalists, who conducted their cause with so much more zeal than wisdom that when the famous Wartburg Festival took place in 1817 Frederick William justly and seriously doubted the expediency of granting the promised liberty.

Amid all this reaction, one ruler, and one alone, stood out as the earnest friend of liberal ideas. Alexander of Russia, too, had made promises. But, unlike Frederick William, he had kept them, had restored the Duchy of Warsaw to independence as the Kingdom of Poland, had given it a constitution and representative assembly, and in the spring of 1818 summoned the Diet. The speech which he addressed to it marked him out as one of the most advanced of Liberals; but the Diet had scarcely ended its session when a great change came over him. What caused it no man knows; but when, in October, 1818, he met the sovereigns and ministers at the Conference of the Powers, Alexander was the despot he ever after lived and died.

By the Quadruple Treaty, signed at Paris in 1815, England, Prussia, Russia, and Austria bound themselves to maintain the Government they had just set up in France, and to hold a Congress of the Powers in 1818. They met, accordingly, in September, at Aix-la-Chapelle, and with that conference a new era opens in the constitutional history of Europe. Then and there was formed the real "Conspiracy of Kings." The reactionary movement of three years had extinguished in the hearts of the best of them the last trace of liberalism, and they all stood together on a common ground of hatred of popular liberty. It was the conference at Aix-la-Chapelle, not the Holy Alliance, that united the sovereigns in the project of a joint regulation of European affairs, and turned the Holy Allies into a mutual association for the insurance of monarchy.

Scarcely had this new purpose been formed when the alliance was called on to act. For ten years past the Spanish colonies in America had been in a state of revolt, first against the rule of Joseph Bonaparte, and then against the tyranny of Ferdinand VII. Every resource of the restored king was used against them and used in vain. The struggle went on till, the last fleet having been fitted out, the last regiment having been sent to perish of yellow fever, and the last dollar having been drawn from the treasury, Ferdinand turned to the sovereigns of Europe for aid. They had restored to him his throne. It is not surprising, therefore, that he should ask them to restore his colonies; but it is amusing to note the impudence with which he intimated that the work of subjugation should be done by Great Britain. She might have acted as mediator. More she would not do, and as subjugation, not mediation, was wanted, Alexander came to the relief of Ferdinand and sold him a fleet of war. When it reached Cadiz it was found that this Emperor, who in 1815 was so eager to see all Europe ruled in accordance with the teachings of Christ, had sold his friend ships so rotten and unseaworthy that not one of them was fit to cross the Atlantic.

The expedition was put off, and the condition of Spanish America was laid before the sovereigns when they met at Aix-la-Chapelle. The dangers which threatened Europe if a federation of republics was allowed to grow up in America were discussed; a proposition was made that a conference between Spain and the powers should be held at Madrid, and that Wellington should preside; but Spain wanted troops, not advice, and was left to subdue her colonies in her own way.

Her way was to gather a rabble at Cadiz in the summer of 1819, call it an army, and send it off to America. Before it could sail, yellow fever broke out, the troops went into camp, and while there, were won over to the cause of constitutional government by the agents of a great conspiracy which had long been growing under the tyranny of the King. On January first, 1820, the day fixed for the outbreak, the troops, led by Colonels Quiroga and Riego, rose and declared for the Constitution of 1812. The rebellion of the soldiers was a small affair in itself, but it set an example; it stirred up others, and on February twentieth the garrison and people of Corunna in their turn proclaimed the Constitution.

And now rebellion spread fast. Town after town followed Corunna. The whole country was up, and Ferdinand in great alarm announced his willingness to assemble the Cortes. His people had long since learned that his word was of no value, and, filling the great squares of Madrid, they clamored all day long for the

Constitution. At length he gave way, and announced his willingness to take the oath to support the Constitution. The next day—the famous eighth of March, 1820—was one of wild rejoicing. The prison of the Inquisition was sacked; the instruments of torture were broken in pieces; political prisoners were set free, and the Constitution carried in procession through the streets. March ninth a mob entered the palace, forced the King to make good his promise, and constitutional government once more existed in Spain.

As tidings of the collapse of absolutism in Spain spread over Europe, all the members of the Holy Alliance save Alexander seemed uncertain what to do. He alone acted with decision, and at once insisted that the great powers should require the Cortes to disavow the revolution of the eighth of March—the revolution to which it owed its existence—and give a pledge of obedience to the King. In such a demand England positively refused to join, and the first proposed attack on Spanish liberty by the Holy Alliance was postponed.

Meantime absolute monarchy fell at Naples. The success of the Liberalists in Spain aroused the Carbonari, a great secret society with lodges in every city and hamlet, and a membership numbering at least one quarter of the male inhabitants of the Kingdom of Naples. They had long been plotting and secretly waiting for the hour of deliverance which now seemed at hand. Ferdinand of Sicily was the uncle of Ferdinand of Spain, and as he might some day be called to the Spanish throne, he too had signed and sworn to support the Constitution of 1812 that his claims to the Crown might not be endangered. If he were willing to have a constitution in a country which he might some day rule, why not force him to give the same constitution to the kingdoms over which he was already ruler? The Carbonari could see no reason, and, rising in armed rebellion, they compelled Ferdinand to proclaim the Constitution of Spain to be the law of the Kingdom of the Two Sicilies, and on July thirteenth, 1820, he took the oath to maintain it.

The men of Portugal were next to awake, and in September, 1820, they deposed the Regency which ruled in the name of the absent King, set up a Junta, and elected a Cortes to frame a constitution. For a moment it seemed not unlikely that France might throw off the yoke of absolutism. But Louis cried out for another meeting of the powers, and in October, 1820, the Emperor of Austria met the Czar and the King of Prussia in the little town of Troppau, in Moravia. England sent an ambassador, but he was instructed to look on and do nothing. France sent two envoys, but they took opposite sides, and her influence counted for nothing. The three founders of the Holy Alliance were thus free to do as they pleased, and very quickly decided what course to take. Ferdinand was to be invited to meet them at Laybach; a summons was to be sent, through him, to the Neapolitans to abandon their Constitution or fight; and a circular explaining and defending this new doctrine of armed intervention was to be issued, in the name of the three powers, to all the Courts of Europe.

The circular went forth on December eighth, 1820, to every foreign court. The events of March eighth in Spain, and those of July second in Naples, had produced, the circular said, a deep feeling of inquietude and alarm, and a desire to unite and save Europe from the evils ready to burst upon her. That this desire should be most keen with governments which not long ago had conquered the revolution, and now see it once more appearing triumphant, is natural. The other powers have therefore availed themselves of an incontestable right, and have decided to take common measures of precaution and restrain such States as, having revolted against legitimate governments and institutions, are seeking by their agents to introduce like disorders and insurrections into other States. As the revolution at Naples strikes deeper root every day, and sensibly menaces the tranquillity of the neighboring powers, it is necessary to immediately apply to her the principles agreed on.

Before resorting to force, however, it was thought best to make one effort of a peaceful character, and summon the King of Naples to meet the allied powers at Laybach.

Thither, in January, 1821, with the consent of the Neapolitan Parliament, the old King, leaving his son to act as regent, accordingly went, only to be told that if the order of things existing since July, 1820, were not at once abolished an Austrian army would occupy Neapolitan soil. The same demand was made known to the Prince Regent at Naples, who stoutly refused to consider it, and summoned the Parliament, which declared that it considered the old King as under restraint at Laybach; bade the Grand Duke of Calabria continue to exercise the Regency, and ordered measures to be taken for the safety of the State. A rush to arms followed. The Prince put himself at the head of most of the troops. The King appealed to the others, but they answered that they would not serve against their fellows, and cried out for the Constitution. Ferdinand, now reduced to impotence, abdicated, and went back to Sicily; and one hundred thousand Austrians entered Italy and crushed the republican uprisings in Naples, in Piedmont, in all Italy, and Ferdinand, in spite of his abdication, was restored to the throne of Naples.

A new declaration and a new circular was now published by the Holy Allies, about to end their conference at Laybach, and in this circular was announced a principle which was to guide them in their future dealings with nations struggling for liberty. Having, in the language of the time, "taken the people of Europe into their Holy keeping," the three autocrats declared that henceforth all "useful or necessary changes in the legislation and administration of states must emanate alone from the free will, the reflecting and enlightened impulse of those whom God has rendered responsible for power!"

Thus committed to the extermination of popular government, the members of the Holy Alliance next turned their attention to Spain. When the Congress at Laybach adjourned in 1821, it did so with the understanding that it should meet again in 1822. That the question of intervention in the affairs of Spain would then come up, and that when it did, Great Britain would have much to say was well known to the powers. What they would do might be doubtful, but the course she should pursue was to her certain. She would leave the revolution in Spain to run its course; she would urge the European powers to do the same, and, following her own interests, would acknowledge the independence of the Spanish South American colonies. A trade so great had sprung up with them that it was impossible to put off the day when she must have in each, if not a minister, at least a diplomatic agent. Such a policy ran so directly counter to the wishes of the Holy Alliance that it was felt to be necessary that it should be upheld by her foremost diplomat, and her Prime Minister, Lord Castlereagh, was accordingly chosen to represent her. In the instructions which he drew up for himself, and which the Cabinet and the King approved, he was commanded to inform the Congress that it was the intention of England to send accredited agents to some of the South American republics, which meant a steady opposition on England's part to any intervention by the Holy Alliance. Unhappily, when the Congress met at Vienna, in September, Castlereagh was dead; Canning was Prime Minister, and the Duke of Wellington was England's representative.

After a short session at Vienna, the Congress adjourned to Verona, where, in October, 1822, the affairs of Spain were carefully considered. No declaration was made in the name of the alliance, but an agreement was entered into that certain changes should be demanded in the Spanish Constitution, and, if not granted, the French army, supported, if necessary, by Russia, Austria, and Prussia, should invade Spain.

The demand was made and was refused; the ambassadors of the members of the Holy Alliance left Madrid, and on April seventh, 1823, a French army, led by the Duke of Angoulême, crossed the frontier and entered Spain.

That moment Canning began to act. He knew, as everybody knew, that when the allies had once settled the affairs of Spain they would go on and settle the affairs of her former colonies, now recognized as republics by the United States. Turning to Richard Rush, who represented our country at London, he proposed that the United States should join with England in a declaration that, while neither power desired the colonies of Spain for herself, it was impossible to look with indifference on European intervention in their affairs, or to see them acquired by a third power. Hardly had the request been made, when Canning received a formal notice that later in the year a Congress would be called to consider the affairs of Spanish America, and again pressed Rush for an answer. Rush had no instructions, but with a courage that did him honor, he replied that "we should regard as highly unjust and as fruitful of disastrous consequences any attempt on the part of any European power to take possession of them by conquest, by cession, or on any other ground or pretext whatsoever," and promised to join in the declaration if England would first acknowledge the independence of the little republics. This she would not do, and the joint declaration was never made.

One of the arguments which Canning used is given in Rush's letter to Secretary Adams, and shows that he at least had no temporary policy in mind. "They" [the United States], said Canning, "were the first power established on that continent, and now confessedly the leading power. They were connected with South America by their position and with Europe by their relations. Was it possible they could see with indifference their fate decided upon by Europe? Had not a new epoch arrived in the relative position of the United States toward Europe which Europe must acknowledge?

Were the great political and commercial interests which hung upon the destiny of the new continent to be canvassed and adjusted on this hemisphere without the co-operation or even knowledge of the United States?"

When Monroe received the letters of Rush he seems to have been greatly puzzled how to act. The suggestion of England that the time had come to make a declaration of some sort admitted of no dispute. But how was it to be made? If he joined with Great Britain would he not be forming one of the "political connections" Washington had denounced in his "Farewell Address"; one of the "entangling alliances" of which Jefferson had given warning in his first inaugural speech? Should he make it alone, would he not be violating that policy of non-interference in the affairs of the colonies which he had himself advised in six messages and two inaugural speeches? Uncertain what to do, he turned to Madison and to Jefferson for advice, and sent the letters of Rush to Monticello. The reply of Madison was long and interesting, and as no editor has ever yet thought it worth while to give the letter a place in his collected writings, I give it in full.*
The answer of Jefferson was written late in October.

"The question presented by the letters you have sent me is the most momentous which has ever been offered to my contemplation since that of Independence. That made us a nation; this sets our compass and points the course which we are to steer through the ocean of time opening on us. And never could we embark upon it under circumstances more auspicious. Our first and fundamental maxim should be, never to

---

* The letter will be found at the end of the essay.

entangle ourselves in the broils of Europe; our second, never to suffer Europe to intermeddle with cisatlantic affairs. America, North and South, has a set of interests distinct from those of Europe, and peculiarly her own. She should therefore have a system of her own, separate and apart from that of Europe. While the last is laboring to become the domicile of despotism, our endeavor should surely be to make our hemisphere that of freedom."

Thus encouraged, not simply to meet an emergency, but to "point the course which we are to steer through the ocean of time opening on us," Monroe consulted his Secretaries. John Quincy Adams was then Secretary of State, and it was at one of these Cabinet meetings that he suggested as a third part of the doctrine the maxim relating to colonization.

In the autumn of 1818, as Mr. J. B. Prevost, the American Commissioner sent out by the President to receive the formal delivery of Astoria, was on his way home he stopped at the port of Monterey, in California. While there he wrote a long report of his mission; described the Columbia River, the climate, soil, and physical features of Oregon, and closed his narrative with an account of an incident which he thought most serious. Until 1816 the Russians, he said, had no settlement south of fifty-five degrees. But in that year, excited very probably by the glowing descriptions of Humboldt, they had established two colonies of an important character. One was at Atooi, on a Sandwich Island, and the other on the California coast a few leagues from San Francisco, the most northerly settlement of Spain. Only two days before he reached Monterey two vessels had left that town for the Russian settlement, carrying to it implements of husbandry and mechanics of every sort. So plain an intention to make a permanent settlement in the Pacific by a race but just emerging from savagery and ruled by a chief who sought not to emancipate but to enthrall, ought surely, Mr. Prevost thought, to excite the serious apprehensions of the United States.

But it did not excite the apprehensions of the United States, and no more was heard of the Russians till one day in February, 1822, when the Chevalier Pierre de Politica placed a most alarming document in the hands of the Secretary of State. It was an edict of the Emperor Alexander, and set forth that the pursuits of commerce, whaling and fishing, and indeed of all other industries whether on the islands or in the ports and gulfs of the northwest coast of America, from Behring Straits to fifty-one degrees, were exclusively granted to Russian subjects. Foreign vessels were therefore forbidden not only to land on the coast and islands, but even to come within one hundred Italian miles of them.

So unexpected an attempt to define the boundary of the two countries aroused the President, who demanded of the Russian Minister the grounds on which it was based. Why had not the boundary been arranged by treaty? Why were vessels of the United States excluded beyond the limit to which territorial jurisdiction extended? He answered that the Russians had long had a settlement at Novo Archangelsk, in latitude fifty-seven, and that fifty-one degrees was about midway between that settlement and Astoria at the mouth of the Columbia. The restriction forbidding an approach to the coast was laid in order to keep out foreign adventurers who, not content with carrying on an illicit trade injurious to the interests of the Russian American Fur Company, had supplied arms and ammunition to the natives of the Russian possessions in America and incited them to revolt. Against these doctrines Adams protested; but Politica cut short the discussion by the statement that he had no authority to continue it, and a year passed before it was resumed. A letter was then received from the Baron de Tuyl, who had succeeded the Chevalier de Politica, asking that the American Minister at St. Petersburg be given power to settle the differences by negotiation. The invitation was accepted, and instructions duly drawn and despatched.

While Adams was busy framing the instructions under which our Minister at St. Petersburg was to act, the Russian Minister called one day in July, 1823, at the State Department, and in the course of conversation Adams announced to him "that we should contest the right of Russia to any territorial establishment on this continent, and that we should assume distinctly the principle that the American continents are no longer subjects for any European colonial establishments." A week after this conversation the instructions were sent off to St. Petersburg, and in giving an account of them to Mr. Rush, at London, Adams reasserted the principle. When the time came for Monroe to write the customary annual message to Congress there were thus three matters to be very seriously considered—the attempt of Russia to colonize in California, and her selection of 51° of north latitude as the south boundary of Alaska; the threatened intervention of the Holy Allies in the affairs of the South American Republics; and the proposition of Canning for a joint declaration against them. Meeting after meeting was held by the Cabinet to discuss these matters; but what was done had best be described by Adams himself. "I remarked," says Mr. Adams, "that the communications recently received from the Russian Minister, Baron de Tuyl, afforded, I thought, a very suitable and convenient opportunity for us to take our stand against the Holy Alliance, and at the same time to decline the overture of Great Britain. It would be more candid, as well as more dignified, to avow our principles explicitly to Russia and France, than to come in as a cock-boat in the wake of the British man-of-war.

"This idea was acquiesced in on all sides.

". . . . Mr. Wirt made a question far more important, and which I had made at a much earlier stage of these deliberations. It was, whether we shall be warranted in taking so broadly the ground of resistance to the interposition of the Holy Alliance by force to restore the Spanish dominion in South America. It is, and has been, to me a fearful question. It was not now discussed; but Mr. Wirt remarked upon the danger of assuming the attitude of menace without meaning to strike, and asked, if the Holy Alliance *should* act in direct hostility against South America, whether this country would oppose them by war. My paper and the paragraph would certainly commit us as far as the Executive constitutionally could act on this point; and if we take this course, I should wish that a joint resolution of the two Houses of Congress should be proposed and adopted to the same purport."

In the end the views of Jefferson and Adams prevailed, and when the message was read to Congress on December second, 1823, the members heard a formal statement of the doctrine which has ever since been known by the President's name.

After reviewing our relations with Russia he said : " In the discussion to which this interest (the rights of the United States on the northwest coast of America) has given rise, and in the arrangements by which they may terminate, the occasion has been judged proper for asserting, as a principle in which the rights and interests of the United States are involved, that the American continents, by the free and independent condition which they have assumed and maintained, are henceforth not to be considered as subjects for future colonization of any ·European powers."

Turning next to the Holy Alliance he said : " We owe it, therefore, to candor, and to the amicable relations existing between the United States and those powers, to declare that we should consider any attempt on their part to extend their system to any portion of this hemisphere as dangerous to our peace and safety. With the existing colonies or dependencies of any European power we have not interfered, and shall not interfere. But with the governments who have declared their independence, and maintained it, and whose independence we have, on great consideration and on just principles, acknowledged, we could not view any interposition for the purpose of oppressing them, or controlling in any other manner their destiny, by any European power, in any other light than as the manifestation of an unfriendly disposition toward the United States.

" Our policy in regard to Europe, which was adopted at an early stage of the wars which have so long agitated that quarter of the globe, nevertheless remains the same, which is not to interfere in the internal concerns of any of its powers; to consider the Government *de facto* as the legitimate Government for us; to cultivate friendly relations with it, and to preserve those relations by a frank, firm, and manly policy; meeting in all instances the just claims of every power, submitting to injuries from none. But in regard to these continents circumstances are eminently and conspicuously different. It is impossible that the allied powers should extend their political system to any portion of either continent without endangering our peace and happiness; nor can any one believe that our Southern brethren, if left to themselves, would adopt it of their own accord. It is equally impossible, therefore, that we should behold such interposition, in any form, with indifference."

The doctrine was for all time, and, put in plain language, was this:

1. No more European colonies on either of the American continents.

2. The United States will "not interfere in the internal concerns" of any European power.

3. "But in regard to these continents (North and South America) circumstances are eminently and conspicuously different," and if any European power attempts at any future time to extend its political system to any part of this hemisphere "for the purpose of oppressing" the nations or "CONTROLLING IN ANY OTHER MANNER THEIR DESTINY," the United States will interfere.

Monroe might have informed the Holy Allies of his doctrine under cover of an official note. But he preferred to announce it before the world, and in his message warned them that any attempt on their part to violate the doctrine would be "dangerous to our peace and safety" and a "manifestation of an unfriendly disposition toward the United States."

At home the declaration was read with pride and satisfaction, and an attempt was at once made by Clay to have so much of it as related to the intervention of the Holy Alliance in the affairs of South America embodied in a joint resolution of the House and Senate. The influence of Clay was great. He was Speaker of the House; he was a candidate for the presidency. But factional spirit ran high. The friends of Adams, of Jackson, of Crawford, of Calhoun had no notion of allowing him to pose as the champion of popular liberty, and the resolution had so little support that Clay, yielding to political necessity, told the House he would let his resolution lie on the table. By this we are told he abandoned the doctrine in its infancy. We think not, and against the act of Clay when Speaker of the House in 1824 would put this act of Clay when Secretary of State in 1825.

During the summer of that year common rumor and the appearance of a great French fleet on our coast gave the republics of South America good reason to believe that France was about to invade Cuba and Porto Rico, with the intention of securing one or both of the islands for herself. Such an event was so much to be dreaded that Mexico called on the United States "to fulfil," in the words of Mr. Clay, "the memorable pledge of the President of the United States in his message to Congress of December, 1823." Clay, with as little delay as possible, acceded to the request, applied the Monroe Doctrine, instructed our Minister at Paris to notify France "that we would not consent to the occupation of those islands by any other European power than Spain, under any circumstances whatever," and bade Mr. Poinsett call on Mexico to assert the Monroe Doctrine " on all proper occasions." *

But in England, according to our Minister then resident in London, the new doctrine was heard with extravagant delight. The English people, English statesmen, and the English press were loud in their praises of the firm stand taken by the United States. "The question," said Mr. Brougham, "with regard to South America is now disposed of, or nearly so, for an event has recently happened than which no event has dispensed greater joy, exultation, and gratitude over all the freemen of Europe: that event, which is decisive of the subject in respect to South America, is the message of the President of the United States to Congress."

The London Courier, the London Times, the Morning Chronicle, Bell's Weekly Messenger, the Liverpool Advertiser, were loud in the praise of the new doctrine, and when the French administration journal L'Étoile denounced the message and called Monroe a dictator, it was the London Times that hastened to defend him.†
The South American Deputies in London were wild with joy, and South American securities of every sort rose in value.

Having thus announced that we would not meddle in European affairs nor suffer the nations of the Old World to interfere with the domestic concerns of the nations of the New, it soon became necessary to define

---

* Clay to Poinsett, March 26, 1825. Clay to Poinsett, Nov. 9, 1825.

† Extracts from these journals will be found at the end of the essay.

our own attitude toward the young republics of South America. One day in the spring of 1825, just after Clay had become Secretary of State, separate interviews were held with the Ministers of Mexico and Colombia at their request. In the course of conversation each announced that his Government was most anxious to have the United States represented at a congress of republics soon to be held at Panama, that he had been empowered to extend such an invitation, but had been instructed before doing so to ask if it would be agreeable to the United States to receive it.

Clay answered, after consulting Adams, that the United States could not be expected to take any part in the war with Spain, nor in any council for deliberating on the means of continuing the struggle for independence, and that before expressing a willingness to receive the formal invitation it would be desirable to know what subjects would be discussed, how the congress was to be organized and act, and what powers were to be given to the diplomatic agents composing it. Each Minister promised to report this answer to his Government, and no more was heard of the matter till November. Then the Ministers replied to Clay, and formally extended the invitation. In answer to the question what was to be discussed, Mexico suggested the kind of opposition to be made to colonization in America by European powers, and the sort of resistance to be offered to the interference of any neutral nation in the war between the young republics and Spain. Colombia approved these and added two more—the independence of the negro republic of Hayti, and a consideration of the means to be used for the abolition of the slave-trade. Guatemala suggested that as the powers of the Old World had formed a continental system, and held congresses to consider their interests, the republics of the New World should meet, form an American system, and discuss American interests.

Though the answers were far from satisfactory, Adams accepted the invitation, and in his annual message to Congress aroused his enemies with the statement that "Ministers *will be* commissioned to attend" the congress. In those days the committees of the Senate were not elected, but were appointed by the Vice-President, and exercising this power, John C. Calhoun, well knowing what was coming, deliberately placed on the Committee on Foreign Relations a majority of senators hostile to Adams. It is needless to say they came from the Southern States.

•The feeling in the Senate over the presumption of the President in sending word that "Ministers will be commissioned" was bitter. What business had he to take such a step without first consulting them? "Will be commissioned," indeed! They would see! So strong was the indignation that it is quite possible that Adams thought it prudent to yield, for the day after Christmas he sent a long message on the subject and the names of three men to be Ministers. His constitutional right to act without the Senate he did not doubt, he said, but as to the expediency of using that authority he was ready to consult Congress. The opposition in the Senate were angry before; now they were furious, and showed their rage in four ways: They endeavored to have the message, which was confidential, considered with open doors; they made a call for information which they knew Adams would not give; they passed a resolution censuring him for his conduct, and finally received from the Committee on Foreign Relations, appointed by Calhoun, a long report, ending with a resolution that it was not expedient for the United States to be represented in the congress at Panama.

It was on this resolution that the Senate debate occurred. But to cite it as a disavowal of the Monroe Doctrine is idle. Other motives produced the opposition. Hatred of Adams, hatred of Clay, but, above all, the many phases of the slave question, were reasons enough why Randolph of Virginia, Hayne of South Carolina, Woodbury of New Hampshire, White of Tennessee, Van Buren, Buchanan, Polk, Berrien, and Calhoun should oppose the congress at Panama. Was it to be expected that any gentleman from the region south of the Mason and Dixon line, the Ohio, and the parallel thirty-six-thirty, would consent to see the United States enter into any kind of a league with republics, or even apply the Monroe Doctrine in behalf of republics that had abolished slavery, that wanted vigorous action to be taken for the suppression of the slave-trade, and were demanding recognition for the negro republic of Hayti?

"Other States," said Hayne, "will do as they please; but let us take the high ground that these questions belong to a class which the peace and safety of a large portion of our Union forbids us to discuss. Let our Government direct all our Ministers in South America and Mexico to protest against the independence of Hayti. But let us not go into council on the slave-trade and Hayti."

"If slavery," said White, of Tennessee, "is an infliction, then all the Southern and Western States have it, and with it their peculiar modes of thinking upon all subjects connected with it. . . . Is it then fit that the United States should disturb the quiet of the Southern and Western States by a discussion and agreement with the new States on any subject connected with slavery? Let us then cease to talk of slavery in this House; let us cease to negotiate upon any subject connected with it."

"Sir," exclaimed Mr. Holmes, of Maine, "under such circumstances, the question to be decided is this: With a due regard to the safety of the Southern States, can you suffer these islands (Cuba and Porto Rico) to pass into the hands of buccaneers drunk with their newborn liberty? . . . What, then, is our policy? Cuba and Porto Rico must remain as they are. To Europe the President has distinctly said we cannot allow a transfer of Cuba to any European power. We must hold a language equally decisive to the South American States. We cannot allow their principle of universal emancipation to be called into activity in a situation where its contagion from our neighborhood would be dangerous to our quiet and safety."

But it is needless to quote more. From Benton, from Randolph, from Berrien in the Senate, and from a host of members of the House, came sentiments of the same sort. It would be unjust to these men, however, to suppose that hostility to emancipation was their sole objection. They were influenced, and influenced, much, by the belief that a purpose of the congress at Panama was to pledge this country to make common cause with the South American republics in carrying out the principles of the Monroe Doctrine. In resisting such action they were right. It was not the intention of Monroe, it is not our policy, to ever make with any nation an agreement of this kind. The House of Representatives did well, therefore, when, in consenting to vote money for the mission, it spread this resolution on its journal:

"It is therefore the opinion of this House that the Government of the United States ought not to be represented at the Congress of Panama except in a diplomatic character, nor ought they to form any alliance, offensive or defensive, or negotiate respecting such an alliance with all or any of the South American republics; nor ought they to become parties with them, or either of them, to any joint declaration for the purpose of preventing the interference of any of the European powers with their independence or form of government, or to any compact for the purpose of preventing colonization upon the continents of America, but that the people of the United States should be left free to act, in any crisis, in such a manner as their feelings of friendship toward these republics and as their own honor and policy may at the time dictate."

Thus was affirmed two parts of the Monroe Doctrine:

1. Not to form any alliance with any foreign nation, nor join with it in any declaration concerning the interference of any European power in its affairs.

2. To act toward them "in any crisis" as our "honor and policy may at the time dictate."

Thus was our true attitude toward the nations of the New World defined, and the Monroe Doctrine completed.

Of the men who took part in that famous debate two are of especial interest to us, for in the course of time each was called on to apply the doctrine he opposed, and each in turn abandoned the position he held in 1826. One is James K. Polk; the other is James Buchanan.

In 1826 Polk in his speech said:

"When the message of the late President of the United States was communicated to Congress in 1823, it was viewed, as it should have been, as the mere expression of opinion of the Executive, submitted to the consideration and deliberation of Congress, and designed probably to produce an effect upon the councils of the Holy Alliance, in relation to their supposed intention to interfere in the war between Spain and her former colonies. That effect it probably had an agency in producing; and, if so, it has performed its office. The President had no power to bind the nation by such a pledge."

When Polk uttered these words he was a member of Congress from Tennessee. But when our country was next called on to apply the doctrine Polk was President of the United States, and had been elected by a party whose cry was, "Give us Texas or divide the spoils!" "The whole of Oregon or none; fifty-four, forty, or fight!" and saw before him a war with Mexico and serious trouble with England. In 1826 the Monroe Doctrine, he thought, had been "designed to produce an effect on the councils of the Holy Alliance" and "had performed its office." Now he found it had still an office to perform, gave his "cordial concurrence in its wisdom and sound policy," and sent this message to Congress:

"It is well known to the American people and to all nations that this Government has never interfered with the relations subsisting between other governments. We have never made ourselves parties to their wars or their alliances; we have not sought their territories by conquest; we have not mingled with parties in their domestic struggles; and, believing our own form of government to be the best, we have never attempted to propagate it by intrigues, by diplomacy, or by force. We may claim on this continent a like exemption from European interference. The nations of America are equally sovereign and independent with those of Europe. They possess the same rights, independent of all foreign interposition, to make war, to conclude peace, and to regulate their internal affairs. The people of the United States cannot, therefore, view with indifference attempts of European powers to interfere with the independent action of nations on this continent."

The cause of these remarks was the dispute—in which we were then engaged with England—regarding the ownership of the Oregon country. She claimed as far south as the Columbia River. We claimed as far north as fifty-four degrees forty minutes. It was as much a territorial dispute as that now going on with Venezuela. Yet Polk did not hesitate to apply the Monroe Doctrine and to assert that, "in the existing circumstances of the world, the present is deemed a proper occasion to reiterate and reaffirm the principle avowed by Mr. Monroe, and to state my cordial concurrence in its wisdom and sound policy. The reassertion of this principle, especially in reference to North America, is, at this day, but the promulgation of a policy which no European power should cherish the disposition to resist. Existing rights of every European nation should be respected, but it is due alike to our safety and our interests that the efficient protection of our laws should be extended over our whole territorial limits, and that it should be distinctly announced to the world as our settled policy, that no future European colony or dominion shall, with our consent, be planted or established on any part of the North American Continent."

Again a little while and Polk applied the doctrine to the purely territorial case of Yucatan. A war had broken out between the Indians and the whites, who, driven to desperation, appealed for help to England, Spain, and the United States, offering in return the dominion and sovereignty of the Peninsula. This was not a case of interference by any foreign power. No effort was being made by any European nation to "extend its system." Two such powers had been invited by a hard-pressed people struggling for life to defend them and receive in return their country. But Polk—taking the broad ground that any European people who by any means gained on our continents one foot of territory more than they had in 1823, though they did so with the consent and at the request of the owners of the soil—sent this message to Congress in 1848:

"While it is not my purpose to recommend the adoption of any measure with a view to the acquisition of the 'dominion and sovereignty' over Yucatan, yet, according to our established policy, we could not consent to a transfer of this 'dominion and sovereignty' to either Spain, Great Britain, or any other European power. In the language of President Monroe, in his message of December, 1823, 'we should consider any attempt on their part to extend their system to any portion of this hemisphere as dangerous to our peace and safety.'"

They would be controlling "the destiny" of the people concerned.

Precisely the same view was taken by Cass, when Secretary of State under Buchanan, in the case of Mexico. The political condition of Mexico was frightful. Since the day Spain acknowledged her independence in 1821 there had never been a moment of quiet. In thirty-three years thirty-six governments had been set up and pulled down, and of them all the worst were those of Miramon and Juarez, by whom such enormities were committed that England, France, and Spain decided on armed intervention in Mexican affairs. Against this, in 1860, both Cass and Buchanan protested.

"While," said the Secretary, "we do not deny the right of any other power to carry on hostile operations against Mexico for the redress of its grievances, we firmly object to its holding possession of any part of that country, or endeavoring by force to control its political destiny."

"I deemed it my duty," said the President in his message in December, 1860, "to recommend to Congress, in my last annual message, the employment of a sufficient military force to penetrate into the interior. . . . European governments would have been deprived of all pretext to interfere in the territorial and domestic concerns of Mexico. We should thus have been relieved from the obligation of resisting, even by force should this become necessary, any attempt by these governments to deprive our neighboring republic of portions of her territory—a duty from which we could not shrink without abandoning the traditional and established policy of the American people."

Three statements are contained in this exposition of the doctrine:

1. That we have a duty resting on us which we cannot shirk without abandoning the traditional and established policy of the American people.

2. This duty is to resist any attempt by a European government to deprive our neighboring republic of portions of her territory.

3. That, if necessary, resistance must go even to the use of force.

This was sound and to the point. But amid the disorder and confusion which marked the closing months of Buchanan's term his views concerning affairs in Mexico were lost sight of. South Carolina had seceded; State after State was following her in rapid succession, and the people on both sides of the Mason and Dixon line were far too busy with their own concerns to know or care what any foreign power might do in Mexico. Yet the three powers were not unmindful of the warning, and before proceeding to meddle in the affairs of Mexico they met at London in October, 1861, made a Convention, and solemnly agreed * not to acquire a foot of soil, nor meddle in any way with the Government of Mexico.

Scarcely had the allies landed at Vera Cruz when

---

* "ART. II. The high contracting parties engage not to seek for themselves, in the employment of the coercive measures contemplated by the present Convention, any acquisition of territory, nor any special advantage, and not to exercise in the internal affairs of Mexico any influence of a nature to prejudice the right of the Mexican nation to choose and to constitute freely the form of its Government."

the intention of Napoleon to violate the Convention and found a French empire in Mexico was disclosed. Spain and England then indignantly withdrew, and left him to go on in that career which closed with the tragic death of Maximilian. To many the invasion by the French seemed the end of the Monroe Doctrine. One writer in the London Times, in 1862, declared Napoleon had done a real service to the world "in extinguishing the Monroe Doctrine." Another in the Westminster Review spoke no more than the belief of all who hated us when he said: "The occupation of Mexico is the extinction of the Monroe Doctrine. That doctrine, it must be owned, is both absurd and arrogant in theory and in practice."

But the doctrine was not extinct. In the long correspondence which followed it is indeed true that Seward does not mention the name of Monroe, yet again and again he asserted the doctrine. In 1862, still trusting to the false assurances of Napoleon, he informed our Minister at Paris that the United States avoided "intervention between the belligerents," because it regarded "the conflict as a war involving claims by France on Mexico which Mexico has failed to adjust."* A year later, when the throne·had been offered to Maximilian and had been accepted, and Napoleon was desirous to have the Empire recognized by us, Seward wrote to our Minister that popular opinion in this country favored "a government" in Mexico "republican in form and

---

*Seward to Dayton, August 23, 1862: "This Government, relying on the explanations which have been made by France, regards the conflict as a war involving claims by France which Mexico has failed to adjust to the satisfaction of her adversary, and it avoids intervention between the belligerents."

domestic in its organization"; that to the mind of Lincoln this "popular opinion of the United States is just in itself and eminently essential to the progress of civilization on the American continent"; that if France ignored it and adopted "a policy in Mexico adverse to the American sentiments," she would prepare the way for a collision between France on the one hand and the United States and the American republics on the other, and that the United States would not recognize any government in Mexico which was not the choice of the Mexican people.

To this view the House of Representatives subscribed, and in April, 1864, not quite two months before Maximilian landed at Vera Cruz, unanimously declared that it did not accord with the policy of the United States to recognize any monarchical government erected in America by any European power on the ruins of a Government once republican. Warnings, protests, notes were of no avail. Maximilian came, and a year passed away before the end of the civil war gave us the time and the means to enforce the doctrine. Then, in the summer of 1865, General Sheridan, with fifty thousand veteran troops, drew up on the banks of the Rio Grande, and for the first time in our history the Monroe Doctrine was backed up with arms. France was notified once more that "the people of every State on the American continent have a right to a Republican Government if they choose," and that any attempt by a foreign power to prevent the enjoyment of such institutions is "in its effects antagonistic to the free and popular form of Government existing in the United States." Napoleon might still have failed to understand the doctrine, but he did not fail to understand the thousand other reasons, armed to the teeth and waiting on the banks of the Rio Grande, and in 1866 the French troops were withdrawn. Since that day the Monroe Doctrine has been in many ways and at many times affirmed and asserted by Presidents, by Secretaries of State, by the people. Secretary Fish upheld and described it in 1870.* Presi-

---

* "1870, July 14. REPORT OF SECRETARY FISH TO PRESIDENT GRANT.

"The United States stand solemnly committed by repeated declarations and repeated acts to this doctrine, and its application to the affairs of this continent. In his message to the two Houses of Congress at the commencement of the present session, the President, following the teachings of all our history, said that the existing 'dependencies are no longer regarded as subject to transfer from one European power to another. When the present relation of colonies ceases, they are to become independent powers, exercising the right of choice and of self-control in the determination of their future condition and relations with other powers.'

"This policy is not a policy of aggression; but it opposes the creation of European dominion on American soil, or its transfer to other European powers, and it looks hopefully to the time when, by the voluntary departure of European governments from this continent and the adjacent islands, America shall be wholly American.

"It does not contemplate forcible intervention in any legitimate contest; but it protests against permitting such a contest to result in the increase of European power or influence; and it ever impels this Government, as in the late contest between the South American republics and Spain, to interpose its good offices to secure an honorable peace. . . .

"It will not be presumptuous after the foregoing sketch to say, with entire consideration for the sovereignty and national pride of the Spanish American republics, that the United States, by the priority of their independence, by the stability of their institutions, by the regard of their people for the forms of law, by their resources as a Government, by their naval power, by their commercial enterprise, by the attractions which they offer to European immigration, by the prodigious internal development of their resources and wealth, and by the intellectual life of their population, occupy of necessity a

dent Grant asserted it in his message asking for the purchase of San Domingo in 1870. The whole country demanded an adherence to it in 1879, when the Interoceanic Canal Congress met under the direction of Ferdinand de Lesseps in Paris. Resolutions declaring that the people of the United States still adhered to the doctrine asserted by Monroe, and could not view the attempt of the powers of Europe to build a canal across the Isthmus of Darien in any other light than a manifestation of an unfriendly disposition toward the United States, were introduced into the House of Representatives by Mr. Burnside in 1879 and by Mr. Crapo in 1880, and were sustained by the Committee on Foreign Affairs. This was a new application. Hitherto the assertion of it had been limited to occasions of political or military interference with the affairs of American powers. Now it was asserted when the enterprise was of a commercial character, and this new position was well explained by Mr. Blaine. The United States, he said, would not interfere with the digging of the canal. But capital so interested must look for protection to one or more of the great powers of the world, and no European power could ever be allowed to extend such protection. This was nothing more than pronounced adherence to principles long since announced, and which, in the belief of the President, were an integral and important part of our national policy.

---

prominent position on this continent which they neither can nor should abdicate, which entitles them to a leading voice, and which imposes upon them duties of right and of honor regarding American questions, whether those questions affect emancipated colonies or colonies still subject to European dominion." — *Senate Executive Documents, 41 Cong., 2 Session,* III, No. 112, pp. 7, 9.

THE MONROE DOCTRINE. 39

In the course of these many years it is indeed true that the doctrine was denied and circumscribed almost as many times as it was affirmed. But the denial had been from within, not from without; that distinction was reserved for our time and for Lord Salisbury.

Many years ago, in a tobacco store in New York city, there was a young man named Robert Schomburgk. For reasons best known to himself, he gave up his position of clerk, went to an island off the coast of South America, studied its flora, its fauna, its physical features, and made a map of it, which he sent to the Royal Geographical Society at London. The map was so well done, and the geography of South America so little known, that the Geographical Society urged Schomburgk to continue his studies on the main-land, and under a grant made by the British Government in 1835 he began the work of exploring the little strip of territory she had obtained from Holland in 1814, and which is now known as British Guiana.

By 1839 the survey was completed, and in his memoir Schomburgk, taking the ground that Great Britain owned the Essequibo River, and was therefore entitled to all the territory drained by its tributaries, drew a line around the sources of the rivers which enter the Essequibo from the west, and urged Great Britain to claim the drainage basin of that river, which she did. It is interesting to note that while she was thus asserting ownership over the water-shed of a river in South America because the Dutch had once had settlements there, she was denying our claim to the water-shed of the Columbia River, which had been discovered, explored, and named by Captain Gray, a citizen of the United States, had been explored by Lewis and Clark, and settled at Astoria by the fur company founded by John Jacob Astor.

But she did more than assert her claim, and in 1840 Schomburgk was sent to mark out on the ground the line, slightly modified, which he had traced on paper. Against this act of aggression Venezuela protested, and by order of Lord Aberdeen the boundary marks came down, and a new line was offered which Venezuela could not and did not accept, and no more was heard of the dispute till 1850. A report was then current at Caracas that Great Britain was about to seize the country between the Schomburgk line and the Essequibo, and to allay the excitement caused by the report the British *chargé*, acting under orders from London, assured the Venezuelan Minister that he must not mistrust for a moment the sincerity of the formal declaration made in the name and by the authority of the home Government that Great Britain did not intend "to occupy or encroach on the territory in dispute." Before the year ended, Venezuela gave a like assurance in almost the same words, and "the agreement of 1850" was completed.

Venezuela had by this time entered on a career of civil commotion and disturbance, and for sixteen years the boundary dispute went unnoticed. During this period each nation accused the other of violating the "agreement of 1850," and the charges seem to be well founded. At length, in 1876, Venezuela again brought up the boundary question, intimated that she would accept a compromise line in lieu of her just rights, and, after four years of effort, received from Lord Salisbury, early in 1880, a statement of "the claims of her Majesty's Government by virtue of ancient treaties with the native races." This was a great surprise. What ancient races were referred to when the treaties were made? By whom these unknown tribes had been recognized and vested with the right to make treaties were matters known to Great Britain and to her alone. These Indians, in fact, had no more right to make treaties with Great Britain than have those who inhabit the United States.

But a greater surprise was yet to come. Lord Salisbury asked Venezuela to suggest a line—which she did—and, waiving all claims east of the Schomburgk line, offered to take that marked out by Lord Aberdeen in 1844. Before an answer could be made, the Beaconsfield Ministry fell from power and Lord Salisbury gave place to Lord Grenville. From him, in 1881, came the astonishing reply that in the course of the five-and-thirty years which had elapsed since Aberdeen drew the line so many settlers had gone into the disputed territory under the belief that it belonged to Great Britain that it was impossible to deprive them " of the benefits of British rule." Lord Grenville then proposed a new line far to the west of those proposed by Schomburgk and Aberdeen.

In the course of thirty years the territory which in 1850 Great Britain had admitted was "in dispute," the territory which she solemnly pledged her word she did not intend "to occupy or encroach" on, had become so full of British subjects that she would not give it up. If this is not an act of aggression, if this is not seeking to control the destiny of a nation, if this is not spreading her system, then what is it? To the offer of a new line thus made by Lord Grenville, no answer was ever returned by Venezuela, and the dispute dragged on for three more years. Meantime more English settlers were going into the territory west of the Essequibo, and when in 1884 Great Britain heard that land grants had been made in it by Venezuela, she dropped all diplomacy, and, in the words of Lord Salisbury, began "to assert their undoubted right to the territory within the Schomburgk line, while consenting to hold open to further negotiation and even arbitration the unsettled lands between that line and what was considered to be the rightful boundary," Venezuela insisted that all or none should be submitted to arbitration; and at last when Great Britain began to fortify the territory covered by the agreement of 1850 she broke off diplomatic relations in 1887.

So the matter stood when in 1895 Congress passed the joint resolution under which Mr. Olney wrote his now famous letter to Mr. Bayard, which called forth Lord Salisbury's yet more famous note to Sir Julian Paunceforte. In this note a foreign government for the first time not only denies the existence of the Monroe Doctrine, but the very right of the United States to assert it. "I must not," says his lordship, "be understood as accepting the Monroe Doctrine on the part of her Majesty's Government. It must always be mentioned with respect because of the great statesman to whom it is due, and the great people by whom it has generally been accepted." But "no statesman," his lordship continues, "however eminent, and no nation however powerful, are competent to insert into the code of international law a novel principle which was never recognized before, and which has not since been accepted by the Government of any other country."

It is not placing a forced meaning on Lord Salisbury's language to say that it flatly denies not only existence, but the very right of existence to the Monroe Doctrine. We have, then, but one of two alternatives: We must take this time-honored doctrine and put it away beside the leather fire-buckets and the tin post-horns of our forefathers as a curiosity—a thing which once served its purpose, but is now, as Lord Salisbury says, utterly inapplicable to the state of things in which we live—or we must so act that no statesman however eminent, no nation however powerful, will ever again have the slightest doubt of its existence and its meaning.

In the assertion that the doctrine has no place in the law of nations Lord Salisbury is right. It does not need to be there. It belongs to a class of facts whose existence does not and must not depend on the consent of nations. When Monroe announced his doctrine he was not inserting, or attempting to insert, a principle into the law of nations. He stated a simple fact. The time to make that fact known to the world had come. But who could make it known? Was it the struggling republics of South America not then recognized by Spain, or England, or any European power? or the republic of the United States, then, as to-day, the leading power in this hemisphere, the great representative of popular government?

The moment was a critical one. It was not Mexico, nor Buenos Ayres, nor Chili that the Holy Allies proposed to attack, but the Republican institutions and the Republican governments of the New World. It was not against the Holy Allies, therefore, that Monroe spoke, but against the destruction of Democratic government in America. His doctrine was not for 1823 merely, but for all time.

For Mexico, for Buenos Ayres, for Central America, for Chili to have made such an announcement in 1823 would have been foolish in the extreme, because they could not have made it good. We alone could declare it because we alone were strong enough to support it.

When in the course of time it was expedient for the people of this country to declare their independence they did so, and our independence is to-day unquestioned because we have maintained it and so compelled the nations of the world to recognize it. When in the course of time it became necessary for our good and for the good of the republics of South America to announce a principle which is to this hemisphere what the balance of power is to Europe, it was announced, and we have maintained it and must continue to do so till every power accepts the Monroe Doctrine just as they accept our national existence.

Either we determine the status of Republican government and Republican institutions in the two Americas, or the nations of the Old World will do it for us.

Lord Salisbury asserts that even if there was a Monroe Doctrine it could not apply to Venezuela because Great Britain is not attempting to colonize or to extend her system. But the Monroe Doctrine is not limited to these conditions. It distinctly declares that no nation of the Old World is to *oppress or in any other manner seek to control the destiny* of any nation in the New. The area now claimed arbitrarily, and with no proof submitted, by Great Britain is one hundred and nine thousand square miles—an area which is exceeded by no States in the Union save Texas, California, and Montana; an area ninety times as large as

Rhode Island, fifty-four times as large as Delaware, thirteen times as large as Massachusetts, and forty thousand square miles larger than the six New England States. Were we to lose so great a tract, were Great Britain to take from us New England and all New York east of Rochester, would she not be controlling our destiny? Would she not be extending her system? And when we recall how much smaller Venezuela is than the United States, and how much larger a part one hundred and nine thousand square miles is of her territory than of ours, we can form some rude conception of how seriously such a loss must affect her destiny for all time to come.

The Monroe Doctrine is a simple and plain statement that the people of the United States oppose the creation of European dominion on American soil; that they oppose the transfer of the political sovereignty of American soil to European powers; and that any attempt to do these things will be regarded as "dangerous to our peace and safety." What the remedy should be for such interposition by European powers the doctrine does not pretend to state. But this much is certain: that when the people of the United States consider anything "dangerous to their peace and safety" they will do as other nations do, and, if necessary, defend their peace and safety with force of arms.

The doctrine does not contemplate forcible intervention by the United States in any legitimate contest, but it will not permit any such contest to result in the increase of European power or influence on this continent, nor in the overthrow of an existing government, nor in the establishment of a protectorate over them, nor in the exercise of any direct control over their policy or institutions. Further than this the doctrine does not go. It does not commit us to take part in wars between a South American republic and a European sovereign when the object of the latter is not the founding of a monarchy under a European prince in place of an overthrown republic. But when a European power rightfully or wrongfully attempts to acquire so immense an area as this, she does, in the language of Monroe, "control the destiny" of a nation; she does, in the language of Polk, "interfere with the independent action of nations on this continent"; she is, as Cass expressed it, "holding possession of that country"; she is seeking "to control its political destiny"; and we are bound, as Buchanan asserted, to resist "the attempt to deprive our neighboring republic of her territory, and the Monroe Doctrine does apply."

NOTES.

MADISON'S LETTERS TO MONROE.

MONTPELLIER, *October 30, 1823.*

To President Monroe:

DEAR SIR: I have received from Mr. Jefferson your letter to him, with the correspondence between Mr. Canning and Mr. Rush, sent for his and my perusal and our opinions on the subject of it.

From the disclosures of Mr. Canning it appears, as was otherwise to be inferred, that the success of France against Spain would be followed by attempts of the Holy Alliance to reduce the revolutionized colonies of the latter to their former dependence.

The professions we have made to these neighbors, our sympathies with their liberties and independence, the deep interest we have in the most friendly relations with them, and the consequences threatened by a command of their resources by the great powers confederated against the rights and reforms, of which we have given so conspicuous and persuasive an example, all unite in calling for our efforts to defeat the meditated crusade. It is particularly fortunate that the policy of Great Britain, though guided by calculations different from ours, has presented a co-operation for an object the same with ours. With that co-operation we have nothing to fear from the rest of Europe, and with it the best reliance on success to our laudable views. There ought not to be any backwardness, therefore, I think, in meeting her in the way she has proposed, keeping in view, of course, the spirit and forms of the Constitution in every step taken in the road to war, which must be the last step if those short of war should be without avail.

It cannot be doubted that Mr. Canning's proposal, though made with the air of consultation, as well as concert, was founded on a predetermination to take the course marked out, whatever might be the reception given here to his invitation. But this consideration ought not to divert us from what is just and proper in itself. Our co-operation is due to ourselves and to the world; and while it must insure success, in the event of an appeal to force, it doubles the chance of success without that appeal. It is not improbable that Great Britain would like best to have the sole merit of being the champion of her new friends, notwithstanding the greater difficulty to be encountered, but for the dilemma in which she would be placed. She must in that case either leave us as neutrals to extend our commerce and navigation at the expense of hers, or make us enemies, by renewing her paper blockades and other arbitrary proceedings on the ocean. It may be hoped that such a dilemma will not be without a permanent tendency to check her proneness to unnecessary wars.

Why the British Cabinet should have scrupled to arrest the calamity it now apprehends, by applying to the threats of France against Spain, "the small effort" which it scruples not to employ in behalf of Spanish America is best known to itself. It is difficult to find any other explanation than that interest in the one case has more weight in her casuistry than principle had in the other.

Will it not be honorable to our country, and possibly not altogether in vain, to invite the British Government to extend the avowed disapprobation of the project against the Spanish colonies to the enterprise of France against Spain herself, and even to join in some declaratory act in behalf of the Greeks? On the supposition that no form could be given to the act clearing it of a pledge to follow it up by war, we ought to compare the good to be done with the little injury to be apprehended to the United States, shielded as their interests would be by the power and the fleets of Great Britain, united with their own. These are questions, however, which may require more information than I possess, and more reflection than I can now give them.

What is the extent of Mr. Canning's disclaimer as to "the remaining possessions of Spain in America"? Does it exclude future views of acquiring Porto Rico, etc., as well as Cuba? It leaves Great Britain free, as I understand it, in relation to Spanish possessions in other quarters of the globe.

I return the correspondence of Mr. Rush and Mr. Canning with assurances, etc.

J. Madison to Monroe.

MONTPELLIER, *December 6, 1823.*

DEAR SIR: I received by yesterday's mail your favor of the 4th, covering a copy of the message and another copy under a blank cover. It presents a most interesting view of the topics selected for it. The observations on the foreign ones are well moulded for the occasion, which is rendered the more delicate and serious by the equivocal indications from the British Cabinet. The reserve of Canning after his frank and earnest conversations with Mr. Rush is mysterious and ominous. Could he have stepped in advance of his superiors? Or have they deserted their first object? Or have the allies shrank from theirs? Or is anything taking place in Spain which the adroitness of the British Government can turn against the allies and in favor of South America? Whatever may be the explanation, Canning ought in candor, after what had passed with Mr. Rush, not to have withheld it, and his doing so enjoins a circumspect reliance on our own councils and energies. One thing is certain, that the contents of the message will receive a very close attention everywhere, and that it can do nothing but good everywhere.

(Indorsed) MONROE, Js.

December 6, 1823.

OPINIONS OF THE ENGLISH PRESS ON THE MONROE DOCTRINE IN 1824.

From the London Courier of December 24th.

The speech of the President of the United States is, in all its bearings, a document of more than usual importance. The latter part, which arrived so late yesterday that we were forced to omit it in a small part of our impression, will be found in our last page to-day; and, waiving every other topic in the speech, we direct our whole attention to that part the most important of all to every European power.

The question of the independence and recognition of the South American States may now be considered as at rest. Great Britain has, as we have repeatedly shown, acknowledged their independence *de facto;* and the United States, their nearest neighbors, have not only acknowledged it, but have given a bold and manly notice to the continental powers that they shall treat "any interposition with a view of oppressing or controlling them in any manner as a manifestation of an unfriendly disposition toward themselves, and as dangerous to their peace and safety"; in other words, they shall view it as affording them just ground for war.

After so clear and explicit a warning, there is not one of the continental powers, we suppose, that will risk a war with the United States—a war in which not only they could not expect to have either the aid or good wishes of Great Britain—but a war in which the good wishes of Great Britain (if she did not choose to give more efficient succor) would be all on the side of the United States. Thus, then, we repeat that the question may be considered to be set at rest; we shall hear no more of a congress to settle the fate of the South American States. Protected by the two nations that possess the institutions and speak the language of freedom—by Great Britain on one side, and the United States on the other—their independence is placed beyond the reach of danger; and the continental powers, unable to harm them, will do well to establish that friendly and commercial intercourse with them which they could never have done had they remained under the yoke of Old Spain.

From the London Morning Chronicle.

The American papers, received yesterday, contain the accounts of the opening of Congress, and the message of the President of the United States. The communication of the chief office-bearer of the great Republic to the Legislature at this critical period, when the ambition of kings, not satisfied with the calamity which it has occasioned in Europe, threatens to rekindle the flames of war throughout the Western Hemisphere—was looked forward to with the utmost anxiety. It is worthy of the occasion and of the people destined to occupy so large a space in the future history of the world.

What a contrast between the manly plainness of this State paper and the Machiavelism and hypocrisy of the declaration of the manifestoes of the Governments of this part of the world!

Whatever lately were the intentions of the French Ministers respecting South America, it is now asserted, from undoubted authority, that English policy has prevailed in Paris over that of Russia, and that not only will France not assist Spain in any attempt to subjugate her former American colonies, but will view, not with indifference, any support which Russia or any other nation may lend her for this purpose. This is certainly a wise resolution on the part of the French Government, for this independence of the new American States must extend their commerce, and thereby increase the prosperity of Frenchmen. Russia, blocked up nearly half the year by impenetrable ice, can never partake of Southern commerce until a port be opened for her in the Dardanelles, and hence the anxiety exhibited by her to involve France in the expensive and hopeless employment of restoring America to the yoke of the Bourbons; for, without this or some other occupation for the French armies and the British navy, she has not the most distant chance of accomplishing the long and ardently cherished designs of her empire against ancient Greece, now in possession. This union of France and England in the great cause of American independence is another strong ground for expecting the continuation of the blessings of peace, and, consequently, an improvement in the public credit of nations. The speech of the President of the United States, so full of wisdom and just ideas, has, however, had more effect on the opinions of the leaders in the national securities than the abundance of money or the changed policy of France, for in it they see a sufficient guarantee for the maintenance of the freedom of the American Continent. There is no part, however, of this speech which can afford more genuine satisfaction to every civilized nation than the notice which it takes of the extraordinary and gallant struggle made, at present, by the Greeks, in the cause of general independence.

From the Liverpool Advertiser of January 3d.

By one short passage in it, is set at rest, we dare presume, whatever may have been in agitation by the continental allies, in reference to the late Spanish possessions in America. There will be no attempt made, it may be confidently affirmed, to interfere with the present condition of those countries, when it is known that such interference would be viewed by the United States as a just cause of war, on her part, with any power attempting such interference.

In regard of the power, prosperity, and resources of the nation herself, also, the language of the speech is very interesting; her revenue, it is affirmed, will, on the first of this year, exceed her expenditure by no less than nine million dollars. Her population is estimated at ten millions, and every branch of industry, every source of revenue, wealth, and power is flourishing.

On its subjects of common interest to all nations, the Government of the United States is enabled to stand forward to suggest and promote what is beneficial, and to crush what is injurious. In the speech is developed a new idea in respect to maritime war, which, if adopted, on this suggestion, by other powers, will greatly tend to lessen the evils of national contention. It is proposed to do away altogether with the system of privateering in so far as it is countenanced by Governments.

It is also suggested, as a means of effectually suppressing the slave-trade, that vessels found by the ships of any nation to be engaged in this traffic shall be treated on the same footing with vessels caught in piracy.

While in her power and resources, as they are illustrated in this speech, the nation of the United States exhibits the vigor of ripe years, she, in those sentiments of active humanity, seems, to our thought, to preserve the fresh feeling of youth, and not to be wholly engrossed, as older States are, in the pursuit or support of purely selfish interests. And we have thus a pleasure from contemplating her less as that metaphysical insentient thing, a State, than as an actual human and feeling being.

From Bell's Weekly Messenger of December 27th.

The main object of any interest during the week now passed is the arrival of the speech of the President of the United States. It is a document of the first interest and importance. It is interesting, because it is a brief, simple, and direct *exposé* of republican government; always true, plain dealing, and sincere. It is important, because, fearing nothing, it conceals nothing, and is totally divested of all trick, artifice, commonplace jargon which renders the diplomacy of Europe so much more than merely nugatory.

Long, very long, have we wished that Canada might be sold or exchanged with the United States. Exchanged for what it may be demanded? Why, for such an annuity for a term of years as would redeem what remains of the English assessed taxes, and redeem them forever.

If America would give us enough for this purpose for five or seven years, the natural progress of our revenue would do what would be required after that time. Add to this that we should save upward of half a million yearly in the expense of the Canada Government, and nearly as much more in the reduction of the army which it would allow. This has long been our own view, and we are persuaded that half, at least, of our best statesmen unite with us in it. As to the right of doing so, there can be no doubt that the Canadians would agree, and for that reason—because it is their decided interest to do so, and because (if we were Canadians) we should not hesitate one moment.

The third point in the speech is where the President asserts that "he owes it to candor, etc., to declare that the United States would consider any attempt on the part of European monarchies to extend their system to any portion of the Western Hemisphere as dangerous to their peace and safety," that "with the existing colonies or dependencies of any European power they have not interfered and will not; but that any interposition for the purpose of oppressing or controlling any of the States whose independence the Republic has, after mature consideration, acknowledged, she would consider in no other light than as the manifestation of an unfriendly disposition toward herself"; in other words, as a just cause of war.

We have long, very long, anticipated that the United States would thus speak, and it puts an end at once to all apprehensions as to any attempt by the allied despots upon South America; for how can these despots assemble any navy which for an instant can meet the American navy, or the South American navy, when manned and commanded by American seamen and American naval officers?

From the Paris Étoile—A Ministerial Paper.

Mr. Monroe, who is not a sovereign, who has himself told us that he is only the first delegate of the people, has taken in his message the tone of a powerful monarch whose armies and fleets are ready to go forth on the first signal. He does more; he prescribes to the potentates of Europe the conduct they are to pursue in certain circumstances if they do not wish to incur his displeasure. Such is the prohibition which he issues against their ever thinking of any new colonization in the two Americas.

Mr. Monroe is the temporary President of a Republic situated on the Eastern Continent of North America. This Republic is bounded on the south by the possessions of the King of Spain, and on the north by those of the Queen of England. Its independence has only been acknowledged for forty years; by what title, then, are the two Americas to be under his immediate dependence, from Hudson's Bay to Cape Horn ? What clamors did he not raise in the United States when the Emperor of Russia wished to trace the demarcation of the part of territory which he claims on the northeast coast as discovered by his subjects! This monarch, however, did not presume to dictate laws to any of the States who have establishments on the same coast. It was reserved for Mr. Monroe to show us a dictator armed with a right of superiority over the whole of the New World.

According to the political system he would establish it would not be permitted to Spain to make the least effort to re-enter on the territory which for three centuries she has possessed. The King of Portugal, as the American papers have observed themselves, could not act as a sovereign and father without exposing himself to the wrath of Mr. Monroe. England would require his previous consent if it suited her interest to make any new military or political establishment either in Canada or Nova Scotia. And yet Mr. Monroe's message contains phrases indirectly hostile to the policy and ambition of the great powers of Europe! But what is that power which professes so proudly maxims opposed to the rights of sovereignty and the independence of crowns? Who is that power which pretends to prescribe to subjects the limits of obedience; who is she, in short, who does not fear to compromise the existence of social order by declaring in the face of heaven that she will not recognize any difference between a government *de facto* and government *de jure* ?

By bringing under one point of view all the assertions and doctrines contained in this message, it is satisfactory to consider that it has not yet received the sanction of any of the authorities, even of the country where it appeared; and, in short, that the opinions of Mr. Monroe are as yet merely the opinions of a private individual.

The London Times of January sixteenth has some very severe and spirited remarks on the extract above given from the Étoile. The following paragraph may serve as a specimen:

"A direct attempt is made by the Étoile to sever the Chief Magistrate of a powerful and enlightened nation from the body of a State which he represents. 'Not a sovereign!' No, but he is the acknowledged—the elected head and organ of a great sovereign people—one whose elevation cost his country neither a drop of blood nor a widow's tear, nor the beggary or banishment, the persecution or corruption of a single human being among ten millions of men. An eminence thus achieved may well appear, at first sight, of questionable origin to an ultra; but let him consider his words. He calls Mr. Monroe a 'temporary president,' but is the power which he exercises a temporary power? It is, on the contrary, a prerogative which never dies, let who will be its trustee for the moment, and which, as Mr. Monroe has on this occasion employed it, has its sanction in the heart of every citizen among those millions who confided it to his hands. Will the Étoile venture to match the durability of any despotic throne in Europe with that of the President's chair in North America? If so, we tell him that he is likely to lose his wager. Or will his patron risk the fate of an expedition on the chance of the policy announced by this 'private individual,' Mr. Monroe being disclaimed by 'the other authorities' of the republics? We believe they are not so rash. The entire commentary of the unfortunate Étoile is an insult on the first article of his own creed—viz., that a Government and the nation for which it speaks must be identified."

THE THIRD-TERM TRADITION.

THE framers of the Constitution of the United States never for a moment supposed that their work could remain unchanged for all time to come. That new conditions which they could not then foresee would arise, and would have to be met by remedies they could not possibly devise, was as well known to them as the fact that such conditions have arisen is known to us. They provided, therefore, that the Constitution may be amended in either of two ways. One of these ways has never yet been used. The other has been used so sparingly that although many hundreds of amendments have been offered in Congress, but nineteen have ever been sent to the States.

That so many have been offered and so few been chosen is because some were trivial, because some were intended to cure ills that were but temporary and soon passed away, and because there has gradually been formed an unwritten constitution which in great measure does away with the need of amendments.

This unwritten constitution is made up of decisions of the Supreme Court, which are regarded as final; of customs and usages which experience has shown to be good and useful; and of certain interpretations and constructions of the written Constitution by the people. In the Constitution, for instance, we read that the President " may require the opinion, in writing, of the principal officer in each of the Executive departments, upon any subject relating to the duties of their respective offices." It is by no means obligatory on him to do so. The language is " he may "—not " he must." Yet upon this slender authority has been founded a council utterly unknown to the Constitution. The first President began the custom of never adopting any policy, never taking any important step, till he had gathered about him for consultation his Attorney-General and his Secretaries of State, Treasury, and War. Every succeeding President has followed his example till the Cabinet —a piece of political machinery the Constitution did not create, nor its framers contemplate—has come to be looked upon as a prime necessity in our system of Federal Government. On no part, again, of the Constitution did the Convention spend more pains than on the sections which define the manner of electing a President. Some members were for having him chosen by the Governors of the States; some by the Senate; some by the legislatures of the States; some by a body of electors especially appointed for the purpose; some wanted an Executive of three men—one from the Eastern, one from the Middle, and one from the Southern States. All were agreed that the choice should not be left to the people—to do which, as one member of the Convention expressed it, would be as foolish as to leave the selection of colors to a blind man. At length they adopted the method of choosing by electors, and, taking the system by which Maryland chose her State senators, modelled after it the Electoral Colleges of the States. Their plain intention was that the presidential electors should do two things—select a suitable man to be President, and then elect him to the office. The people were to have no direct part in the matter. But our Constitution was not very old when the need of unity of action among the electors of the same party became apparent, and presidential candidates began to be nominated first by the Congressional Caucus, then by State legislatures, and at last by the National Nominating Convention. As every elector is expected to give his vote for the nominee of his party, the Electoral Colleges are practically stripped of all power in the election of a President, are reduced to mere boards for registering and formally transmitting the result of the popular vote, and a highly important provision of the written Constitution is reversed and nullified by a custom which forms a part of the unwritten constitution.

Much the same thing has taken place with regard to the President's term of office. Every phase of that question, from the expediency of a short term with re-election to a long term without re-election, seems to have been carefully considered. At the outset the general opinion of the delegates was that Congress should elect the President; that his term of office should be three years; and that he should be re-eligible, as the doctrine of rotation would tend, it was said, to throw out of office the men best fitted to execute its duties. On the other hand, many of the members were very earnest for a term of seven years and no re-election. The Executive, said they, is to be chosen by the Legislature, and will be absolutely dependent on it, as its creature and the Executive of its will and of the laws it passes. A long term with no succession to office will prevent a false complaisance on the part of the Legislature toward an unfit man, and the temptation on the part of a bad Executive to intrigue with the Legislature for reappointment. One member begged hard for triennial election with ineligibility after nine years: but the States by a vote of five to four decided that the President's term should be seven years, and by a vote of seven to two made him ineligible to re-election. Later on in the debate the members changed their minds, struck out this prohibition, and, by a vote of six States to four, declared him to be eligible to re-election. Ten days later, however, on the motion of Mason of Virginia, this decision was set aside, and the resolution passed that the "Executive be appointed for seven years, and be ineligible a second time."

This seemed to be final. But when the Committee of Detail made its report there was another struggle to take the election from Congress. So earnest was the effort that the Convention could come to no conclusion, and in despair sent the matter, with a great many others, to a committee of one from each of the eleven States, which in time reported a plan for a choice by an Electoral College—or, in case the College failed to elect, by the Senate—and fixed the term at four years. In the debate which followed, a member of the committee told the Convention that the sole purpose of the plan offered by the Committee of Eleven was to get rid of the provision, in the report of the Committee of Detail, that a President could not be re-elected, and so make him independent of Congress. He was assured that the College would never elect; that the Senate would always make the choice; and that the President would be the creature of one branch of Congress. But the idea of re-election to many terms carried the day, and with some slight changes the recommendation of the Committee of Eleven was incorporated in the Constitution.

From all this it is quite clear that the intention of the framers was that a President might be elected over and over again as many times as the electors saw fit to choose him. This was no carelessly formed decision, but was the result of a long and bitter experience under the old Articles of Confederation they were about to overthrow. At the outbreak of the Revolution the belief was general that the liberties of the people and the rights of the State would not be safe under any system of general government if the members of the Federal Legislature held their offices for a long term, or were repeatedly elected to it. The Articles of Confederation therefore carefully provided that the members of the Continental Congress should be chosen annually; that they might be recalled at any time by the States that sent them; and that no delegate should hold his office for more than three years in any term of six. The result was disastrous. Congress was a small body. The duties thrust on each member were diverse and important. Yet the moment he began to be fairly familiar with his duties, the moment he began to be a really efficient servant of the people, his term expired, and he returned, in the language of the time, "to the body of the people," lest another term in Congress should "breed a lust of power." It was with the intention of preventing this loss of the services of valuable and experienced men that the fathers carefully abstained from placing any limit on the time of service of senators and representatives, and, after due consideration, reversed their action and removed a limit they had placed on the number of times a citizen could be elected President.

But again their purpose has been defeated and their judgment condemned by that great tribunal—the people—before which, in our country, all public issues must sooner or later be tried. Again the unwritten constitution has amended the written, and no task is now quite so hopeless as that of re-electing a President to a third term. For much of this, precedent is alone responsible. Had our first President been willing to accept a third term—and the people would gladly have given it—he would in all likelihood have been followed by a long line of Presidents each serving for twelve instead of eight years. But he was weary of office and gladly laid it down. His motive for this act is so often forgotten that it is well to quote from his "Farewell Address":

> The acceptance and continuance hitherto in office, to which your suffrages have twice called me, have been a uniform sacrifice of inclination to the opinion of duty, and to a deference to what appeared to be your wishes. . . . I rejoice that the state of your concerns, external as well as internal, no longer renders the pursuit of inclination incompatible with the pursuit of duty or propriety.

No scruples about a third term troubled him in the least. He went back to private life solely because he was tired of the presidency, and because the state of the country did not demand a further sacrifice of his comfort. Yet this act set an example which for many years was followed implicitly by his successors, though it was long before the people saw anything wrong in the suggestion of a third term. Mr. Jefferson was the first to point this out. More than two years before his second term ended, the Legislature of Vermont on November fifth, 1806, formally invited him to become a

THE THIRD-TERM TRADITION. 61

candidate for a third term, and the great Republican strongholds made haste to follow her. Georgia joined in the request in December; Maryland in January, 1807; Rhode Island in February; New York and Pennsylvania in March; and New Jersey in December. North Carolina joined later. So far Jefferson had made no reply, but the time had now come to speak out, for in a few weeks it would be the duty of the Congressional Caucus to nominate—or, as the phrase went, recommend—a candidate. On the tenth of December, 1807, therefore, he replied to the invitations of Vermont, New Jersey, and Pennsylvania, and gave his reasons for declining a third term. He said:

> That I should lay down my charge at a proper period is as much a duty as to have borne it faithfully. If some termination to the services of the Chief Magistrate be not fixed by the Constitution, or supplied by practice, his office, nominally for years, will in fact become for life; and history shows how easily that degenerates into an inheritance. Believing that a representative government responsible at short periods of election is that which produces the greatest sum of happiness to mankind, I feel it a duty to do no act which shall essentially impair that principle; and I should unwillingly be the first person who, disregarding the sound precedent set by an illustrious predecessor, should furnish the first example of prolongation beyond the second term of office.

The enemies of Mr. Jefferson have asserted that his long silence was due to policy and not to indifference, that the thirteen months which elapsed between the November day, 1806, when the Legislature of Vermont invited him to run again, and the tenth of December, 1807, when he answered with his famous letter, were spent in a careful nursing of what in the political language of our time would be called "his boom"; and that he did not say No till he was quite sure that it would be folly to say Yes. The charge is unfair and unjust; yet the fact remains that he could not possibly have been elected. There were then seventeen States in the Union, casting a hundred and seventy-six electoral votes, making eighty-nine necessary for a choice. On the tenth of December, 1807, these votes stood:

For Jefferson and a third term.		Federalist States.		Republican States not declaring for third term, and supporting Madison.	
Vermont	6	New Hampshire	7	Virginia	24
Rhode Island	4	Massachusetts	19	South Carolina	10
New York	19	Connecticut	9	Ohio	3
Pennsylvania	20	Delaware	3	Kentucky	8
New Jersey	8	Maryland	2	Tennessee	5
Maryland	9				
Georgia	6		40		50
North Carolina	14				
	86				

It will be observed that in the list of third-term States the full electoral vote of each is given to Jefferson, except in the case of Maryland, which in 1804 and in 1808 cast two Federalist votes. These, therefore, have been taken from him in the table, leaving him eighty-six, or just three short of a bare majority. As a matter of fact, the third-term States, when the election took place, cast but seventy-nine Republican votes, for Rhode Island was carried by the Federalists, who also secured three votes in North Carolina.

Mr. Jefferson's chances in the Caucus, which met on the twenty-third of January, 1808, were very poor. They were poorer still before the people, who, the land over, most heartily indorsed his anti-third-term principles. The Democratic citizens of Adams County, Pennsylvania, in public meeting assembled at Gettysburg, approved "that manly and sublime effort which dictated your determination to retire from public life at the close of the next elective period of your authority.". At a meeting of delegates from the wards of Philadelphia an address was drawn up in which the President was assured that—

—in yielding homage to the motives which have induced your voluntary retirement from public life, while surrounded by the warmest affections of the people, we derive consolation from the consideration that your example may operate on all future Presidents to pursue a course which has added lustre to your character, already dear to liberty and to your country.

The Senate of Maryland in a long address told him:

While we daily appreciate the motives which induce you to decline being considered among the number of those out of whom the choice of our next President is to be made, and while we revere the patriotism which dictated those motives, permit us still to indulge the pleasing hope that when the next period of presidential election approximates [1812], should the united voice of your countrymen require it, those same motives and that same patriotism will induce you to sacrifice your private wishes and convenience to your country's good.

Even the Legislature of the far-away Territory of Orleans was moved to address the President and to heartily commend his wise decision. Their address said:

However we may regret, in common with our fellow-citizens of the United States, this determination to decline being a candidate for the highest office in the gift of the people, the motives which induce it afford another proof of your patriotism, and must command the approbation of the country.

The Tammany Society of Philadelphia, while celebrating its anniversary in May, 1808, drank to the toast, "President Jefferson—Rotation in office is the bulwark of freedom. His precedent deserves our homage and our gratitude, and traitors would alone refuse them." On the Fourth of July his conduct was very generally approved in some such toast as this: "Jefferson—May his successor imitate his virtues and follow his motto, rotation in office."

That his virtues had any influence on his successors is exceedingly doubtful; but his bold assertion that two terms were all that it was safe to give any President had a deep and lasting influence on the people, and did far more than the example of Washington to establish the unwritten law which for more than sixty years none of his successors was hardy enough to defy.

It must not be supposed, however, that during these sixty years the third-term tradition was forgotten. Indeed, it was rarely lost sight of. Presidents referred to it in their messages; senators, representatives, political parties called for a constitutional amendment embodying it, and on more than one occasion it seemed not unlikely that such an amendment might be secured. The question first came up in 1823, when the absolute certainty of a contested election in 1824 led to a desperate attempt to defeat certain candidates by means of an amendment to the Constitution. One that was offered provided that no man could be President or Vice-President if he had held any office under the Constitution within four years of the day of election. This would have cut off Adams, Crawford, and Calhoun. Another was to the effect that no member of Congress could be a candidate. This would have cut off Clay. A third was designed to take the choice of presidential electors from the State legislatures and give it to the people.

This would have assured the election of Jackson. While the friends of the various candidates differed as to who should be President, they agreed most heartily on one point, and in 1824, by a vote of 36 to 3, the Senate sent a joint resolution to the House providing that no President should have more than two terms. The House did not act; but the failure of the Electoral Colleges in 1824 to choose a President, and what it pleased many to consider the defeat of the will of the people by the House of Representatives in 1825, brought about another serious effort to change the constitutional provisions regarding the President. Some wanted a method by which he could be elected without the intervention of the House of Representatives; some were for an election by a direct vote of the people; others, as the whole question of the presidency was under discussion, proposed to so amend the Constitution as to make it read: "No person who shall have been elected to the office of President of the United States a second time shall again be eligible to that office."

This was popular in the Senate, and passed, with no opposition, by a vote of 25 to 4. In the House the joint resolution was sent to a committee and never heard from. Still, the idea would not down, but year by year, session after session, came up as vigorous as ever. In 1828, in 1829, in 1830, in 1831, in 1832, in 1833, in 1835, during both Jackson's terms, it was never absent from the journals for a session. Indeed, as Jackson's administration progressed, as his popularity grew stronger on the one hand, and hatred of him became more intense on the other, men began to think that one term was enough, and joint resolutions providing for such a limitation were introduced over and over again.

Of our later Presidents, Jackson was the only one who could have defied the tradition. He was the first "man of the people" to be raised to the office of Chief Magistrate. In his day Democracy was indeed triumphant, and he was the ideal Democrat. No one else has ever closed a second term more honored, more truly beloved by the people than on the day whereon he began his first term. He had but to say the word, and he would surely have been thrice President of the United States. But he, too, would not break through the unwritten law, and with the beginning of his first term we enter on a long period which might well be called the one-term era. Joint resolutions providing for such a term limitation were introduced into Congress in 1828, 1829, 1830, and 1832. Jackson proposed such a restriction in his message in 1833, and the House and Senate again listened to demands for such a constitutional amendment in 1835, 1836, 1838, and 1840. When the Whigs in 1841 read John Tyler out of the party they asserted in the manifesto that "one term for the President" was Whig doctrine, and they put the same pledge into their national platform in 1844.

About this time a reaction set in, and in 1844 and 1846 the constitutional amendments proposed in Congress provide for a term of six years and no re-election. Then follows a blank period during which nothing is heard of it, for the custom of giving even a second term had gone out of fashion. From Jackson to Lincoln no President was given a second term, and none save Van Buren were ever renominated. But at length, in 1872, the third-term question came up in a very definite form. The second election of Grant, it will be remembered, took place in the autumn of that year, and was scarcely over when the New York Herald raised the cry of Cæsarism, and loudly proclaimed that our Republican institutions were threatened with ruin by the probable re-election of Grant in 1876. The possibility of such an event was four years away; yet so great was the dread of it that the third-term question became a real political issue. Other newspapers echoed the cry. Public men were called on to define their position. Political conventions declared against it in their platforms, and finally, as the presidential year drew near, Mr. Springer, of Illinois, moved this resolution in the House of Representatives:

Resolved, That, in the opinion of this House, the precedent established by Washington, and other Presidents of the United States, in retiring from the presidential office after their second term, has become, by universal concurrence, a part of our Republican system of government, and that any departure from this time-honored custom would be unwise, unpatriotic, and fraught with peril to our free institutions.*

How perfectly the resolution expressed the sentiments of the people is made manifest by the treatment it received at the hands of their representatives, who, without a moment's hesitation, suspended the rules and passed it, on the very day it was introduced, by a yea-and-nay vote of 234 to 18. Thirty-seven did not vote.

This ended for the time being all hope of renominating Grant, who retired at the close of his term and began his famous journey around the world. But it was only for the time being, and, as that journey drew

---

* Journal of the House of Representatives, December 15, 1875, pp. 66, 67.

to a close, the masters of the Republican party—Mr. Conkling, Mr. Cameron, and Mr. Logan—determined to renew the old effort to re-elect him. The time seemed opportune. One of those periods of despondency—of political blues—which occasionally afflict us, had set in. The contested election of 1876; the troubles in the South; the pacific policy of Hayes; the attempt to steal the State government in Maine; and, above all, the desperate condition of the Republican party—had aroused serious doubts as to the permanency of "our free institutions." Men were beginning to talk of a strong government, or at least of a government administered by a strong man—such as Grant, who just at this time landed on the Pacific coast. The reception given him by his countrymen was such as has never been accorded to any other citizen, and, mistaking this outburst of gratitude for a sure sign that the people had again turned to Grant for political leadership, the effort of the machine to renominate him began in serious earnest. The struggle which followed is too recent to need description. We all remember how the dominating power of Conkling in New York, of Cameron in Pennsylvania, and of Logan in Illinois extorted from the conventions of those States a demand for the nomination of Grant; how other States followed this lead; how the friends of the movement were denounced as "Restorationists" and "Imperialists"; how they persisted in their effort to the very last; how in the Chicago Convention they never cast less than 303 votes and once cast 313; and how by their persistence they forced that compromise which resulted in the nomination of Garfield. All these things are still fresh in our memories, and, being so, it is not a little strange that a

THE THIRD-TERM TRADITION. 69

serious effort should be on foot to give a third term to Mr. Cleveland.

The fears which tormented the founders of the Republic have long since vanished. We do not believe that our democratic institutions can ever be subverted by any occupant of the White House. We stand in no dread that the day will come when some successful general or some unscrupulous politician will first seize the presidency and then use its great power to set up a life-long dictatorship, or establish a kingdom, on the ruins of the Republic. Yet there is no reason to believe that the old-time antipathy to a third term is one whit less strong than it ever was. Any sane man will admit that the bank, or the railroad company, or the corporation of any sort that should dismiss a tried and able president merely because the stockholders had twice placed him in the executive chair, would deserve financial ruin. No tendency in the business world is more marked than the constant effort to find men preëminently fitted to carry on certain lines of business, and to place the management of such concerns entirely in their hands. But the common-sense rules which govern the selection of the president of a corporation do not apply in the election of a President of the United States. Our Presidents are not chosen because of their fitness, but because of their availability. Some are dark horses; some are nominated because they alone can reconcile contending factions; some because they can carry pivotal States. Others are forced on the voters by the machine. In theory this is all wrong. In practice no harm comes from it. Under our system of government we do not want, we do not need, a President of extraordinary ability. The average man is good enough, and for him two terms is ample. We want a strong government of the people by the people, not a government of the people by a strong man, and we ought not to tolerate anything which has even the semblance of heredity. The advocates of a third term for Mr. Cleveland will do well to remember the doctrine of the illustrious founder of their party, that "in no office can rotation be more expedient."

THE POLITICAL DEPRAVITY OF THE FATHERS.

IN times like the present, when the boss is everywhere, and when the high places of many State and municipal governments are filled by men who have secured them by methods greatly to be condemned, it may afford the honest citizen some consolation to know that these evils have always existed. Whoever reads the magazines and newspapers, whoever listens to the oratory of the pulpit and the after-dinner speeches of political reformers, is well aware of the existence of a widespread belief that politicians and legislators and public men are more corrupt to-day than they were in the time of our ancestors three generations ago, and that the cause of our political debasement is a free and unrestricted ballot. This, most happily, is a pure delusion. A very little study of long-forgotten politics will suffice to show that in filibustering and gerrymandering, in stealing governorships and legislatures, in using force at the polls, in colonizing and in distributing patronage to whom patronage is due, in all the frauds and tricks that go to make up the worst form of practical politics, the men who founded our State and national governments were always our equals, and often our masters. Yet they lived in times when universal suffrage did not exist, and when the franchise was everywhere guarded by property and religious qualifications of the strictest kind. In New England, ninety years ago, a voter must have an annual income of three pounds, or a freehold estate worth sixty pounds. In New York he must be possessed of an estate worth twenty pounds York money, or rent a house for which he paid forty shillings annually. In New Jersey the qualification was real estate to the value of fifty pounds, in Maryland and South Carolina fifty acres of land, and in Georgia ten pounds of taxable property. But many a man who could vote was hopelessly debarred from ever holding office. No citizen could be a Governor in Massachusetts who did not own a thousand pounds of real estate, nor be a senator unless he had a freehold worth three hundred. In North Carolina senators must own three hundred acres of land, and a Governor lands and tenements to the value of a thousand pounds. Here the qualification for a representative was one hundred pounds of real property; there it was one hundred acres of land; elsewhere it was two hundred and fifty acres of land, and open profession of the Protestant religion.

Religious restrictions were almost universal. In New Hampshire, in New Jersey, in North Carolina, in South Carolina and Georgia, the Governors, the members of legislatures, and the chief officers of State must all be Protestants. In Massachusetts and Maryland they must be Christians. In North Carolina and Pennsylvania they must believe in the inspiration of the Old and New Testaments, in South Carolina in a future state of rewards and punishments, and in Delaware in the doctrine of the Trinity.

From the standpoint of those who, in our day, disapprove of universal suffrage, this ought to have been a time of great political purity. The voters were taxpayers, Christians, and owners of property. The officeholders were men of substance, while the qualifications for holding office increased with the dignity of the place. Yet it was, in truth, a period of great political depravity. Indeed, it may well be doubted whether, in all our annals, there can be found a finer example of filibustering than that afforded by the Assembly of Pennsylvania in 1787.

The Legislature of that State then consisted of one House, which met at Philadelphia, and at the session in the autumn of 1787 had resolved to adjourn, *sine die*, on the twenty-ninth of September. As the question of the day was the ratification of the Federal Constitution, just framed, a member of the Assembly, on the morning of the twenty-eighth, moved that a Convention be called to consider the Constitution, and that a time be fixed for the choice of delegates. The enemies of the Constitution opposed the motion, and, in the midst of the debate which followed, the Assembly adjourned for dinner. The opponents of the call were in the minority; but without the presence of at least three of them there would be no quorum. All resolved, therefore, to stay away, and when the Assembly met again, at four o'clock in the afternoon, and the clerk called the roll, no quorum was present. The sergeant-at-arms was thereupon sent to summon the absentees; but not one would obey, and the Assembly was forced to adjourn till the following morning. One of the reasons given for objecting to a call for a Convention was that Congress, to which the Constitution had been transmitted by the framers, had not submitted it to the States, and that to act before it was sent out by Congress was indecent and disrespectful. It so happened, however, that Congress, then in session at New York, had submitted the Constitution to the States, and that an express, riding post-haste, brought the resolution to a member of the Assembly early on the morning of the twenty-ninth.

When the Assembly met on that morning, the factious members being still absent and no quorum present, the sergeant and the clerk were again sent to bid them attend, and were ordered to show the resolution of Congress, in hope of removing their objections. But every one the sergeant summoned replied, "I will not attend." Meantime a report of their conduct had spread abroad, and the people, hearing that there was no quorum, went to the tavern, seized two of the absentees, dragged them to the State-House, thrust them into the Assembly Chamber, and blocked the doors. This completed a quorum, and the Convention was called.

But it must not be supposed that all that was good was confined to one party, and all that was bad to the other. The Convention then called met in the State-House late in November, 1787, and took the Constitution into consideration. As the members would not bear the expense of employing an official stenographer, the labor of reporting the debate from day to day was undertaken by two young men. One, Alexander James Dallas, attended in behalf of the Pennsylvania Herald. The other, Thomas Lloyd, announced that he would take down the proceedings "accurately in shorthand," and when the Convention had adjourned would publish them in one small octavo volume. But the debate had not gone on very long before the reports of Dallas in the Herald attracted attention, were copied far and wide, and furnished such material for opposition in States yet to consider the Constitution that the Federalists became alarmed and suppressed them. To do this it was necessary to buy the Pennsylvania Herald, which was done, and the report of the debate stops abruptly with November thirtieth. The Convention sat till December fifteenth, but not another word of its proceedings nor a line of explanation appears in the Herald. It was necessary, in the next place, to dispose of Mr. Lloyd, who, though he had published nothing as yet, had promised to do so, and had secured subscriptions. But he too succumbed, and when, to satisfy his subscribers, he issued his book, in place of the debate accurately taken in short-hand, as he had promised, there appeared but two speeches—one by Thomas McKean and one by James Wilson, both ardent supporters of the Constitution. As a consequence, there does not exist to-day anything more than a fragment of the proceedings of the Pennsylvania Convention which ratified the Constitution.

When ten other States had followed the example of Pennsylvania, the Continental Congress, sitting at New York, selected the first Wednesday in January, 1789, as the day when the electors of President should be chosen in the eleven ratifying States.

In most instances the business of choosing them was easily and rapidly transacted. But the Legislature of New York was the scene of a bitter contest. The Assembly had passed a bill defining the manner of electing senators and presidential electors, according to which each House was to nominate two men to be United States senators, and then the Houses were to meet in joint session and compare lists. If there was either complete or partial disagreement, a joint ballot was to be held on the names of the unsuccessful candidates. Now, in the Assembly, the Antifederalists had a great majority, while in the Senate the Federalists had a small majority. Had the bill passed the Senate and become a law, the nominees of each House would have been different, a joint session would have been necessary, and at that joint session the Antifederalists of the Assembly, greatly outnumbering the Federalists of the Senate, would have elected both senators.

For this reason the Senate disliked the bill, and so amended it that, in case the nominees of the House were not those of the Senate, the House should choose one from the two offered by the Senate, and the Senate one from the two proposed by the House. To this the House refused to agree, and a conference followed; but as neither would yield, New York had no senators during the first session of the first Congress.

By another section of the same bill provision was made for the choice of presidential electors in a manner similar to that for the election of senators. Each House was to prepare a list of eight names, a joint session was to follow, the lists were to be compared, and men whose names were on both were to be declared elected. If the two lists were utterly different—and they were absolutely certain to be so—eight of the sixteen nominees were to be chosen by joint ballot, in which event the eight proposed by the Assembly would have been elected. The Senate, of course, refused to hear of such a plan; and as the Assembly would not yield, no electors were chosen, and New York cast no vote for President in 1789.

This stubborn contest between the two Houses over the choice of electors and senators was followed, three years later, by the theft of the governorship. The candidates were, John Jay for the Federalists and George Clinton for the Republicans. Each had been long in public life; each had rendered many and distinguished services to the State; and, as a consequence, the election was close—so close, indeed, that the loss of a few votes would decide it either way.

In those days, when men were without the telegraph, the railroad, or the steamboat, and when the centre of New York State was the frontier, the counting and canvassing of a State vote was a slow and tedious matter. The law required that as soon as the vote of a town was counted the inspectors should send the ballots to the sheriff of the county, who should put them in a box, and, when every town in the county had been heard from, should carry the box to Albany and deliver it to the Secretary of State. As the votes in the eastern and southern counties were announced one by one, the majority for Clinton dwindled till it stood at one hundred and eight, with two strong Jay counties to be heard from. If Clinton was not to be defeated, it was clear that an excuse must be found for throwing out the returns of some Federalist county, and, happily for the Republicans, an opportunity to do so existed. The box from Tioga County, which contained a good majority for Jay, had been given by the sheriff to his deputy to carry to Albany. But the deputy fell sick by the way, and sent the box on by a sub-deputy of his own appointment. This the Clintonians decided was illegal, and insisted that the vote of Tioga should not be counted. But even with Tioga left out, Jay would have a majority if Otsego was counted.

Now, in Otsego, the sheriff had been appointed in February, 1791, to serve one year, and just before the close of his first term had written to the Council of Appointment declining a second. One month after the end of his year a successor was appointed, but had not qualified nor acted when the election took place. In this state of things the old sheriff continued to act, and, gathering up the ballots cast in the towns of his county, sent them by his deputy to Albany. Scarcely had he done this when he found that the ballots of one town had been left out, and these he sent wrapped up in paper. The Clintonians, availing themselves of these irregularities, insisted that the returns of Otsego should not be counted. There was, in the first place, no sheriff. In the second place, the law required that the vote of *every* town should go in the box; but as one had not gone into it, all the others must be lost. To this the Federalists made an elaborate answer, and supported their reasoning by the published opinion of eight of the most distinguished lawyers then practising in New York city.

The votes, after being received by the Secretary of State, were to be canvassed by a joint committee of six members of the Senate and six members of the Assembly. As some were Federalists and some Republicans, they very naturally differed as to receiving and canvassing the votes of Otsego and Tioga, and, after many stormy sessions, agreed to refer the whole matter to a commission consisting of the United States senators from New York, Rufus King and Aaron Burr.

Colonel Burr, knowing that the Clintonians had a majority of the canvassing board, proposed to give no opinion. But when King declared that he should advise the canvassers to count the votes of Tioga and Otsego, Burr immediately advised them not to do so. Thus left to themselves, the majority rejected the returns from the two counties as irregular, and declared Clinton Governor.

A storm of indignation swept over the State. The Federalists, in their fury, held public meetings, denounced the Governor as a usurper, declared the board of canvassers was corrupt, and described the policy of the Republicans as Machiavellian. But when the next election gave them the House and Senate, they showed very quickly that they too could be Machiavellian when it was expedient. By the Constitution of New York as it then was, every office not expressly elective was filled by appointments made by a board of five men, known as the Council of Appointment. These five men were the Governor and four senators chosen by the Assembly, one from each group of six senators from the four senatorial districts into which New York was divided. As the elective offices were confined to the Governor, the Lieutenant-Governor, State Treasurer, members of the Legislature, and congressmen, the list of appointments was a long one, and included the Secretary of State, the comptroller, the judges, the Attorney-General, the clerks of the courts, the sheriffs of the counties, the coroners, the mayors of the cities, the county court judges, and the justices of the peace. In making these appointments the Governor had merely the casting vote; but as the law said he must "with the advice and consent of the said Council appoint all the said officers," the Governor had always held that he alone could nominate. While the Governor and the Council were of the same political stripe, this claim was freely allowed. But in 1794 the revolt against Clinton made the Council a Federalist body, which naturally declined to put into office Republicans named by the Governor, and for the first time in its history the members asserted an equal right to nominate. Clinton protested, and the matter was dropped, to come up again during the administration of John Jay. In 1795, while Mr. Jay was in London, where he had just concluded the treaty that still bears his name, he was triumphantly elected Governor, without his consent and almost without his knowledge, and was re-elected in 1798. But the Federalist success of this latter year was followed by the sweeping Democratic victory of 1800, and in 1801 Jay found himself in a condition similar to that of Clinton in 1794: a majority of his Council of Appointment were Democratic.

This was no trifling matter, for in February, 1801, the civil commissions of the office-holders in eleven counties and of the mayors of four cities expired, and it may well be believed that the workers in the victorious party became clamorous for their rewards.

The Assembly having elected the Council, the Governor convened it in February to fill the vacancies, and, according to custom, asserted his sole right to nominate. But at the board sat De Witt Clinton, and, led on by him, the Republicans rejected in rapid succession eleven of the Governor's nominations, refused to vote on several more, and then began to make nominations of their own. This was too much for Jay, who adjourned the Council, and, as it could not meet unless summoned by him, the places went unfilled. Jay then appealed to the Legislature, which called a convention, that amended the Constitution and gave to each member a right to nominate. Thus was the spoils system introduced into New York, and from that day a change in the political complexion of the Council of Appointment was sure to be followed by a proscription of office-holders.

But it is to Massachusetts that we owe the introduction of the most infamous piece of party machinery this century has produced. In 1812 the Jeffersonian Republicans of that State elected not only a Governor and a majority of the House, but, after years of persistent effort, secured control of the Senate. By the Constitution of Massachusetts it was decreed that the Senate should consist of forty men, chosen annually from such districts as the General Court should mark out, and that until such districts were created the senators should be chosen from the counties. But the General Court had never used this power, and the temporary provision that each county should be a senatorial district became in time an established usage, with all the force of law. This usage, however, the Republicans now laid violent hands on, rearranged the districts without regard to county lines, overcame Federalist strongholds by connecting them to Republican strongholds, cut Worcester County in two, joined Bristol and Norfolk, attached some of the towns of Suffolk to those of Essex, and in the next General Court had twenty-nine senators out of forty.

The story is told that a map of the Essex senatorial district was hanging on the office wall of the editor of the Columbian Centinel when the artist Stuart entered.

Struck by the peculiar outline of the towns forming the district, he added a head, wings, and claws with his pencil, and, turning to the editor, said: "There, that will do for a salamander." "Better say a Gerrymander," returned the editor, alluding to Elbridge Gerry, the Republican Governor who had signed the districting act. However this may be, it is certain that the name "gerrymander" was first applied to the odious law in the columns of the Centinel, that it came rapidly into use, and has remained in our political nomenclature ever since. Indeed, a huge cut of the monster was prepared, and the next year was scattered as a broadside over the Commonwealth, and so aroused the people that in the spring of 1813, despite the gerrymander, the Federalists recovered control of the Senate and repealed the law; but not before the progeny of the monster had sprung up in New Jersey.

At the October elections in 1812 the Federalists, with the aid of the peace party, elected a majority of both branches of the Legislature. This success was quite unexpected, and, greatly elated over their victory, they proceeded to gather its fruits when the Legislature met a few weeks later. As the law then stood, it would become the duty of the people of New Jersey, early in November, to choose eight presidential electors by a general ticket, a manner of election which would surely end in a Republican triumph, for the party majority on a State vote was twenty-five hundred. But the Federalists were determined that their opponents should not triumph, and six days before the election was to take place they repealed the old law, deprived the people of a vote, gave the choice of presidential electors to the

Legislature, and, when the time came, chose eight Federalist electors.

Their next act was to gerrymander the congressional districts. The custom so familiar to us—the custom of having in each State as many districts as the State has members of the House of Representatives—was not then in general use, and the six representatives from New Jersey were elected by a general ticket. Here again the Republican majority in the State insured a Republican delegation; but it was overcome on the eve of election by a bill which established three congressional districts, with boundaries so carefully marked out that four of the six representatives were secured by the Federalists.

In New York the district system had long been in use. But the apportionment of representation, under the census of 1810, made a redistricting act necessary, and the Republicans gladly seized the opportunity to apply the gerrymander. Two wards of New York city were joined to Long Island. The towns of Red Hook, Rhinebeck, and Clinton were taken out of Dutchess County and attached to the county of Columbia, and a number of long, rambling, irregular districts were laid out.

The bad example set by Massachusetts, New York, and New Jersey was soon imitated by Maryland. The opportunities for the use of the gerrymander were very limited, for the House of Delegates was composed of four men from each county and two from Annapolis and Baltimore, while the Senate was elected, not by the people, but by a body of electors chosen in each county for that particular purpose. Presidential electors, however, were chosen in districts, and to these, in order to get a Republican elector, the gerrymander was most shamefully applied. Montgomery County, which lay on the Potomac River and touched the District of Columbia, was cut in twain, and the piece which was strongly Federalist was joined to the city of Baltimore, which was strongly Republican, by a long and narrow strip of territory running the whole length of the county of Anne Arundel.

We have said that Maryland could not then have been gerrymandered for the purpose of securing State senators; but the Federalists now proved that they might be elected by a judicious planting of colonies. Once in every five years the voters of each county met and elected two men to be electors of the Senate. The inhabitants of Baltimore and Annapolis chose one for each city. The men so selected then assembled and proceeded to elect by ballot, either from their own body or from the people at large, fifteen senators. Now, it so happened that in 1816 the Federalists needed but one elector in order to control the College, and so secure a Federalist State Senate. As Annapolis sent one elector, and was Republican by about thirty majority, they decided to colonize the city, and for this purpose, during the last days of February and the first weeks of March, 1816, they hurried in bands of laborers and mechanics till forty men in all had arrived and put up at the lodging-houses and the tavern. The new-comers said they were in search of work. But when it was observed that, although no work was to be had, they still lingered, paying their bills and showing little concern that none were busy, the party leaders of the Republicans began to suspect that it was politics, and not work, that had caused this singular migration, and soon unearthed the plot. Indeed, they proved that the pretended laborers were hired, for twenty dollars a month and their board, to go to Annapolis, acquire residence, and vote the Federalist ticket. Such an outburst of indignation followed this discovery that the men were discharged and the attempt was abandoned.

In New York, meantime, the Republicans had stolen the Assembly. There were, in 1815, one hundred and twenty-six members of the Assembly; but so close had the election been that each party secured sixty-three. Before the meeting of the Assembly one Republican died, another went abroad for his health, and as one Federalist was too sick to attend, the numbers of the two parties became, Federalist sixty-two, Republicans sixty-one. It happened, however, that Mr. Henry Fellows, a Federalist of Ontario County who had received seven votes more than Mr. Allen, had been refused a certificate of election by the county clerk, because in the town of Pennington forty-nine ballots were cast for "Hen. Fellows" when they should have been cast for "Henry Fellows." This gave the Republicans a majority of one, and they openly declared that, when the Assembly met, they would elect a Speaker and Council of Appointment and secure the patronage of the State, an announcement which so incensed the Federalists that on the first day of the session they refused to attend, stayed out in a body, and prevented a quorum. On the second day, fearing their constituents would not approve such conduct, all were present; but, despite every effort and argument they could make, the certificate of Allen was recognized and a Republican Speaker and clerk were elected. It was then moved to expel Mr. Allen instanter. But the Republicans defeated the motion, and, with the aid of Mr. Allen's vote and the casting vote of the Speaker, chose a Republican Council of Appointment. Having thus secured the patronage of the State, they consented to examine into Mr. Allen's right to a seat, and in time, by a unanimous vote, unseated him and gave his place to Mr. Fellows. The Federalist members of the Assembly now addressed the voters and called on them to drive from power the party which had been guilty of so gross a fraud. The voters, unhappily, were as depraved as their representatives, and in 1816 the Republicans carried the Assembly by a large majority.

THE RIOTOUS CAREER OF THE KNOW-NOTHINGS.

IT is much to be regretted that no student of our history has yet seen fit to place before his countrymen as truthful and impartial a biography of political parties in the United States as it is possible for an honest man to write. To suppose that such a narrative would be dry and tedious is a mistake, for it would be the story of a great people made up of men from every civilized race and land, experimenting in self-government on a stupendous scale, and dealing with moral, social, financial, and industrial issues of the gravest importance. But the most readable part would be the account of the innumerable third parties : of the conditions of national life from which they sprang ; of the high aims, or selfish purposes, or impracticable ends they sought to accomplish ; of their triumphs ; or, as has so often been the case, their quiet and ignominious disappearance. They have been the expressive features of our political life, and have reflected every gust of passion, every unreasonable prejudice, every ennobling purpose, every patriotic sentiment that has appealed strongly to the people. Sometimes the membership has been confined to a single section of our country, as was that of the Anti-Masonic party, which never spread beyond the

New England belt of westward emigration. Sometimes they have had followers everywhere, as the Greenback party and the Populists of our own day. Sometimes their purpose has been accomplished, as was that of the Liberty party, the Free Soilers, and the Abolitionists. Sometimes their purposes, while never accomplished, have never been abandoned, and they have periodically appeared before the country seeking support. Such a one is that party which under many names and at many times has come forward as the defender of American institutions when endangered by the presence of foreigners.

It is safe to say that this dread of the naturalized citizen has never been wholly absent from our political life, and that its outbreaks have always followed periods remarkable for the great numbers of new-comers to our shores. The Irish risings, the French Revolution, the massacre in San Domingo and the establishment of the Negro Republic, drove to this country, during the last decade of the eighteenth century, thousands upon thousands of Frenchmen and Irishmen, who, availing themselves of the liberal naturalization laws, became citizens, and entered political life in the land of their adoption. Those were the days when the franchise was most restricted: when property qualifications and religious qualifications were required of every man who cast a vote or held an office; when an elector must have a freehold estate or a specified amount of yearly income, or pay a certain annual rent; and when no one could be a governor, or a judge, or a member of the Legislature who was not a Christian or a member of a particular Protestant sect, and who did not believe in the Trinity, or the divine inspiration of the Testaments, and a future state of reward and punishment. Yet, in spite of these limitations, the sudden appearance in large numbers of naturalized citizens to whom the past history and traditions of the country were as nothing, and who eagerly supported the party bent on overthrowing the Federalists, aroused serious alarm for the safety of American institutions. Then for the first time fear was expressed that the founders of the Republic had been too liberal; that it was not safe to invest the new citizen so early in his career with all the rights of the native; and in 1798 the term of residence prior to naturalization was changed to fourteen years.

The Republicans, who secured control of affairs in 1801, repealed this law and reduced the term to five years, and a whole generation passed away without any further signs of hostility to the foreigner.

Yet this same party, which courted and invited the man from abroad, was no friend to the institutions he was supposed to leave behind him, and again and again broke out into open hostility to them. It attempted to drive the common law of England from the courts; in three States it succeeded in forbidding any case, any decision, any law-book decided or made or written in England since the Revolution, to be cited or read in court; it expelled the mace from the House of Representatives of Pennsylvania because it was a symbol of monarchy; and it sent out to the States an amendment to the Federal Constitution which forbade a citizen of the United States to receive any title of nobility or honor, or accept any gift or office from an emperor, king, prince, or foreign power, under penalty of loss of citizenship. Had one more State approved the proposed amendment, it would have become law. Indeed, many persons thought it was law, and in school-books published as late as 1860 it may be seen at the end of the Constitution as Article Thirteen of the Amendments.

Fortunately the period during which this feeling was strongest was that during which immigration was smallest. But with the end of the Napoleonic wars the tide again set strongly toward America; foreigners came to us at the rate of twenty thousand a year; and with their appearance the old spirit of Native Americanism revived —a spirit which many new causes tended to intensify and embitter. Since the days of Washington and Adams the franchise had been greatly extended; religious qualifications had been removed; property qualifications had been abolished or reduced; the number of elective officers had been increased; the free-school system had been established; and the power of the naturalized citizens greatly enlarged, for they settled almost entirely in the cities, where they formed a class by themselves. Though naturalized, they were not Americanized. Our history, our principles, our welfare concerned them not. The Declaration of Independence, the Fourth of July, Bunker Hill, Evacuation Day, the Constitution—were events and days and instruments of which they knew nothing, and for which they cared nothing. They celebrated their own days, spoke their own language, cast a united vote in behalf of whichever party would buy it at the highest price; and—what was far more offensive —were all members of the Roman Catholic Church, which was looked on as a foreign institution.

The Episcopal Church in America had no connection with the Established Church of England. The Methodists, the Baptists, the Presbyterians looked up to no church-head resident beyond the sea. But every

Roman Catholic—layman, priest, or bishop—was a member of a great church hierarchy whose ruler was a foreign prince claiming and exercising both spiritual and temporal jurisdiction. That a people who could not abide the common law of England, and had all but forbidden an American citizen to receive even a title of honor at the hands of a foreign ruler, should look with alarm on the rapid increase in the number of aliens strongly attached by birth, by language, and by religion to monarchical institutions, is not surprising. In their eyes this sudden and steady inflow of Catholics was not the work of hard times, but of a deliberate and well-planned purpose on the part of the Catholic powers to destroy the free institutions of America.

Many well-known events encouraged and strengthened this belief. The rise of the Holy Alliance; the hostility which it showed toward Republican institutions; the eagerness with which it stamped out popular movements in Naples in 1820 and in Spain in 1823; the desire of the Catholic powers to reduce the revolted provinces of Spain on this continent; and especially the recent formation of the St. Leopold Foundation in Austria, and the revival of the Order of the Jesuits, were all cited as indisputable evidence of the hatred felt by foreign governments—and by foreign Roman Catholic governments in particular—for the principles of freedom and the rights of man. Did any one inquire the cause of this hostility, he was instantly referred to the lectures delivered in 1828 by Frederick Schlegel, a devout Roman Catholic, the profoundest of German scholars, the friend and adviser of Metternich, and Counsellor of Legation in the Austrian Cabinet. In the course of his lectures Schlegel labored to prove that Protestantism favored democracy, while Popery supported monarchy; that the political revolutions to which European governments had so long been subject were the natural results of the Reformation; that the great nursery of these destructive principles—the revolutionary school for France, and Spain, and all of Europe—was North America; and left his hearers to draw the conclusion that democracy should be destroyed in America by establishing Catholic missions. When, therefore, at the conclusion of his lectures, the St. Leopold Foundation was organized in Austria and spread to Hungary, Italy, Piedmont, Savoy, and France, the charge was openly made that its purpose was to build up the power of Rome in the United States by encouraging the emigration of Roman Catholics from Europe, and by establishing missions in the various States.

To this, color was given by the appearance of Roman Catholic orders, churches, and institutions in places where within the memory of men then living all such things had been proscribed. Bishops, cathedrals, sisters of charity, sisters of mercy, convents, nunneries, colleges, schools, orphan asylums, and newspapers devoted to the Church of Rome, were now to be seen in every great city which had been the recipient of foreign emigration. By such arguments, supported by visible signs of the presence of a Church whose head was crowned and owed no allegiance to the United States, the Native-American spirit, which by 1830 was rising high against foreigners, became at the outset closely allied with an anti-Catholic feeling, and the two have never parted company.

The decade covered by the 'thirties is unique in our history. Fifty years of life at high pressure had brought the people to a state of excitement, of lawlessness, of mob rule, such as had never before existed. Intolerance, turbulence, riot, became the order of the day. Differences of opinion ceased to be respected. Appeals were made not to reason but to force; reforms, ideas, institutions that were not liked were attacked and put down by violence; and one of the least liked and first to be assaulted was the Church of Rome. In 1831 St. Mary's Church in Sheriff Street, New York, was robbed and burned by incendiaries. In 1833 Miss Rebecca Reed fled from the Ursuline Convent at Charlestown, Mass., and told such tales that when, in 1834, Sister Mary John escaped from the same institution in a dazed and hysterical condition, the people rose and gave the convent to the flames.

With these deeds of violence the anti-Catholic excitement seemed to go down. But that hostility to foreigners which went hand in hand with it grew stronger and spread wider year after year. The stream of immigrants that entered New York city every twelvemonth would now seem small indeed, but it was then thought to be portentous. From thirty thousand in 1830 the number grew steadily till it passed sixty thousand in 1836. In the decade between 1830 and 1840 more than five hundred thousand were landed at New York alone, a number often greatly surpassed in our times by the arrivals in one year. But when it was asserted that one white person in every twenty of the population was of foreign birth, then these arrivals began to assume an alarming significance.

Hurrying westward, the new-comers moved into the Mississippi Valley and startled the men of the new States by the appearance of a population that could neither read, write, nor speak our language. In Cincinnati, by 1840, half the voters were of foreign birth. Twenty-eight per cent. were Germans, sixteen per cent. were English, and one per cent. French or Italian. In Dubuque County, Iowa, the natives of one foreign nation cast one third of all the votes given at local elections. In St. Louis and in New Orleans the influence of foreigners was felt still more, and from the men of the West now came the cry that they were being swamped by the dregs of Europe; that their institutions, their liberties, their property were at the mercy of voters steeped in the ignorance, the prejudices, the vices of the Old World. A demand was now made for a reform in the naturalization laws and the extension of the term of residence to twenty-one years. But both Whigs and Democrats, in their platforms and in the political tracts, indorsed the cause of the immigrant, and the question became, Shall a new party be founded or the old parties reformed? Here and there, as at Germantown in 1837, at New York city, and in the District of Columbia, even during the campaign of 1840, symptoms of a new party movement were visible. But it was not until 1841 that the people of Louisiana called a State Convention and founded the American Republican party, or, as it soon came to be called, the Native-American party. From that Convention issued an address urging national organization for the protection of American principles and the exclusion of foreigners from office—a piece of advice which found ready listeners, and at the next election in New Orleans a large part of the municipal ticket was carried by the American Republicans. At St. Louis, at Lexington, at Philadelphia, and at New York the interest in the movement grew daily, and was once more joined with anti-Catholicism. The principles of the new party were:

1. Extend the term of naturalization to twenty-one years.
2. Nominate no man to office who is not a native born.
3. Guard from corruption and abuse the proceedings necessary to obtain papers of naturalization.
4. Prevent the union of church and state.
5. Keep the Bible in the schools.
6. Resist the encroachment of a foreign civil and spiritual power upon the institutions of our country.

For the spread of these sentiments the naturalized citizens—the "patented citizens" as they now were called—were in large part responsible. No opportunity that could serve to remind the native of the presence of the unassimilated foreigner was suffered to go by unused. Laborers combined to force contractors to employ no Americans. Old-World vendettas were fought out in our streets, and Americans for the first time became familiar with such terms as "Orangemen," "Ribbonmen," "Corkonians," "Fardowns," and with such airs as "Croppies, Lie Down!" and "Boyne Water." Then were seen the harp of Ireland and the thistle of Scotland glittering on the uniforms of troops enrolled by law among the citizen soldiery of the United States. Then were made those two demands of the Catholics for a share in the school funds, and for the exclusion of King James's Bible from the public schools. Then were seen at the polls "No Catholic Irish Ticket!" and on the fences handbills headed "Irishmen! To your Posts!" "Catholics! Vote for Mr. Lott!" "Irishmen and all Catholic Voters!" or, in one instance, the cross, and under it the words "In union is our strength!"

In a community excited by reminders such as these, and by the foolish and intemperate appeals and abusive charges made by the press of both parties, some local incident was all that was needed to bring about the instant union of the natives, and this incident was furnished by the political leaders in New York. For years past the elections in that city had been closely contested by the Whigs and Democrats; and when, with the aid of the Irish vote, the Democrats won in 1843 and gave a large proportion of the patronage to citizens of foreign birth, both Whigs and Democrats bolted their party, joined with the feeble American Republicans, and in April, 1844, chose a native mayor and board of aldermen. Meantime the excitement in New York spread to New Jersey and to Philadelphia, where the efforts to organize a party produced the dreadful riots of May and July, during which many lives were lost and many churches and buildings burned—deeds which nothing but the coolness of the leaders prevented from being repeated in New York. In both cities the success of the Americans was due to a determination on the part of earnest and patriotic Democrats to punish their party. The punishment inflicted, they went back to their allegiance, elected a Democratic mayor of New York in 1845, and, after enabling the Americans to send six representatives to the Twenty-ninth Congress, so weakened the party by their desertion before 1846 that but one American Republican sat in the Thirtieth Congress, and he came from Pennsylvania. In 1847 such districts as still maintained an organization went through the form of sending delegates to a national convention which met at Pittsburg in February, and, after nominating a Vice-President, recommended Zachary Taylor for President. The campaign which followed served but to exhibit their weakness, and in the Thirty-first Congress not one American Republican found a seat.

For the moment the excitement seemed over. The great issues raised by the Mexican War; the attempt to extend slavery into the Territories; the split which the Wilmot Proviso produced in both the Whig and Democratic parties; the discovery of gold, and the rush to California; the Free-Soil movement, and the intense excitement which went before and followed the Compromise of 1850—dwarfed all other issues. The result of that Compromise and the deaths of Clay and Webster in 1852, and the crushing defeat of Scott at the polls, laid the Whigs prostrate; and in their efforts to reorganize they called in the aid of what was left of the American Republicans, to whom a new series of events had given renewed life.

The political disturbances in Europe from 1848 to 1850, and the discovery of gold in California, once more turned the stream of emigration westward and poured such a volume of foreigners into the Eastern cities as had never been known. Almost as many now came in three years as had ever at any previous time arrived in ten years. From 1840 to 1850 the sum total of arrivals was one million five hundred thousand. But in 1851, six hundred thousand; in 1852, three hundred and eighty thousand; and in 1853, three hundred and seventy thousand foreigners entered the United States. The old feeling of dread revived, and the natives once more joined the anti-Catholic party and some time, and somewhere in New York city, in 1852 founded a secret oath-bound association which spread over the country like wildfire.

The state of affairs was ripe for such a growth. In the first place, the fugitive-slave law, and the man-hunting, mobbing, and rioting it produced, had destroyed the Whig and badly injured the Democratic organizations, and had released thousands of voters from all allegiance to party. In the next place, the anti-Catholic feeling had never been suffered to subside. The "awful disclosures" in 1845 concerning the imprisonment of Edward Wilson in a religious institution at Cincinnati; the founding of a "No-Popery" newspaper named The North American Protestant in 1846; the so-called disclosures and lectures on auricular confession by Giustiniani—did their work so thoroughly that from 1846 to 1852 many an aspirant for office was called on to purge himself of the accusation of hostility to Catholics. The charges made by the Democrats against Scott in 1852, that he had been an American Republican in 1841; that in 1840 he had taken part in the attempt made at the Astor House in New York to found a Native-American party; and that neither in 1844 nor in 1848 had he been a friend of Catholics—were among the most serious that his supporters had to answer, were the subject of elaborate pamphlets, and cost him the vote of many a Whig State. No task was found harder by the Democrats than to explain why New Hampshire, the native State of Pierce, would not amend her Constitution and admit Catholics to office.

In the next place, the arrival of Father Gavazzi, an apostate Barnabite monk, marked the beginning of a new anti-papal crusade. He described the priests as given to every form of low debauchery; he declared that sisters of charity were prostitutes the world over, and declared that parents who sent their daughters to a convent sent them to a brothel. Under his influence street preaching was revived, and by 1854 there was no city of any importance but had an anti-popery preacher holding forth from curbstones and barrel-tops. That those denounced should turn upon the traducer was no more than human, and a new era of mob violence opened —in Boston, in New York, in Pittsburg, in Cincinnati, in Louisville, in Baltimore—directly due to the anti-popery preachers.

That nothing might be wanting to increase the excitement, the Papal Nuncio, Mgr. Gaetano Bedini, landed at New York in the autumn of 1853 and gave a new opportunity to Gavazzi to stir up hatred and strife. The apostate priest, putting himself at the head of the movement against Bedini, travelled the country over, making charges no rational man ever for a moment believed, and which were soon proved to be utterly false. But the people were in no frame of mind to be reasoned with; the priest was believed, and the Nuncio was insulted, abused, mobbed, burned in effigy, and threatened with assassination. As he travelled westward the excitement grew more and more intense, and, when Cincinnati was reached, became so great that the militia were called out to keep order. A howling mob two thousand strong paraded the streets, carrying transparencies inscribed "No Priests! No Kings! No Popery!" "Down with Bedini!" and when, as they drew near the home of the Archbishop, the police attempted to interfere, a running fight began.

To the northward and eastward the agitation was carried on by a street preacher who called himself the "Angel Gabriel." He began his career in the streets of Boston, holding forth against popes, priests, nuns, and Catholics generally, and so excited a crowd that heard him one night in May, 1854, that it attacked the Irish settlement at Chelsea and the Bellingham Catholic Church, and set an example that was followed wherever he went. In June the Catholic church at Coburg was burned; on July third an armed mob attacked the Irish quarter of Manchester, N. H., and expelled a peaceful population. On July fourth the Catholic church at Dorchester was blown up by gunpowder, and on the fifth the "Angel Gabriel," by preaching, caused the sacking and destruction of the Catholic church at Bath. But the list is too long to complete. It is enough to know that such was the state of the public mind when "The Supreme Order of the Star-Spangled Banner" began its invisible, resistless, mysterious career. It was a network of local secret associations or councils, whose members were bound together by secret oaths, and recognized one another by signs, grips, and passwords. The councils of each State were arranged in four degrees, and over these degrees presided a Grand Council of the United States of North America, with its President, its Vice-President, Secretaries, Inside Sentinel, Outside Sentinel, and Chaplain. Every member of a council was required to be twenty-one years old, to believe in the existence of a God, and to obey without question the will of the Order. Highly organized, thoroughly in earnest, it did its work with a precision of movement and a concert of action hitherto unknown in American politics. Its nominations were made by secret conventions of delegates from the various lodges in the city or the district the candidate was to represent; they were generally of the best men irrespective of party, and were voted for by the members of the

Order under penalty of expulsion. No public indorsement was ever made; but the result, when viewed the day after the election, left no doubt that a powerful secret body of voters was at work defeating the schemes and setting at naught the calculations of the politicians.

To the old party leaders the situation was embarrassing, and became most serious when in 1854 the Kansas-Nebraska bill split the Northern Whigs and sent those who opposed, not slavery, but slavery in the Territories (and who could not therefore join either the Democrats or Republicans), into the ranks of the new and secretly working party. The charm of mystery brought others, and in 1854 the accession of voters was believed to be five thousand a week. With them went in that element which was at once the strength and the weakness of the party; for hundreds of thousands of the new-comers had no sympathy with the movement against the Catholics, and, after contributing to success at many an election, split off and formed a wing derided as the "Mountain Sweets."

At first all was harmony, and in 1854 the new Native-American party carried the elections in Massachusetts and Delaware, and in New York State secured some congressmen and polled 122,282 votes. By this time the party had thrown off much of its secrecy. The name of the Order had been discovered. Its secret alphabet was known. It did not hesitate to indorse men and to put forth candidates of its own. The meeting places of its councils were no longer concealed, and it had received from its opponents the popular name of Know-Nothings. It is said that the true name and purpose of the Order were known to none save those who reached the highest degree; and that, as members of the lower degrees, when questioned about their party, always answered, "I don't know," the nickname "Know-Nothings" was given it, and at once accepted. But its avowed purposes were well known, and in the Know-Nothing almanacs of 1855 were declared to be—

anti-Romanism, anti-Bedinism, anti-Papistalism, anti-Nunneryism, anti-Winking-Virginism, anti-Jesuitism. Know-Nothingism is for light, liberty, education, and absolute freedom of conscience, with a strong dash of devotion to one's native soil.

As described in more sober and responsible publications, the Know-Nothing was a man who opposed not Romanism, but political Romanism; who insisted that all church property of every sect should be taxed; and that no foreigner under any name—bishop, pastor, rector, priest—appointed by any foreign ecclesiastical authority, should have control of any property, church, or school in the United States; who demanded that no foreigner should hold office; that there should be a common-school system on strictly American principles; that no citizen of foreign birth should ever enjoy all the rights of those who were native-born; and that even children of foreigners born on the soil should not have full rights unless trained and educated in the common schools.

These were the principles which appealed to the South. That great section of our country was almost without a foreign-born population, was full of nativist feeling in its best form, and when, in 1854, the Whig party was wrecked by the Kansas-Nebraska bill, the remnant of it in the South turned willingly to its Native Americans. So strengthened, the new party in the elections of 1855 secured the Land Commissioner of Texas, the Legislature and Comptroller of Maryland, and all but carried the States of Virginia, Georgia, Alabama, Mississippi, Louisiana, and Texas. In the North the triumph was complete, and the governors and legislatures of New Hampshire, Massachusetts, Rhode Island, Connecticut, New York, California, and Kentucky were Know-Nothings. That this victory in the North was largely due to a great uprising against Catholicism is beyond dispute. The demand for a part of the school funds for the purpose of supporting Catholic schools; the vast accumulation of property by the Church, and the peculiar manner of holding it; the ease with which church legislation was secured; and the long controversy between Senator Brooks, of New York and "John, Archbishop of the Province of New York," went far to arouse even the cool-minded. "Who gave John Hughes this title?" it was asked; "Who was it that had so kindly marked out the 'Province of New York'?"—who but the Pope and "King of the States of the Church"? and "Is not this just the course to make America another State of the Church?" As the time was one of intense political excitement over Kansas, over slavery, over the fugitive-slave law, over the attempt to secure Cuba, the elections were attended by Know-Nothing riots, in which life and property were destroyed. But it was an age of riot, and what was then done to Catholics and their churches was no more than many a Catholic had been doing for years past to Abolitionists and Free-Soilers, or than foreign-born citizens have in our day done to Chinamen.

The success at the elections in 1855 encouraged the Grand Council to prepare the Order to enter the presidential campaign of 1856 as a national party. A secret meeting was accordingly held at Philadelphia in February, and there the first and only native platform of the Know-Nothings was adopted. Horace Greeley had described them as possessing about "as many elements of persistence as an anti-cholera or anti-potato-rot party would have," and the proceedings of that one Convention proved that his description was correct. Into it had by this time been drawn men of every shade of opinion on every question of the day, and to frame such a platform as would satisfy these was hopeless. As presented by the Grand Council and adopted by the Convention, the platform declared the following principles:

3. Americans must rule America; and to this end native-born citizens should be selected for all State, Federal, and municipal offices of Government employment in preference to all others.

5. No person should be selected for political station who recognizes any allegiance or obligation of any description to any foreign prince, potentate, or power.

6. The unqualified recognition and maintenance of the reserved rights of the several States . . . and to this end the non-interference by Congress with questions appertaining solely to the individual States.

7. The recognition of the right of native-born and naturalized citizens of the United States, permanently residing in any Territory thereof, to frame their constitution and laws.

9. A change in the laws of naturalization, making a continued residence of twenty-one years an indispensable requisite for citizenship.

10. Opposition to any union between church and state; no interference with religious faith or worship; and no test-oath for office.

12. The maintenance and enforcement of laws constitutionally enacted until said laws shall be repealed or declared null and void by judicial authority.

The third, seventh, and ninth planks were put in to please the old-time Native-Americans; the fifth and tenth were for the anti-Catholics; the sixth and twelfth, which related to the enforcement of the fugitive-slave law, were to satisfy the South; the seventh, and a hearty condemnation of the President and the Kansas Bill, it was expected would win votes in the North. In reality it pleased no one, and after a short struggle fifty "North-American" delegates, from seven free States, quit the Convention, which then nominated Millard Fillmore and Andrew Jackson Donelson. The Whigs, a few months later, indorsed the nominees. But it was too late: a wave of Republicanism was sweeping eastward from the Northwest, and in November, 1856, swept Know-Nothingism out of the North. In a popular vote of 4,053,967, the American party cast but 874,534; of 296 electors it secured but eight, and sent but twenty representatives and five senators to Congress. In 1858 it suffered still more, and to the Congress which met in December, 1859, not one Native-American came from any State north of the Potomac and the Ohio save Maryland. There it was still an anti-Catholic party, and in Baltimore, drawing to itself all the ruffians, "plug-uglies," and "tigers," held the polls, and for three years gave such an exhibition of lawlessness as can be found in the history of no other city.

A lingering trace of the Know-Nothings is to be seen in the Constitutional party of 1860, and in those secret, oath-bound Ku-Klux-Klan and White-Cap organizations which have terrorized the South since reconstruction days. But it has been reserved for the present to witness a true revival of the American Protestant Association of 1840 in the American Protective Association of 1894, with the secret methods of the Know-Nothings thrown in. Never was the name "American" more misapplied. Such parties and such methods are wholly foreign. They belong to the days of the Inquisition, the Star Chamber, the Bastille, and the poisoned flower; not to the close of the nineteenth century in America.

THE FRAMERS AND THE FRAMING OF THE CONSTITUTION.

ON the eleventh of June, 1776, the Continental Congress, then sitting at Philadelphia, chose two committees to perform two pieces of important work. One was to draw a declaration of independence; the other was to frame articles of perpetual union. The Committee on the Declaration finished their work and gave it to the world on July fourth, 1776; the Committee on Articles of Confederation reported a plan four days later; but it was not till March first, 1781, that the articles were finally adopted.

The government that went into effect on that day was bad from beginning to end. There was no executive, no judiciary, and only the likeness of a legislature. Congress consisted of one House presided over by a president chosen each year by the delegates from among their number. The delegates could not be more than seven nor less than two from any State, were elected yearly, and could serve but three years in any term of six. On the floor of Congress all voting was done by States, and the assent of nine was necessary to declare war, to make peace, to coin money, to pass any ordinance of the least importance. To such trivial questions as came up from day to day—when should the House rise; who should be geographer for the next year ?—the assent of the majority of the States was enough, and it was a white day whereon six did not make a majority.

To this body the States had given a few powers, and had given them grudgingly as of necessity. Congress had power to declare war, make peace, issue bills of credit, keep up a navy and army, contract debts, enter into treaties of commerce and alliance, and settle disputes between the members of the confederation. But it could not enforce a treaty nor a law when made, nor impose any restriction on commerce, nor lay a tax of any kind for the purpose of raising a revenue. Bad as the articles were, they were made worse yet by the provision that to amend them required the consent of each one of the thirteen members of the Union.

The evils of this system were not slow to appear. Acting on States, and not on individuals, Congress never secured a hold on the people, was always looked on as a revolutionary body, and was treated, first with indifference, and then with contempt.

The large vote needed to pass a weighty measure often made it impossible to legislate at all. Two States, Georgia and Rhode Island, were seldom represented. Of the eleven others, more than eight were rarely present, and Congress was thus forced to adjourn again and again for want of a quorum. Repeatedly these adjournments covered a space of thirteen consecutive days. As nine of the eleven States had but two delegates each, the powers of Congress passed into the hands of three men, who, by their negative votes, could defeat any measure requiring the assent of nine.

Lacking power to enforce its acts, Congress made treaties which the States set at naught, called for money which the States never paid, and saw article after article of the confederation broken in the most defiant way. The States were forbidden to wage war and make treaties. Yet Georgia waged war and made a treaty with the Creeks. The States were forbidden to keep troops in time of peace. Yet Pennsylvania sent troops that drove the Connecticut settlers from the valley of Wyoming; Massachusetts raised an army and put down Shays's rebellion. The States were forbidden to enter into compacts. Yet Maryland and Virginia made a compact. Indeed, Congress itself was more than once driven to exercise powers to which, by the articles, it had no right whatever.

Having no power to manage trade, Congress could not, by commercial restrictions, force Great Britain to enter into a trade treaty. British goods came over in immense quantities, the balance of trade turned against us, and, to settle the balance, the coin of the country went over to England in boxes and barrels. The States, deprived of a circulating medium, put out paper money; with paper money came tender laws and force acts, and in Massachusetts open rebellion against the Commonwealth.

Many of these evils had long been felt. Indeed, the Articles of Confederation were not in force before it was proposed to amend them. The Hartford Convention of 1780 urged the States to suffer Congress to tax them according to population and spend the revenue so raised in paying the interest on the public debt. Congress accordingly asked for such an amendment, and twelve States consented. But Rhode Island would not, and it failed. Again a little while and Congress asked for specific duties and a permanent revenue, and again twelve States consented. But this time New York stood out, and the second proposed amendment was a failure. At last, made desperate, Congress asked for power to regulate trade for twenty-five years. Once more twelve States consented. Once more New York refused. Once more the attempt to amend the articles was a failure. Then, every other means having been tried, Congress approved the call already sent out for a Convention of the States at Philadelphia.

Such a Convention had twice been asked for. New York wanted one in 1782; Massachusetts was equally eager in 1785. But the origin of the Constitutional Convention of 1787 goes back to the action of a joint commission which sat at Mount Vernon in March, 1785. There were then no concerted regulations between Maryland and Virginia touching the jurisdiction and navigation of Chesapeake Bay and the Potomac River. Trouble had arisen in consequence, and the commission had been chosen to frame a compact that would serve as a remedy. But they had not been very long at work when they saw that common duties and common principles for explaining the meaning of commercial laws and settling disputes about the currency were just as necessary as well-defined rights on the river and bay. With these things, however, the commissioners had no right to meddle. Yet they ventured to draw up a supplementary report setting forth the need of legislation on the currency, the duties, and commerce in general, and urging the appointment each year of two commissioners to arrange such matters for the next year.

Maryland readily accepted the report, and asked Delaware and Pennsylvania to come into the scheme. But Virginia went further, and asked all the States to a trade Convention at Annapolis in September, 1786. New York and New Jersey, Pennsylvania, Delaware, and Virginia alone attended, spent two days in discussing the low state of trade and commerce, in lamenting their want of powers, and then called a new Convention, to meet at Philadelphia in May, 1787. This was the call that Congress approved in February, 1787; and it was high time, for seven States had already chosen delegates.

Virginia was first to act, and sent up her seven most noted citizens. Jefferson was then Minister to France; Patrick Henry and Richard Henry Lee would not serve; but in their places came George Washington and James Madison, Edmund Randolph, the Governor, George Mason, George Wythe, John Blair, and James McClurg, a professor in William and Mary College.

New Jersey came next, and on November twenty-third chose William Livingston, eleven times her Governor; William Paterson, ten times her Attorney-General; David Brearley, her Chief-Justice, and William Houston, her delegate to Congress. Houston fell sick, and Jonathan Dayton took his place. Scarce a month went by but the name of some State was added to the list. In December came Pennsylvania; in January came North Carolina; in February came Delaware, Massachusetts, and New York. South Carolina and Georgia came in April, and Connecticut in May. New Hampshire would gladly have acted promptly, but her treasury was empty, her delegates could not bear the cost of the journey themselves, and the Convention was half through its work when John Langdon and Nicholas Gilman appeared in her behalf. Rhode Island alone refused to attend.

The day chosen for the meeting of the Convention was the second Monday in May, which, in that year, fell on the fourteenth of the month. But so tardy were the delegates in setting out, and so great were the hindrances met on the way, that the twenty-fifth of May came before seven States were present in the State-House. This made a quorum. The Convention at once called Washington to the chair, chose William Jackson secretary, appointed a committee to prepare rules, and adjourned, to meet again on the twenty-eighth. Nine States then answered to their names. The doors were then closed, a solemn pledge of secrecy was laid on the members, and thenceforth for many years what took place in the Convention was never fully known.

The delegates thus bound to secrecy were assuredly a most remarkable body of men. Hardly one among them but had sat in some famous assembly, had signed some famous document, had filled some high place, or had made himself conspicuous for learning, for scholarship, or for signal services rendered in the cause of liberty. One had framed the Albany plan of union; some had been members of the Stamp-Act Congress of 1765; some had signed the Declaration of Rights in 1774; the names of others appear at the foot of the Declaration of Independence, and at the foot of the Articles of Confederation; two had been presidents of Congress; seven had been, or were then, governors of States; twenty-eight had been members of Congress; one had commanded the armies of the United States; another had been Superintendent of Finance; a third had repeatedly been sent on important missions to England and had long been Minister to France.

Nor were the future careers of many of them to be less interesting than their past. Washington and Madison became Presidents of the United States; Elbridge Gerry became Vice-President; Charles Cotesworth Pinckney and Rufus King became candidates for the presidency, and Jared Ingersoll, Rufus King, and John Langdon candidates for the vice-presidency; Hamilton became Secretary of the Treasury; Madison, Secretary of State; Randolph, Attorney-General and Secretary of State, and James McHenry, a Secretary of War; Ellsworth and Rutledge became Chief-Justices; Wilson and John Blair rose to the supreme bench; Gouverneur Morris, and Ellsworth, and Charles C. Pinckney, and Gerry, and William Davie became ministers abroad. Others less fortunate closed their careers in misery or in shame. Hamilton went down before the pistol of Aaron Burr; Robert Morris, after languishing in a debtor's prison, died in poverty; James Wilson died a broken-hearted fugitive from justice; Edmund Randolph left the Cabinet of Washington in disgrace; William Blount was driven from the Senate of the United States.

Blount sat for North Carolina, and with him were Alexander Martin, a soldier of the Revolution; Richard Dobbs Spaight, a native of Ireland; Hugh Williamson, and William Davie. South Carolina sent Pierce Butler, John Rutledge, and the two cousins, Charles and Charles Cotesworth Pinckney. Butler was an Irishman, was descended from the Dukes of Ormond, and, when the Revolution opened, was a major in the Twenty-ninth Regiment of Foot. The Twenty-ninth was one of the regiments stationed at Boston, and furnished the soldiers who did the shooting in the famous Boston massacre. Disgusted at the treatment of the colonists, and convinced that justice was on their side, he threw up his commission when the war opened, joined the Continental army, fought through the war, and then settled in South Carolina. Another man of Scotch-Irish ancestry was John Rutledge. He too had been educated abroad, had studied law at the Temple, and had been sent at the age of twenty-six to the Stamp-Act Congress of 1765. Nine years later he sat in the first Continental Congress, and was pronounced by Patrick Henry the most eloquent speaker in that body. Fearless, resolute, a man of fine parts, he was unquestionably the foremost man South Carolina produced till she produced Calhoun.

Georgia sent up William Houston, William Pierce, a Virginian, William Few, and Abraham Baldwin, a Connecticut man. The Connecticut delegation was, as a whole, the ablest on the floor. Save Benjamin Franklin, no man who came to the Convention had made for himself so instructive and so useful a career as Roger Sherman. He was a man of the people. Born near Boston, he got his education at the common school, and was early apprenticed to a shoemaker. His apprenticeship over, he set out on foot, with his tools on his back, for New Milford, in Connecticut. There he kept store and read law till he was admitted to the bar, when he moved to New Haven. At New Haven he rose rapidly in the estimation of his townsmen, was made treasurer of Yale College, represented the town in the Legislature, and when New Haven became a city, was chosen first Mayor, and remained Mayor for the rest of his life. He was fourteen times sent to the Legislature. He was twenty-three years a judge. Connecticut elected

FRAMING THE CONSTITUTION. 115

him to the Congress of 1774, and re-elected him repeatedly till he died. He signed the Declaration of Rights in 1774; the Declaration of Independence, which he was one of the committee to write; and the Articles of Confederation, which he helped to frame.

With him came William Samuel Johnson and Oliver Ellsworth. Johnson had been a judge and a member of Congress; but he enjoyed a distinction rarer still, for he was a scholar of high rank. Indeed, the fame of his learning reached England, where Oxford made him a Doctor of Laws, and the Royal Society a member.

Massachusetts sent up Caleb Strong, Nathaniel Gorham, a rich Boston merchant; Elbridge Gerry, a signer and a member of Congress; and Rufus King, a congressman and a fierce hater of slavery. Alexander Hamilton, John Lansing, and Robert Yates represented New York. Yates and Lansing were men of ability; but they held the narrow and selfish views then so prevalent in New York State, became mere obstructionists in the Convention, and when they could not succeed in setting up State-rights government, left the Convention and went home. The departure of Yates is much to be lamented, for, while he stayed, he was busy taking notes of the debates and proceedings. Five men came from Delaware—Gunning Bedford, Jr., Richard Bassett, Jacob Broome, George Read, who signed the Declaration, and John Dickinson, who would not. The largest delegation was that from Pennsylvania. On her list are the names of Jared Ingersoll, who led the bar and whose father had been driven from New England for trying to serve as Stamp agent in 1765; George Clymer, another signer; Thomas Fitz Simons, a great merchant; Robert and Gouverneur Morris; Thomas

Mifflin, a general of the Revolution, a member of Congress, and once a member of the infamous Conway Cabal; James Wilson, a Scotchman and the best-read lawyer in the Convention; and Benjamin Franklin. Maryland sent up Daniel of St. Thomas Jenifer, Daniel Carroll of Carrollton, John Mercer, Luther Martin, and James McHenry.

It is a sure sign of the high respect in which this famous body of men was held, that not one word was uttered by the people against their secret sessions. Profound secrecy, it was said, could not be kept by men who quarrelled. Secrecy was kept, and this meant that the delegates were of one mind on all Federal measures. Had the world, it was asked, ever beheld such a sight? When before had a people without strife and without bloodshed deputed a band of patriots, that would have adorned the best days of Greece and Rome, to cure the evils of its Government? That evils existed was lamentable; but they were unavoidable. The Confederacy was like a hut or a tent put up in time of war and fit for the needs of war. But peace was come, and it was now time to build a suitable and durable dwelling, with tight roof, substantial bolts, and strong bars, to shield the States from every kind of harm.

The simile of a house and a roof was a favorite, and was used again and again. The United States was like an old man and his wife who with thirteen sons landed in America. There they built a spacious dwelling and lived happily for several years. But the sons grew weary of the company of their parents, and each put up a cabin for himself near their old home. At once trouble began. One had implements of husbandry stolen; another lost a crop; a third had his sheep eaten by the wolves; a fourth nearly died of cold from the roof of his cabin being blown away; a fifth saw his flock swept off by floods. At last twelve of the brothers met on a plain and resolved to ask their father to take them back. He did so gladly, and the old house, mended and enlarged, was made more beautiful than ever. The thirteenth son stood out, and, after three years, hanged himself by his garters in the woods.

This son was Rhode Island. His flocks, in the language of the simile, were indeed being eaten by wolves. Wholly given over to the party of Shays, the party of legal-tender acts, of force acts, of paper money, the State had sent no delegates to Philadelphia and was not at any time represented in the Convention. This contempt for the wishes of the country was warmly resented. She was denounced as the cause of the failure of the impost. To her charge was laid the suffering of the soldiers in the Revolutionary War, the heavy taxes, the bankrupt treasury, the poverty of the whole nation. Let her, it was said, never again be suffered to defeat a Federal measure. Drop her from the Union. Turn her out from the company of States. Or, better still, apportion her to Massachusetts and Connecticut. Vermont would more than take her place. As the Fourth of July drew near, the Governor of New Jersey was said to have expressly ordered that no more than twelve cannon be fired, and no more than twelve toasts be drunk. At Trenton and a few places elsewhere this was done. The Convention, it was asserted, was determined that Rhode Island should be considered out of the Union. The government about to be set up would hold her responsible for a fair share of the Federal debt, and would first seek by gentle means to collect it. But, if these failed, the sum would be taken from her by force.

As to what this new and vigorous government would be, the people made all manner of guesses. Many plans, it was thought, had been talked of. One was said to keep the form but not the spirit of Democracy; another parted the States into three republics; another gave a strong executive power without even the semblance of a popular constitution. The Convention was accused by some of having a plan to set up a king. A constitution, the knowing ones asserted, had been made, titles, orders, and social distinctions established, and a commission would soon be sent to offer the crown to the Bishop of Osnaburgh, the second son of King George. This idle tale was more than half believed, and each post brought letters to the delegates begging to know if it were true. The answer invariably was, "While we cannot affirmatively tell you what we are doing, we can negatively tell you what we are not doing; we never once thought of a king."

For our knowledge of what they did think of doing we are indebted to the journals of the Convention, to the notes taken down by Yates and Madison, and to the "Genuine Information" of Luther Martin. From these sources it appears that the serious work of the Convention was opened by Randolph on the morning of Tuesday, the twenty-ninth of May. In a speech of great force he summed up the weak points of the Articles of Confederation, showed how unsuited they were to the needs of the country, and urged all present to join in setting up a strong national government. As a plan of such a government, he read fifteen resolutions which the Virginia delegate had framed while waiting for the Convention to assemble.

This, which came in time to be known as the Virginia plan, provided that there should be a national Executive, a national Legislature, a national Judiciary and Council of Revision; that the Executive should be chosen by the Legislature and be ineligible a second time; that the Legislature should consist of two branches, with power to coerce refractory States and veto all State laws contrary to the Articles of Union; that the people should choose the members of the first branch; that the first branch should choose the members of the second from men nominated by the Legislatures of the States; that the representation of each State should be proportioned to the inhabitants on its soil or to the share it bore of the national expenses; that the judiciary should be elected by the national Legislature; that the Executive and the judges should form a council to revise all laws before they went into force; that provisions should be made for admitting new States, for amending the Articles of Union, for assuring to each State a Republican form of government and a right to its soil.

The resolutions read and explained, Randolph moved a Committee of the Whole on the State of the Union, and to the committee the Virginia plan was sent. No sooner was this done than Charles Pinckney, of South Carolina, presented a second plan for a constitutional government. This too went to the committee, was never heard of again, and is now hopelessly lost.

Next day the Virginia plan came formally before the committee, and during two weeks was carefully debated. Each resolution was taken up. Some were amended, some were dropped, and others put in their stead. But the feeling of the delegates seemed to be that there should be an executive, legislative, and judicial branch of government; that the Legislature should consist of two Houses, and that the members of one should be elected by the people. When the number of the Executive and the way of choosing came up, there were almost as many opinions as States on the floor. Some wanted an Executive of three, one from each part of the country; some were for a single Executive with a council of revision; some for a single Executive without a council of revision. He was to be elected directly by the people. He was to be chosen by electors, or by State Legislatures; by the State Governors; by one branch of the national Legislature; by both branches on a joint ballot; by both branches on a concurrent vote; he was to be chosen by lot. For three days no other business was done. It was then determined that the Executive should be chosen as the national Legislature decided, should hold office seven years, and should not be re-elected.

This decision was reached on Monday, the fourth of June. The debates up to that time had been most amicable. But, before the week ended, the delegates began to wrangle, sectional spirit began to appear, and those lines which again and again divided the Convention before it rose became plainly visible. There were parties made up of individuals and parties made up of States. There were men who wished for a Federal government not much unlike that they were trying to better, and there were men who did not want a Confederacy at all. There were men eager to see a centralized government set up, and men insisting that State sovereignty should be carefully maintained. There were the Southern States against the Northern States, the commercial States against the agricultural States; and what proved far more serious still, there were the great States against the small.

Out of these party divisions came in time the three compromises of the Constitution. The fear in which the little States stood of the great secured the compromise giving representation to States. The hatred felt by the slave States for the free caused the second compromise, giving representation to slaves. The jealousy between States agricultural and States commercial brought about the third compromise, on the slave-trade and commerce.

The great States were Massachusetts, Pennsylvania, and Virginia; New York, New Jersey, and Delaware were the small. The great States were for a strong national government on the Virginia plan; the little States were for the old confederation mended and improved, and made their first firm stand on Saturday, the ninth of June. The second resolution of the Virginia plan, that suffrage in the national Legislature ought to be in proportion to wealth or free inhabitants, had been postponed, and this, on motion of Paterson, of New Jersey, was now taken up.

The Convention, he said, had no power to make a national government. Congress had assembled them to amend the Articles of Confederation. The articles were, therefore, the proper basis for all proceeding. Bad as they might be in some ways, they were excellent in others. They acknowledged the sovereignty of the States, treated them all alike, and gave to each the same vote and the same weight when assembled in

Congress. On no other plan could a confederacy of States be maintained. Representation as proposed, representation in proportion to wealth or numbers, looked fair in the face; but it was unfair and unjust at heart. Suppose it adopted, suppose the States to send delegates to the first branch according to the sums of money they paid to the Board of Treasury, and see what would happen. Virginia would have sixteen votes and Georgia one. Was this just? Was it safe? Did any one think New Jersey would risk her independence, her sovereignty, her well-being in a Congress in which she had but five votes while Virginia had sixteen? There was no more reason for giving a State paying a large quota more votes than a State paying a small quota than there was for giving a rich man more votes at the polls than a poor man. New Jersey would never confederate on such a plan. She would be swallowed up. She would rather submit to a despot than to such a fate.

The great States took a different view. It was true, they admitted, that each State was sovereign, and that all were therefore equal. It was also true that each man is naturally a sovereign over himself, and that therefore all men are naturally equal. But could he keep this sovereignty when he became a member of a civil government? He could not. Neither could a State keep her sovereignty when she became a member of a Federal government. All government came from the people. Equal numbers of people ought therefore to have an equal number of representatives, and different numbers of people a different number of representatives. The people, not the States, were to be represented. And did any one think that one hundred and fifty Pennsylvanians should have no more representation than fifty Jerseymen? Six States thought not, and voted that in the first branch representation should be according to some equitable ratio. An equitable ratio was next decided to be the rule by which, in April, 1783, Congress fixed the quotas of the States. This rule was that quotas should be laid according to the whole number of free white inhabitants of both sexes, of every age, occupation, and condition, and three fifths of all other persons save Indians not taxed.

The small States had lost the day. But they were not discouraged, and, led on by Connecticut, made a stout fight for an equal vote in the Senate. Again they were defeated, again population was made the basis of representation, and, this done, the committee hurried on to the consideration of the remaining resolutions of the Virginia plan. By the thirteenth of June they had all been passed; the committee had reported them to the House, and the House was about to name a day for considering the report, when Paterson rose and asked leave to bring in a totally different plan. Alarmed at the strong display of national feeling, the delegates from Connecticut and New Jersey, Delaware and New York, with Luther Martin, of Maryland, had framed a plan and chosen Paterson to lay it before the Convention; a plan which Hamilton well described as "pork still, with a little change of the sauce." Congress was to consist of a single House, with power to regulate trade and commerce, and raise a revenue by duties on imports, postage on letters and newspapers, and stamps on paper and vellum. There was to be an Executive of several persons not eligible to a second term, and removable by Congress at the request of a majority of the Governors of the States. There was to be a Supreme Court, uniform laws of naturalization, and, when necessary, requisitions on the States for money, according to the rule of April, 1783; officers were to be sworn to support the Constitution, and the Constitution and its laws and treaties were to be "the supreme law of the land."

This plan, it was said, had two great merits—it fully agreed with the powers of the Convention; it would be gladly accepted by the people. These were important; for the duty of the Convention was not to frame such a government as might be best in theory, but such as the people expected and would approve. If the confederation was really so bad, let the Convention say so, go home, and get power to make such a government as they wished. But to assume such power was not to be justified on any ground. If, as some held, the confederation had fallen to pieces, if no general Government really existed, then the States were once more independent sovereignties, and should stand on the footing of equal sovereignties. All then must agree or none could be bound. If the confederation did exist, then by the terms of the articles no change could be made without the consent of all. This was the nature of all treaties. What had been unanimously done must be unanimously undone. It was said that the great States consented to this equality, not because it was just, but because, at the time, it was expedient. Be it so. Could they, therefore, take back that assent? Could a donor resume his gift without the leave of the donee?

It was now the turn of the great States to make an attack, and they did so vigorously. Wilson drew a long comparison between the Virginia plan and the Jersey plan. By the Virginia plan there were to be three branches of government; by the Jersey plan but one. By the Virginia plan the people were to be represented; by the Jersey plan the States. By the one a majority of the people would rule; by the other a minority. The Virginia plan provided for a single Executive; the Jersey plan for an Executive of many. The Virginia plan provided for a negative on the laws of the States; the Jersey plan for the coercion of the States.

Madison demanded to know in what respect the Jersey plan was better than the old articles. It could not prevent violations of the laws of nations, nor of treaties, nor prevent encroachments on the Federal authority, nor trespasses of the States on each other, nor secure internal tranquillity, nor give good governments to the States, nor guard the Union from the influence of foreign powers. It could cure none of the evils that had long grown intolerable.

Hamilton, who liked neither of the plans, now read to the committee his own thoughts on the best form of Republican government. The supreme legislature, as he called it, was to consist of two branches—the Assembly and the Senate. Members of the Assembly were to be chosen by the people for three years. Members of the Senate were to be elected by electors chosen by the people and serve as long as they behaved well. The Executive was to be one man chosen by electors for good behavior. He was to have a veto on all laws about to be passed, was to conduct war when once begun, make treaties with the leave of the Senate, and appoint the heads of the departments of war, finance, and foreign affairs without consulting any one. There was to be a supreme judiciary, and in each State there were to be courts to try all matters of general concern. State laws contrary to the laws and Constitution of the United States were to be void. To prevent, if possible, such being passed, the general Government was to appoint the Governors of the States.

The committee had now before them the Virginia plan, the South Carolina plan, the New Jersey plan, and the thoughts of Hamilton on government, which he distinctly declared were thoughts, and nothing more. But they gave no heed to any schemes save those sent in by Virginia and New Jersey. The question, therefore, at once became which of the two should be reported. We must, said the State-rights party, report the Jersey plan. Our powers are limited, and this is the only plan that comes within them. Our powers, said the Virginia party, extend to everything or to nothing. We are free to support any plan and to reject any plan. The people are bowed down under intolerable burdens. They look up to this Convention with fond hopes, and expect from it a government that will cure the ills of which they complain. A strong national government alone can do so, and such a government the Virginia plan will give them. The committee heartily agreed to this, voted the Jersey plan inadmissible, rose, and reported the Virginia plan to the Convention.

This much settled, the debating went smoothly on for a week. Put in good humor by the adoption of their plan, the great States now began to make some idle concessions to the small. The word "national" occurred twenty-six times in the resolutions, was hateful to the little States, and was therefore graciously dropped. But the questions that took up the time of the Convention till the last of June were: Should the Legislature consist of one branch or two? Should there be one Executive or three? Should the members of the first branch be twenty-five years old or thirty? Should the members of the second branch serve for nine years, for seven years, for five years, during good behavior? Then was reached that question which never once came up for discussion without provoking a violent display of sectional feeling and a long and rancorous debate. The question was, Should suffrage in the Legislature be according to the rule established by the Articles of Confederation, or according to some other?

Defenders of the State-rights theory asserted that the general Government ought to act on States, and not on individuals. The States were sovereign. Being sovereign, they were equal, and being equal, they ought to have equal votes. If the large States did indeed have the same interests as the small, there could be no harm in giving equal suffrage to all. If the great States did not have the same interests as the small, then unequal suffrage would be dangerous to the last degree. Once given votes in proportion to population or to wealth, it would be all the same whether the delegates were chosen by the people or by the legislatures. The great States would combine; the little States would be enslaved.

The defenders of the Virginia plan pronounced these fears and reasons absurd. It was the great States that fell out and the small ones that combined. This had always been the case in the Old World, and it would be so in the New. Massachusetts and Pennsylvania and Virginia could never combine. They were far apart. Their manners, customs, religions, were unlike. They had nothing common even in trade. They were, however, rich, populous, and would surely be called on to bear the largest part of the cost and burdens of the Government about to be set up. If, therefore, they consented to equality of suffrage, they would be out-voted, and their money and their property would be completely at the mercy of the little States.

Between these two contending parties now appeared for the first time a party of compromisers, made up chiefly of Connecticut men. Both the State-rights and the Virginia party went, they held, too far. One looked on the States as so many separate political societies; the other looked on the people as one great political society of which the States were merely districts of people. The truth was, the States did exist as political beings, and a Government to be good and lasting must be formed for them in their political capacity as well as for the individuals composing them. The well-being of each was to be considered. The true plan was, therefore, to give the people representation in the one branch and the States representation in the other. New York, New Jersey, and Delaware were in no mood for a compromise and would hear nothing of such a plan. But the great States had their way, and voted that in the first branch representation ought to bear some proportion to the population of the States. This was final. Thenceforth no attempt was ever made to set it aside.

Greatly elated, the compromisers now redoubled their efforts, and insisted that, in the second branch, the voting should be by States. But the defenders of

FRAMING THE CONSTITUTION.

the Virginia plan again flew into a passion, another rancorous debate took up two days, and when the vote was finally reached, the ballot stood five to five. Never before had the members been so angry, nor the speeches so personal and bitter. Reflections, recrimination, taunts, threats of secession, were heard on every side. In this pass, at the suggestion of Charles Cotesworth Pinckney, the whole matter of representation was sent to a grand committee, and the Convention adjourned for three days.

But the debates in the Committee of Eleven were as stormy as the debates in the Committee of the Whole. Again a compromise was offered and again it was refused. You propose, said the State-rights party to the Virginia party, to consent to an equal representation in the second branch of the Legislature if we will consent to an unequal representation in the first. We will not. This is merely offering, after a bitter struggle to put both your feet on our necks, to take one off if we will quietly suffer the other foot to remain. But we know well that you cannot keep even one foot on unless we are willing, and we know well that, having one firmly planted, you will be able to put on the second when you please. Riches will come to you; population will come to you, and with them power. Will you not then force from us that equality of representation in the second branch which you now deny to be our right, and yield only from necessity? You tell us that you will enter into a solemn compact with us not to do so. But did you not years ago enter into a solemn compact with us, and are you not now treating it with the utmost contempt? Do you think that while we see you wantonly violate one, we will meekly enter into another?

Franklin most happily was a member of the committee, and brought his colleagues in time to a better mind and persuaded them to agree to a report. This recommended that each State should be given one representative in the first branch of the Legislature for every forty thousand inhabitants, and that in the second branch each State should have an equal vote. As the price of the concession by the great States, it was insisted that all money bills should originate in the first branch and not be amended in the second, and that no money should be drawn from the Treasury except by bills originating in the first branch.

Thus was the first compromise ended. The report, indeed, did not pass the Convention for two weeks, and then by a close vote. But it was not again disputed that in the second branch the States should have an equal vote.

Meanwhile the Committee of the Whole took up the report in detail. The clause fixing representation at one to forty thousand was recommitted, and reported back with the provision that in the first House of Representatives there should be fifty-six members, and that for the future representation should be based on wealth and population. The provision of one representative for forty thousand inhabitants was dropped as too unsafe. It would enable the West in time to outvote the East. By making a general and not a specific rule, the East would keep the Government in its own hands, take care of its own interests, and deal out representation in safe proportion to the West.

But wealth and population were ever changing, and to find this change Randolph proposed an estimate and a census. The idea seemed a good one. There were,

FRAMING THE CONSTITUTION. 131

however, below the Mason and Dixon line thousands of human beings who might with equal justice be considered as population or as wealth. They could be bought and sold, leased and mortgaged, given away, or bequeathed by will. They held no property, acquired no estates, and to the delegates from the North and East seemed to be of no more account in the South than a black horse or a black ox in New England. They insisted, therefore, that slaves should be looked on as property. By the delegates from the South, however, a slave was held to be a man, for by doing so they hoped to increase their representation. No sooner, then, was it moved to take a census, than Williamson moved that the census should be of all free whites and three fifths of all others.

Instantly the old division of great States and little States disappeared, and the Convention was parted on the new basis of North and South. On the one hand were Delaware, South Carolina, and Georgia, demanding that slaves should have an equal representation with the whites; on the other hand were Massachusetts, Pennsylvania, and New Jersey, demanding that slaves should not be represented at all. Between the two, but leaning more toward the North, were Virginia, Maryland, and North Carolina. New York was no longer represented. Yates and Lansing, enraged at the passage of the Connecticut compromise, had gone home in a huff. Hamilton could no longer vote, and New York ceased to be considered a member of the Convention.

The labor of slaves, such was the argument of delegates from the South, is as productive and as valuable in South Carolina as the labor of freemen in Massachusetts. They put up the value of land; they increase the amount of imports and exports; they may, in emergency, be turned into soldiers and used for defence; they ought therefore, in a Government set up chiefly for the protection of property and to be supported by property, to have equal representation with the whites.

What, said their opponents, is the principle of representation? It is an expedient by which an assembly of certain men chosen by the people is put in place of the inconvenient meeting of all the people. Suppose such a meeting to take place in the South, would slaves have a vote? They would not. Why, then, should they be represented? Had a master in Virginia a number of votes in proportion to the number of his slaves? He had not. Why, then, if there is no slave representation in the States Legislature, should there be slave representation in the National Legislature? What, in plain language, did it mean? It meant that the man from South Carolina who went to the coast of Africa, and in defiance of the most sacred laws of humanity dragged away his fellow-creatures from their dearest connections and damned them to the most cruel bondage, should have more votes, in a Government formed for the protection of the rights of man, than a citizen of Pennsylvania or New Jersey who viewed such a nefarious practice with horror.

Between the two was a third party, made up of men holding a variety of views. One could not consider the negro equal to the white; yet the negro was a man, was a part of the whole population, and ought to have some representation. Another thought the Continental rule of three fifths about right. A third was for giving slaves representation in the second branch but not in the first. They could do nothing, however, in the way of compromise, and, when a vote on the resolution for a census was taken, every State present answered *No*.

Matters were now just where they were when the report of the committee was presented. But they did not long remain so. Gouverneur Morris, in an evil hour, moved that taxation should be in proportion to representation. In the form of direct taxation the motion passed. Upon this a Southern member cried out that an attempt was being made to deprive the South of all representation of her blacks, and warned the Convention that North Carolina would never confederate unless she had at least a three-fifths representation for her slaves.

The threat was indeed formidable. Whatever form of government the Convention might frame would, it was well known, have to be submitted to the States for approval. It had long seemed doubtful whether enough would approve to enable any plan to go into operation. Rhode Island had refused to join the Convention. The delegates from New York had gone home disgruntled. Massachusetts was not to be counted on. Were North Carolina added to the number, the Convention might as well break up, for their labors could accomplish nothing.

To appease her, therefore, the lost resolution for a census of whites and three fifths of the blacks was again moved, and the whole matter of slavery was once more before the Convention. How it should be settled was for the South to say, for of the ten States present the North could command but four. The South decided on a compromise, and the compromise offered was, to proportion representation according to direct taxation, and both representation and direct taxes according to population, counting as population all free whites and three fifths of the negroes. When the ballot was taken

North Carolina and Georgia voted yea; South Carolina was divided, and the second compromise was accepted.

On the sixteenth of July the report of the committee containing the two compromises came before the Convention. The day was a great one, for on the vote then taken hung the fate of the Constitution. On one part of the report the States had been divided into the great against the small. On another part they had taken sides as the slaves against the free. But the vote was now on the whole report, and the States were forced to take their stand accordingly. The four little States supported it because of the compromise giving equal representation in the Senate. Two of the large States opposed it for the same reason, and were joined by South Carolina and Georgia, who still insisted on a full representation of slaves. Massachusetts was divided, for King and Gorham stoutly refused to support any plan of government that gave recognition and encouragement to slavery. Everything, therefore, turned on the vote of North Carolina, who, to save the Constitution, deserted the great States, joined with the small, and the report passed by five votes to four.

Now each party grew very angry. Randolph was for an adjournment, that the great States might have time to decide what steps to take next, and that the small States might arrange some plan of conciliation. He was sharply answered by Paterson that it was high time to adjourn, and to adjourn *sine die*. The rule of secrecy ought to be taken off and the people consulted. As for conciliation, the small States would never conciliate except on the basis of equality of representation.

The indignation of the members from the great States at this was extreme, and early the next morning a number of them met to consider what to do. It was clear that the little States were fixed in their opposition. They had again and again asserted that they would never give way, and they were still showing a front as determined as ever. Since, then, this partition of the Convention into two parties of opposite opinions seemed inevitable, the duty of the great States was, some said, quite plain. They represented the majority of the people of the United States. Let them, then, make ready a plan of government of their own. If the small States agreed to it, well and good. If not, so much the worse for them. Others were for yielding, though, by so doing, they did give way to a minority rule. But the conference came to nothing, and when the hour for the meeting of the Convention arrived the members went to their seats in no amiable frame of mind.

The next ten days were spent in distributing power between the States and the General Government; in determining how the judges should be appointed; where impeachments should be tried; what jurisdiction the Supreme Court should have; how many senators should be given to each State; whether a man must own land before he could be eligible to Congress, to the Supreme Bench, to the Executive office; in what manner the Constitution should be ratified. This done, the Jersey plan, the South Carolina plan, and the twenty-three resolutions of the Convention on a national government were sent on July twenty-sixth to a committee with instructions to report a constitution. The Convention then adjourned for two weeks.

On the committee were Gorham, Ellsworth, James Wilson, Randolph, and John Rutledge. Of their doings nothing is known save that, when the Convention assembled on the morning of Monday, August sixth, each member was given a copy of a draft of the Constitution, neatly printed on a broadside. The type was large. The spaces between the lines were wide, that interlineations might be made, and the margin broad for noting amendments. A few of these broadsides have been preserved, and, when compared with the Constitution, show that the amendments were many and important. The draft provided that the President should be chosen by Congress, should hold office during seven years, and should never, in the whole course of his life, have more than one term; the Constitution intends the President shall be chosen by a body of electors, and puts no limit to the number of his terms. By the draft he was given a title and was to be called "His Excellency"; the Constitution provides for nothing of this kind. By the draft he could be impeached by the House of Representatives, but must be tried before the Supreme Court; by the Constitution he must, when impeached, be tried before the Senate. By the one he need not be a native of the United States; by the other he must. The one made no provision for a Vice-President; the other does. The one provided that members of Congress should be paid by the States that sent them; the other provides that they shall be paid out of the National Treasury. In the draft, senators were forbidden to hold office under the authority of the United States till they had been one year out of the Senate; the Constitution makes no such requirement. By the draft, Congress was to have power to emit bills of credit, to elect a Treasurer of the United States by ballot, to fix the property qualifications of its members, to pass navigation acts, and to admit new States if two thirds of the members present in each House were willing; none of these powers are known to the Constitution. The draft provided but one way of making amendments; the Constitution provides two. Nothing was said in the draft about the passage of *ex post facto* laws, about the suspension of the habeas corpus, about granting patents to inventors and copyrights to authors, about presidential electors, or about exclusive jurisdiction over an area ten miles square. Provision was made for a clumsy way of settling quarrels between States concerning jurisdiction and domain.

As soon as the delegates had read their broadsides the work of the revision began. To the Government was now given the name " United States of America." The Legislature was called " The Congress "—the first branch the " House of Representatives," and the second branch the " Senate." The Executive was named the " President." Power to emit bills of credit was stricken out. An attempt to limit representation to free inhabitants failed. An attempt to secure the return of fugitive slaves succeeded. A long series of resolutions giving Congress power to regulate affairs with the Indians; set up temporary governments for new States; grant charters of incorporation; establish a university; give a copyright to authors; encourage discoveries; advance the useful arts; have exclusive jurisdiction over the seat of government; provide for departments of war, marine, finance, commerce, domestic affairs, foreign affairs, and State; assure the payment of the public debts; guarantee the right of habeas corpus and the liberty of the press; prevent the quartering of troops on the people in time of peace; and give a privy council to the President—were readily agreed to. Indeed, but little debate was provoked till the fourth and sixth sections of the seventh article were reached.

These sections forbade Congress to lay a tax on articles exported from any State, or to tax slaves imported, or to hinder the importation of slaves in any way whatever, or pass a navigation act, unless two thirds of the members present in each House were willing. So much as related to a tax on exports was quickly disposed of. Southern members, indeed, protested. They declared that if the power to tax exports was not given to the General Government it would remain with the States; that if it remained with the States, those agricultural would be at the mercy of those commercial; that the whole South would be made tributary to the North. But their fears were pronounced unreasonable, the power was not given to Congress, and another relic of the political economy of the ancients was swept away forever. So much as related to taxing and hindering the importation of slaves had been put in to please South Carolina and Georgia. Except these two, every State was willing and eager to stop the importation of slaves. But the Convention was reminded that the staples of South Carolina and Georgia were indigo and rice; that these could not be raised without slave labor; that the toil in the rice swamp and the indigo field was more than even the brawniest negro could long endure; that, if they could not bring in negroes from abroad, their industry and their property were gone; and that, sooner than submit to this, they would quit the Union.

The moment, therefore, that Luther Martin moved that the fourth section be so changed that the importation of slaves could be taxed, South Carolina declared that she would never agree to it. If the men from other States thought she would, they were greatly mistaken; they were, indeed, simply standing in their own light. Let the South have more slaves, and more rice, more indigo, more pitch and tar would be produced; and the more produced, the more for the ships of the New England men to carry. In this demand for the free importation of slaves South Carolina was joined by Connecticut. Ellsworth and Sherman both declared that the clause ought to be left as it was. The old Confederation had not meddled with slavery, and they did not see any reason why the new one should. What enriched a part of the Union enriched the whole, and as to what enriched them, the States were the best judges.

That slavery could enrich any land was flatly denied. Wherever it existed, Gouverneur Morris asserted, the arts languished and industry fell into decay. Compare New England, it was said, with Georgia; compare the rich farms and prosperous villages of Pennsylvania with the barren and desolate wastes of Maryland and Virginia, and see what a difference it made whether a land was cultivated by freemen or by slaves. The wealth, the strength, the prosperity of the country depended on the labor of whites, and there could be no white labor where slavery existed.

Convinced of this truth, Maryland and Virginia had forbidden slaves to be carried to their ports. North Carolina had done almost as much. But all this would be useless if South Carolina and Georgia were free to bring in as many as they chose. Already the settlers in the growing West were clamorous for slaves to till their new lands, and would fill that country with negroes if they could be had through South Carolina. But did any one suppose they would stop when every farmer had a full supply? Were not slaves to be represented? Were not five negroes to be counted as three whites? Would not the political power of the South increase with the increase of her slaves? Here, then, was a new incentive for a free importation, a new encouragement to the traffic. More than this, slavery corrupted manners, turned masters into petty tyrants, and was utterly inconsistent with the principles of the American Revolution and dishonorable to the American character.

All this, it was admitted, might be so. But honor, religion, humanity, had nothing to do with the question. The question was, Shall or shall not the Southern States be parties to the Union? With the slave-trade prohibited, South Carolina, for one, never would. To this it was answered, If two States will not take the Constitution, if the importation of slaves is taxed, there are other States that will not take the Constitution if the importation of slaves is not taxed. The exemption of slaves from duty when every other import is taxed is an inequality to which the commercial States of the North and East will not submit.

At this point Gouverneur Morris proposed that the taxation of exports, of slaves imported, and the question of a navigation act should be sent to a committee. They were, he said, fit subjects for "a bargain among the Northern and Southern States." Sherman, and Randolph, and Pinckney, and Ellsworth, and a dozen more thought so too, and the fourth and fifth sections went to a Committee of Five.

The sixth section soon followed them. This provided that no navigation act should be passed without the assent of two thirds of the members present in each House, and was as hateful to the East as a restriction on the importation of slaves was to the South. The committee, therefore, had not been long in session before it was apparent that the New England States, despite the sentiments they held on slavery, were ready to make just such a bargain as Morris proposed. If the South would consent to strike out the sixth section and give Congress power to pass navigation acts, the East would consent to the importation of slaves for a limited time. The South did consent. The bargain was struck, and the committee advised that the sixth section should be stricken out, that the fifth should be left as it was, and that the fourth should be so changed that the importation of slaves should not be forbidden before 1800.

Having obtained so much, the South wanted more, and insisted that the time should be extended till 1808. The East readily agreed, and so made good their part of the bargain. It now remained for the South to do likewise; but the South began to object. Much was said about being in the minority, about being bound hand and foot, about having Southern trade at the mercy of the ship-owning States. If a majority of Congress could pass a navigation act, the New Englanders would shut out foreign ships, get all the carrying trade of the country for themselves, and then demand ruinous prices for carrying tobacco, rice, and indigo to Europe. Congress ought not to have any power over trade. The most, therefore, that the South would yield was that a two-thirds vote should be necessary for the exercise of this power.

The Eastern States protested that the restriction must be taken off; that it would ruin them not to be able to defend themselves against foreign regulations. If the new Government were to be so fettered as to be unable to relieve the commerce of the Eastern States, what motive could there be for them to join it? Disunion was to be lamented; but, if it came, the South would be the chief sufferer.

The majority of the Southern members had been put in good humor by the two concessions of the East, that exports should not be taxed and that slaves should be imported till 1808, and by their influence the third compromise was carried.

The Convention then went on for a week striking out words here, putting in resolutions there, and bringing the draft nearer and nearer the Constitution as we now have it. On the last day of August the postponed sections and the parts of committee reports not acted on were sent to a Committee of Eleven. This committee reported from time to time till September eighth, when all that had been done was sent to a Committee on Arrangement and Style. Saturday, the fifteenth, their work was accepted and ordered to be engrossed. On that day, as the question was about to be put for the last time, the delegates who disliked the Constitution began to make excuses for withholding their support. Mason lamented that a bare majority of Congress could pass a navigation act, and moved that no such act should be passed prior to 1808. But nothing came of it. Randolph asked that the State conventions to which the Constitution was to be submitted might submit amendments to a second Federal Convention. Mason approved this. The Constitution, he said, had been formed without the knowledge of the people. It was not right to say to them, Take this or nothing. A second convention would know their wishes. Gerry named nine features which he especially disliked.

Alarmed at this opposition, Franklin spent Sunday in preparing a little speech to be read to the dissenters. But, when Monday came, when the members were in their seats, and the Constitution, ready for signature, lay upon the table, he found himself too weak, and James Wilson read the paper for him. He was, he said, an old man, and had often, in the course of a long life, been forced to change opinions he was once sure were right. As he grew older, therefore, he had learned to doubt his own judgment and to pay more respect to the judgments of others. Steele in one of his dedications told Pope that the only difference between the Church of England and the Church of Rome in their opinion on the certainty of their doctrine was this: The Church of Rome was infallible; the Church of England was never in the wrong. He had heard of a certain French lady who, in a quarrel with her sister, said: "I do not know how it is, sister, but I meet with nobody but myself that is always in the right." Doubting his own opinion, he agreed to the Constitution with all its faults, if it had any. He had expected no better, and he was not sure that it was not the best. He hoped that each member who still had objections would do likewise—doubt a little of his own infallibility and sign the document. As a good form he would propose, "Done in convention by the unanimous consent of the States present, etc." Gouverneur Morris drew up this form, in hopes that men who would not sign as individuals would sign as State delegates. He gave it to

Franklin to bring before the Convention, thinking that, supported by him, it would have great weight.

As soon as Wilson had finished reading, Gorham rose and moved that the ratio of representation be changed from one for every forty thousand to one for every thirty thousand. No debate followed, and as Washington was about to put the question, he expressed a hope that the change would be made. The smallness of the proportion of representatives had always seemed to him an objectionable part of the plan.

The change was made, the form of ratification proposed by Morris was carried, the journals and papers deposited in the hands of the President, and toward evening the members began to sign. Sixteen refused. Luther Martin had followed the examples of Yates and Lansing, had quit the Convention and gone home to Maryland in disgust. Gerry feared a civil war; Randolph was convinced the consent of nine States could never be obtained; Mason was sure they were about to set up a monarchy or a tyranny, he did not know which, and none of them would sign. The rest of the sixteen carefully kept out of the room.

Washington was first to sign. When he had done so, the other delegates went up one after another in the geographical order of their States, beginning with the East. Hamilton alone signed for New York. As the Southern members were affixing their names, Franklin, looking toward the President's chair, on the back of which was cut a sun, said to those about him that painters had found it difficult to distinguish a rising from a setting sun. "I have," said he, "often and often in the course of the session, and the solicitude of my hopes and fears as to its issue, looked at that behind the President without being able to tell whether it was rising or setting. But now at length I know that it is a rising and not a setting sun."

When the Convention rose that evening, it rose never to sit again.

As early as possible on the eighteenth of September, Major Jackson, the Secretary, set out for New York to lay the Constitution, the accompanying resolutions of the Convention, and the letter of Washington before Congress. But that body was not to be the first to receive it. The Legislature of Pennsylvania was in session, and to it the Constitution was read on the morning of the eighteenth. Copies were at once given to the printers in the city, and on the nineteenth, long before Major Jackson reached New York, the people of Philadelphia were reading it in the Packet, the Journal, and the Gazetteer. September twentieth, the documents were laid before Congress and the next day were published in the newspapers at New York.

Meanwhile such delegates to the Convention as were members of Congress were hurrying back to New York; and well they might, for in Congress the enemies of the Constitution were many and bitter. The delegation from New York opposed it to a man; and with them were joined Nathan Dane, William Grayson, of Virginia, and R. H. Lee. Congress, they held, could give no countenance to the Constitution. That document was a plan for a new government. A new government could not be set up till the old Confederation had been pulled down, and to pull down the Confederation was not in the power of Congress, for that body could not destroy the Government by whose authority it owed existence. The answer was that Congress had sanctioned the Convention, and that, if it could sanction the call for the Convention, it could sanction the work the Convention did. But Lee and his followers would not listen to argument, and on September twenty-sixth he moved that a bill of rights and a long list of amendments should be added to the Constitution. He would have no Vice-President, more congressmen, more than a majority to pass an act regulating commerce, and a council of state to be joined with the President in making all appointments. Congress, however, would not seriously consider his amendments, and the next day it was moved that the Constitution be sent to the executives of the States, to be by them submitted to their respective legislatures. Instantly it was moved to add the words, "in order to be by them submitted to a convention of delegates to be chosen agreeably to the said resolution of the Convention," and the motion was carried. It was now quite clear that neither party could have all that it wanted. The Federalists wished to send the Constitution to the States by the unanimous vote of Congress; but this they could not do so long as the delegates from New York held out. The Antifederalists wished to send it to the States without one word of approval; but this they could not do unless the Federalists consented. When, therefore, Congress met on the twenty-eighth, each party gave up something. The Antifederalists agreed to unanimity; the Federalists agreed to withhold all marks of approval. The amendments offered by Lee on the twenty-sixth, and the vote on the twenty-seventh, were then expunged from the journal, and the Constitution, the letter of Washington, and the resolution of the Convention, were sent to the States. Twenty hours later the Legislature of Pennsylvania called a State Convention to consider the Constitution.

By the provisions of that instrument the ratification by nine States was to put it in force. Before the year closed, Delaware and Pennsylvania and New Jersey had done so. Georgia and Connecticut followed in January, 1788. In February came Massachusetts with nine amendments. In April came Maryland, and in May South Carolina with four amendments. In June New Hampshire ratified with twelve amendments, and the list of nine States was complete. "The Good Ship Constitution," as the Federalists delighted to call that instrument, was now fairly launched. "The New Roof" was up, finished, and firmly supported by nine stout pillars, and, while the rejoicings over its completion were still going on, news came that it was to be upheld by two pillars more. Virginia and New York had ratified. Virginia offered twenty amendments and a bill of rights; the amendments offered by New York numbered thirty-two.

Nowhere else had the contest been so long and so bitter. In some States the people disliked the Constitution because the liberty of the press was not secured, because there was to be no trial by jury in civil cases, because the name of God was not to be found in it, because there was to be no more rotation in office, because there was no bill of rights, because there was no religious qualification for office, because there were to be slave representation and the importation of slaves for one-and-twenty years. But in New York the Constitution was hated from beginning to end. Nor would the Convention ratify it till the Federal members solemnly agreed that the States should be invited to a new Federal Convention, to which it should be submitted for amendment. Clinton accordingly issued the call. But the States most happily did not favorably respond. Some malcontents of Pennsylvania did, indeed, hold a Convention at Harrisburg in September, 1788, and there drew up some amendments which they referred to the Convention called by New York. But of this action, also, nothing came. September thirteenth, 1788, Congress fixed upon the first Wednesday in January, 1789, as the day for choosing presidential electors, the first Wednesday in February for the meeting of the electors, and the first Wednesday in March as the day the Constitution was to become law. Five weeks later the Congress of the Confederation expired ignominiously for want of a quorum.

As yet the Constitution was without amendments. But the first session had not closed when Virginia sent in a petition begging Congress not to rise till action had been taken on those offered by the States. Madison accordingly drew up and presented to the House nine amendments, which are almost identically the nine suggested by the minority of the Pennsylvania Convention in an address to their constituents. Of these in time the House made seventeen. Of the seventeen the Senate made twelve, and of the twelve, the States adopted ten, which were declared in force December fifteenth, 1791. Another was added in 1798, and still another in 1804; after which, though many were offered, none were accepted till the close of the civil war.

The amendments proposed by the first Congress removed, in great part, the objections of the Antifederalists, and the two States that were still refractory began to show signs of giving way. In November, 1789, North Carolina consented to join the Union. But six months passed, and Rhode Island held out. Then, when the United States was about to treat her as a foreign power, when the revenue laws were about to be enforced against her, when it seemed likely that a great exodus of her most worthy citizens would take place, the Federalists carried the ratification of the Constitution by a vote of thirty-four to thirty-two. But the victory was not with them alone, for their opponents added a long bill of rights and twenty amendments, which, it was jeeringly said elsewhere, was more than one for each town in the State.

WASHINGTON'S INAUGURATION.

The Constitution of the United States, as every one knows, was framed by a Convention of delegates from twelve States, sitting behind closed doors in the old State-House at Philadelphia. After a stormy session of four months the "Dark Conclave," as the Anti-federalists delighted to call the Convention, ended its labors September seventeenth, 1787, signed the Constitution, and sent the document to Congress, to be in turn transmitted to the States. This done, the States began to act at once, and, when the year closed, Delaware, Pennsylvania, and New Jersey had accepted the Constitution without amendments. Georgia and Connecticut ratified in January, 1788, and were followed in quick succession by Massachusetts, Maryland, South Carolina, New Hampshire, and Virginia. Under the Articles of Confederation the assent of nine States in Congress assembled was necessary to pass an ordinance of any importance. This rule the Convention had adopted, and had provided that the assent of nine States should dissolve the old Confederation, should set up the Constitution, and make it the supreme law for each of the ratifying States. When, therefore, on July second, 1788, the President of Congress rose and announced the ratification by New Hampshire, he reminded the members that the needed number was complete, that the new plan of government was approved, and that it remained for Congress to make such provisions and to take such steps as were necessary to put it into force. An ordinance was thereupon passed, and a committee chosen to examine the notices of ratification and report an act for putting the Constitution into operation.

The duty of the committee-men seemed simple enough. They were to name a day on which the States should choose electors of President and Vice-President, a day on which the electors should vote, and a day and a place for the meeting of the Senate and House, and the beginning of government under the new plan. But, simple as it seemed, the committee found it hard to perform. Indeed, two weeks went by before they reported an act providing for the needed days, but leaving the place of meeting blank. Nor did Congress succeed in filling that blank till a great display of sectional feeling had been made, and a long and bitter contest ended. Every one agreed that the place should be central, and that central should mean somewhere between the shores of Chesapeake Bay and the mouth of the Hudson River. Within these limits, however, were many large and opulent towns, and which had the best claim to be considered central, Congress was long unable to say. Some members insisted that population should be considered, pointed out that more people dwelt south of the Potomac than north of it, and thought Baltimore or Annapolis would be a good town. Others were for considering distances, and urged Wilmington and Lancaster and Philadelphia as places no farther from the eastern border of the province of Maine than the southern border of Georgia. Still others, on the ground of policy and economy, stood out for New York. To be constantly shifting the government from place to place was to make it seem weak and unstable, and sure to bring it into contempt among the people. To pack up cart-loads of books and tons of papers and drag them over the country, unless they went forth to that Federal city which was to be the lasting home of the new Congress, was a piece of wanton extravagance.

These arguments fell on dull ears. For a time all was jealousy, local bias, petty spite. September was almost half gone when Congress finally decided that the States should choose electors on the first Wednesday in January, 1789, that the electors should cast their votes on the first Wednesday in February, and that the new Congress should meet on the first Wednesday in March in the city of New York.

The history of the Congress thus about to expire is worth recalling. It begins with the meeting of the fifty-three colonial delegates who, in September, 1774, assembled at Philadelphia. Gathered in response to the call of Massachusetts, they passed the non-intercourse, non-importation, non-consumption agreement; issued the colonial Declaration of Rights; drew the famous address to the King and the address to the People of Great Britain, and after a session of eight weeks called a new Congress to meet in May, 1775, and adjourned. But long before the tenth of May arrived the crisis in the quarrel with the mother country was reached, the stores at Concord were destroyed, the battle of Lexington was fought, and the new Congress, seizing authority that had not been given, entered at once on the conduct of the war.

Between the day when this Congress met and the

day when the Articles of Confederation were put in force a period of seventy months went by. During these seventy months the Congress of the United States acted under no constitutional authority whatever. The States were parties to no instrument of government, and every act committed by their delegates was done with the tacit or express consent of the States. No system of representation was in use. To the secret deliberations of the little body that bore the name of the Congress came delegates chosen in such a way and in such numbers and bearing such instructions as best pleased the States that sent them. Once seated in Congress, these men found themselves members of what a few years later would have been denounced as a "dark and secret conclave." The doors were shut, no spectators were suffered to hear what was said, no reports of the debates were taken down in short-hand or longhand; but under a strict injunction of secrecy they went on deliberating day after day. From month to month so much of the journal as Congress thought fit was indeed given to the people; but Congress thought fit to give merely a dry record of ordinances passed, of motions made, of reports read, of committees chosen. Over these deliberations presided a President elected by the Congress, and looked up to as the representative of the sovereignty of the States united for common defence. As such, his house, his table, his servants, were all provided at public cost. But the expense of every other delegate was borne by the State that sent him.

Thus formed, the Continental Congress no sooner met in 1775 than it proceeded, without any authority, to raise armies, equip navies, to borrow money, to set up a post-office, to send out ministers, to make treaties, and to do innumerable acts of sovereignty in the name of the States. It was the Continental Congress that commissioned Washington; that sent Franklin to the court of France; that voted the Declaration of Independence; that framed the Articles of Confederation; that advised the colonies to throw off all allegiance to the King and "take up civil government."

The Articles of Confederation went out to the States in 1777, but it was not till the first of March, 1781, that the thirteenth State signed and put them into force. Meanwhile the Congress was fast sinking into open contempt among the people. The great things which it did were soon forgotten; the things which it did not do were long remembered. Most of its dealings were with the States. In but a few ways did it touch the people, and in the most delicate of these its record is that of disaster after disaster. The bills of credit which no one would take, the loan offices set up in every State, the Congress lottery that failed so miserably, the forty for one act, the old tenor and the new tenor, commissary certificates, quartermaster certificates, hospital certificates, interest indents, were constant reminders of the financial imbecility of Congress, and did far more to bring it into contempt than any of its great acts did to bring it into honor. Every other expression of contempt, "not worth a farthing," "not worth a tinker's dam," gave way to the new expression of worthlessness, "not worth a continental."

Happily, at this juncture, the Confederation was finished, and Congress, for the first time in its history, met under the shadow of constitutional authority. Great things were expected of the Union, and for a time it seemed likely that the expectations would be fulfilled.

But when Congress organized under the newly ratified Articles of Confederation in November, 1781, Cornwallis had surrendered, the war had virtually ended, and the Confederation began at once to fall in pieces. By the Articles the character of the Congress was little changed. The President was still chosen by the members. The members were chosen annually; could not serve more than three years in any term of six; could not be more than seven nor less than two from any State, and were paid by those who sent them. As the charge of maintaining them was not light, as no delegation, however large, could cast more than one vote, a strong incentive was created to keep the delegations down to two, and in time to send none at all. Twenty delegates, representing seven States, were present when Washington resigned command of the army. Twenty-three delegates, from eleven States, voted to ratify the treaty of peace with Great Britain. Thenceforth, to the end of its career, Congress rarely consisted of twenty-five members. Again and again it was forced to adjourn day after day for want of a quorum. Once these adjournments covered thirteen consecutive days. Ordinances of trifling importance could be passed by the assent of a majority of the States. But no measure of importance, no ordinance to provide for the issue of money, the payment of the debt, the ratification of a treaty, the raising of a body of troops, could pass unless nine States assented. Most of the time but eleven States were represented. Of these eleven it often happened that nine had but two delegates each, and it thus became possible for three men to defeat the weightiest measures.

Acting on the States and not on the people, Congress never won the affections of the people, but was looked on, was spoken of, was treated, as a foreign government rather than a creature of their own making. When a band of ploughmen gathered under the window of its room at Philadelphia and broke up its sitting with taunts and threats, not a citizen could be found willing to aid in defending it. Driven from the city, it fled to Princeton, and there found a refuge under the guns of fifteen hundred soldiers. From Princeton it soon adjourned to Annapolis. There, disgusted at the perpetual sitting of Congress, the Rhode Island delegates, acting under instructions from their Legislature, moved a recess. This was carried, and, as the Articles of Confederation required, a committee of the States was chosen to sit during the recess. But the members quarrelled, separated with bitter words, and for two months the country was without a general government of any kind. In November, 1784, the Congress reassembled at Trenton, and from Trenton in time they adjourned to New York. In the taverns, meanwhile, the wits were expressing their contempt in the popular toasts, "A hoop for the barrel," "Cement for the Union." In the newspapers Congress was likened to a wheel rolling from Dan to Beersheba and from Beersheba to Dan. Neglected by its members, insulted by the troops, a wanderer from town to town, the subject of jest by the people, the Congress of the Confederation sank rapidly to the condition of a debating club. It made requisitions that never were heeded, voted monuments that never were put up, rewarded great men with sums of money that never were paid, planned wise schemes for the payment of the debt that never were carried out, and looked on in helplessness while English troops held and fortified American forts, while State after State openly violated the Articles of the Confederation, refused it power to regulate trade, refused it power to lay a tax on imported goods, and finally called that Convention which, in 1787, framed the Constitution and gave to Congress the duty of fixing the day when it should cease to exist.

Having thus fixed the day of its death, the Continental Congress of the Confederation began to die fast. When the ordinance passed, on the thirteenth of September, 1788, nine States were present. September eighteenth, this number had dwindled to six. October fourteenth, there were but two in attendance, and all government was ended. Day after day a few delegates —sometimes six, sometimes two—would saunter into the hall, have the secretary take down their names, and then go off to their favorite tavern. But no sittings were held, no business was done, and the Congress whose name is bound up with so much that is glorious in the annals of our country expired ignominiously for want of a quorum.

While these few men, true to their trust, were striving to keep up the semblance of a Congress, the first Wednesday in January, 1789, arrived, and electors were chosen in all of the ratifying States save New York. In that great Commonwealth the choice was to be made by the Legislature, and the Legislature was divided against itself. The Assembly was in the hands of the Clinton men, and strongly Antifederal. The Senate was in the hands of the friends of Hamilton, and was by a small majority Federal. The bill which the Assembly framed provided that the Senate and Assembly, having each nominated eight electors, should meet and compare lists, that men whose names were in both lists should be considered elected, and that from those whose names were not in both lists one half of the needed number should be chosen by each branch of the Legislature. The Senate amended the bill by proposing that the two branches of the Legislature should not meet, but should exchange lists, and that, if the lists differed, each branch should propose names to the other for concurrence, and should go on doing so till all the electors were chosen. The Assembly promptly rejected the amendment; a conference followed; the Senate stood firm, and no electors were chosen. New York, therefore, cast no vote in the first Presidential election, and had no representative on the floor of the Senate during the first session of the first Congress under the Constitution.

Very similar was the quarrel that took place in New Hampshire. There the law gave the people the right of nominating, and the Legislature the power of appointing, but was silent as to the way in which the appointment should be made. The Assembly was for a joint ballot. This the Senate would not hear of, and stood out for a negative on the action of the Assembly as complete and final as in the cases of resolutions and bills; a wrangle followed, and midnight of the seventh of January was close at hand, when the Assembly gave way, made an angry protest, and chose electors, each one of whom was a Federalist.

In Massachusetts the General Court chose two electors at large, and eight more from a list of sixteen names sent up from the eight congressional districts. In Pennsylvania the choice was by direct vote of the people, and the counties beyond the mountains being strongly Antifederal, two general tickets were promptly in the field. On the Lancaster ticket were the names of ten Federalists well known to be firm supporters of Washington. On the Harrisburg ticket were the names of men who had signed the address and reasons of dissent of the minority of the Pennsylvania Convention, had been members of the Antifederal societies and committees of correspondence, had labored hard to defeat the Constitution, and, even after nine States had ratified, had sat in the famous Harrisburg Convention which petitioned the Legislature to ask to have the Constitution sent for amendment to a new convention of the States. These men, the Federalists declared, were planning to make Patrick Henry President, and though some were given a great vote, not one secured election.

In Maryland, where the choice was also made by the people, the excitement became intense, for the lines which parted the Federalists and Antifederalists were precisely those which a few years before parted the non-imposters and the paper-money men from the men who wished for honest money and the prompt payment of the Continental debt. All over the State meetings were held, addresses were issued, and each party accused of fraud. But, when the votes were counted, the Federalists were found to have carried the day. Virginia likewise left the choice with the people, and in that State some fights took place and some heads were broken. But these were of common occurrence, often happened when members of the House of Burgesses were elected, and were thought nothing of. In Connecticut, New Jersey, Delaware, South Carolina, and Georgia the electors were chosen by the Legislatures of the States. In Rhode Island and North Carolina no elections were held; they had not accepted the Constitution, and were not members of the new Union.

Of the sixty-nine electors thus appointed, not six were formally pledged to the support of any man. In Baltimore and Philadelphia, where the contest was close, a few had been charged with Antifederalist leanings, and had issued cards declaring that if elected they would cast their votes for Washington and Adams. But the others gave no pledges, and none were wanted. Differ as men might touching the merits of the Constitution, there was no difference of opinion touching the man who should fill the highest office under the Constitution, and voters and electors alike united on General Washington.

There all unanimity ceased, for no other name was a charmed name with Americans. That of Franklin stood high, but Franklin had passed his eightieth year, was sorely afflicted with an incurable disease, and was justly thought too old and feeble for the second place. The services and the claims of Samuel Adams were almost as great, but he had begun by opposing the Constitution, had ended by accepting it with much reluctance, and was accordingly passed over by the Federalists, who brought forward the name of John Adams in his stead.

John Adams was a native of New England, and this was given out by some as a good and sufficient reason why Southern Federalists should oppose him. He had lived long abroad, and was declared by others to have come home less of a Republican than he went out. He had, his enemies admitted, written a book called "A Defence of the Constitutions of Government of the United States of America." But it ought, they said, to be called an insidious attack. Could any man read such stuff as this—" The rich, the well-born, and the able will acquire an influence among the people that will soon be too much for simple honesty and plain sense in a House of Representatives "—and call it Republican? Was the author of such nonsense a fit man to rule over a free people? A better reason for opposing Adams came from the Antifederalists of New York. Eleven States, these men argued, have ratified the Constitution, yet six sent with their ratifications long lists of proposed amendments. These amendments are not trivial; they are very serious. The new Government will have to consider them. It is highly important, therefore, to have in the new Government some man who will do his best to further them. Such a man is Governor George Clinton. His name is not written at the foot of the Declaration of Independence; he has never sat in Congress, nor gone on a mission to foreign parts to caper before dukes and princes, and dance attendance in the antechambers of kings; he has no theory about the place to be given to the rich and the " well-born " in the State; but he is a stanch Republican, a friend to the liberty of the press, an enemy of standing armies, a hater of consolidated governments in every form, a man in whose hands the interests of the six States proposing amendments will be safe. So eager were his friends to see him Vice-President that they formed clubs, took the name of Federal-Republican, and, while electors were yet to be chosen, canvassed, corresponded, and sent out a circular letter in his behalf. For a time his chances of success were good; but when it was known that Clinton could not carry his own State, that New York had chosen no electors, all hope of success was given up. And well it might be, for when the electors met on the first Wednesday in February, Clinton got but three votes, and these three were cast by Virginia. Washington, on that day, was given sixty-nine; John Adams received thirty-four. Thirty-five more votes were thrown away on ten men, no one of whom received more than nine.

STATES.	Washington.	Adams.	Huntington.	Hancock.	Jay.	Clinton.	R. H. Harrison.	Rutledge.	John Milton.	James Armstrong.	Telfair.	Benjamin Lincoln.
New Hampshire....	5	5										
Massachusetts......	10	10										
Connecticut........	7	5	2									
New Jersey.........	6	1			5							
Pennsylvania.......	10	8		2								
Delaware...........	3				3							
Maryland...........	6						6					
Virginia............	10	5		1	1	3						
South Carolina.....	7			1				6				
Georgia.............	5								2	1	1	1
Total..........	69	34	2	4	9	3	6	6	2	1	1	1

That a vote or two should be thrown away was necessary. As the Constitution then read, it was the duty of each elector to write down on his ballot the names of two men, without indicating which he wished should be President. The man receiving the greatest number of electoral votes was to be President, and the man receiving the next highest, Vice-President. Had every elector who voted for Washington also voted for Adams, neither would have been elected, and the choice of a President would have devolved on the House of Representatives. So great a scattering, however, was unnecessary, and is to be ascribed to a fear that Washington would not be given the vote of every elector—a fear Alexander Hamilton did all he could to spread.

The choice of representatives was left with the people. By the Constitution, any man who could vote for a member of the lower branch of his State Legislature could vote for a member of Congress. But not every man could on election day write a ballot and bring it to the polls, or stand in the crowd that shouted "Aye!" when the name of his candidate was called. Suffrage was far from universal. The elective franchise belonged to the rich and well-to-do, not to the poor. The voter must own land or property, rent a house, or pay taxes of some sort. Here the qualification was fifty acres of land, or personal property to the value of thirty pounds; there it was a white skin and property to the value of ten pounds. In one State it was a poll-tax; in another, a property tax; in another, the voter must be a quiet and peaceable man with a freehold worth forty shillings, or personal estate worth forty pounds. To vote in South Carolina a free white man must believe in the being of a God, in a future state of reward and punishment, and have a freehold of fifty acres of land; to vote in New York, he must be seized of a freehold worth twenty pounds York money, or pay a house-rent of forty shillings a year, have his name on the list of taxpayers, and in his pocket a tax receipt.

The effect of restrictions such as these was to deprive great numbers of deserving men of the right to vote. Young men just starting in life, sons of farmers whose lands and goods had not been divided, wandering teachers of schools, doctors and lawyers beginning the practice of their profession, might count themselves fortunate if at the age of twenty-eight they could comply with the conditions imposed by the constitutions of many of the States. Of the mass of unskilled laborers —the men who dug ditches, carried loads, or in harvest-time helped the farmer gather in his hay and grain—it is safe to say that very few, if any, ever in the course of their lives cast a vote, for they were thought well paid if given food, lodging, and sixty dollars a year.

While such as could vote were choosing their representatives, fit meeting-places for the senators and representatives were being made ready by some public-spirited citizens of New York. Driven from Philadelphia in 1783 by the threats of a band of mutinous soldiers, the Congress of the Confederation at last found a refuge at New York, and had been given quarters in the City Hall, which then stood on the corner of Nassau and Wall. The Congress room was on the second story at the east end, and would not even now be thought mean. Travellers who came to the city and, prompted by curiosity, visited the room where the Congress sat, never failed to go away much impressed by the pictures, the furniture, the hangings, it contained. The railed-in platform on which the President sat; the great chair of state; the crimson silk canopy with its curtains of heavy damask; the mahogany tables; the chairs, rich with carving and gorgeous with seats of crimson morocco; the great curtains of damask that hung at the windows; the long line of portraits of officers who died in the war; the huge canvases from which, when the curtains were pulled aside, the King and Queen of France seemed ready to step to the floor beneath—drew from every visitor exclamations of admiration and surprise. Yet neither this room nor the building were thought fine enough for the use of the new Congress, and money to put the building in better form was soon being asked for at every coffee-house in the city. Thirty-two thousand five hundred dollars was quickly collected, and the work of alteration was given to Major L'Enfant, who deserves to be remembered as the man to whom is due all that is good and nothing that is bad in the plan of the city of Washington.

No time was lost; yet the masons and carpenters were still busy when the fourth of March arrived. This mattered little, however, for no President was to be inaugurated, no Senate, no House was ready to take possession; nothing was to be done to mark in any way the fact that the weak and crumbling Confederation had given place to a strong and vigorous Government. Toward sunset on the evening of the third a salute was fired at the Battery as a long farewell to the old Confederation. At daylight on the morning of the fourth, at noon, and at six in the evening, salutes were again fired and all the church bells rung out a welcome to the Constitution. But no celebration was attempted, for the new Congress seemed to have inherited all the sloth, all the indifference, all the torpor of the old. The Senate was to consist of twenty-two members and the House of fifty-nine. Yet while the bells were ringing and the cannon firing there were but eight senators and thirteen representatives in the city. This seemed quite as it should be. The terrible condition of the roads in February, the long distances many would have to ride, the late day on which the elections were held, might, it was urged, account for the absence of many. When, however, a week went by and not one more senator came, the patience of the eight gave way, and they issued a strong appeal to the absentees to hurry.* But another week passed, and another address was issued, before the ninth senator crossed the Hudson to take his seat. The tenth came two days later, the eleventh a week later, and the twelfth, who made a quorum, reached the city on the fifth of April.

The House of Representatives meanwhile had been more fortunate—had secured a quorum, had chosen a Speaker, and was hard at work on a tariff act, when a messenger from the Senate knocked at the door and informed the Speaker that the Senate was ready to count the electoral vote.

This duty done, the Houses parted, and Charles Thomson was sent to carry a certificate of election to Washington, while Sylvanus Bourne went on a like errand to John Adams at Braintree. The journey of these two men from their homes to the seat of Congress

---

* The following is a copy of such an appeal, sent to the Hon. George Read:

NEW YORK, March 11, 1789.

The Honorable George Read, Esqr.:

SIR: Agreeably to the Constitution of the United States, eight Members of the Senate and eighteen of the house of Representatives have attended here since the 4th of March. It being of the utmost importance that a Quorum sufficient to proceed to business be assembled as soon as possible, it is the opinion of the Gentlemen of both houses, that information of their situation be immediately communicated to the absent Members.

We apprehend that no Arguments are necessary to evince to you the indispensible necessity of putting the Government into immediate operation, and therefore request that you will be so obliging as to attend as soon as possible.

was one long ovation. Adams set out first, and was accompanied from town to town along the route by troops of soldiers and long lines of men on horseback, was presented with addresses, was met at Kingsbridge by members of Congress and the chief citizens of New York, and escorted with every manifestation of respect to the house of John Jay. His inauguration took place on April twenty-second, and was attended by one incident, unnoticed at the time, but serious in its consequences. In the crowd that stood about the doors of Federal Hall to catch a glimpse of Mr. Adams as he went in were John Randolph, of Roanoke, and his elder brother Richard. The lads were students at Columbia College, and, pressing too close to the Vice-President's carriage, Richard, in the language of his brother, "was spurned by the coachman." In a healthy-minded lad the wrath which the "spurning" called forth would surely have gone down with the sun. But John Randolph was far from healthy-minded. To him the act was past all forgiveness, and to the last day of his life he hated, with a fierce, irrational hatred, not the coachman, but John Adams himself.

Washington set out on the sixteenth of April. But he had not gone a mile from his door when a crowd of friends and neighbors on horseback surrounded his carriage and rode with him to Alexandria. There the Mayor addressed him, in the fulsome manner of the time, as the first and best of citizens, as the model of youth, as the ornament of old age, and went with him to the banks of the Potomac, where the men of Georgetown were waiting. With them he went on till the men of Baltimore met him, and led him through lines of shouting people to the best inn their city could boast.

That night a public reception and a supper were given in his honor, and at sunrise the next morning he was on his way toward Philadelphia.

In size, in wealth, in population, Philadelphia then stood first among the cities of the country, and her citizens determined to receive their illustrious President in a manner worthy of her greatness and of his fame. The place selected was Gray's Ferry, where the road from Baltimore crossed the lower Schuylkill—a place well known and often described by travellers. On the high ridge that bordered the eastern bank was Gray's Inn and gardens, renowned for the greenhouse filled with tropical fruit, the maze of walks, the grottos, the hermitages, the Chinese bridges, the dells and groves, that made it "a prodigy of art and nature." Crossing the river was the floating bridge, made gay for the occasion with flags and bunting and festoons of cedar and laurel-leaves. Along the north rail were eleven flags, typical of the eleven States of the new Union. On the south rail were two flags: one to represent the new era; the other the State of Pennsylvania. Across the bridge at either end was a triumphal arch, from one of which a laurel crown hung by a string which passed to the hands of a boy who, dressed in white and decked with laurel, stood beneath a pine-tree hard by. On every side were banners adorned with emblems and inscribed with mottoes. One bore the words, "May commerce flourish!" On another was a sun, and under it, "Behold the rising empire." A third was the rattlesnake flag, with the threatening words, "Don't tread on *me*." On the hill overlooking the bridge and the river was a signal to give the people warning of the President's approach.

Toward noon on the twentieth of April the signal was suddenly dropped, and soon after Washington, with Governor Mifflin and a host of gentlemen who had gone out to meet him at the boundary line of Delaware, was seen riding slowly down the hill toward the river. As he passed under the first triumphal archway the crown of laurel was dropped on his brow, a salute was fired from the cannon on the opposite shore, and the people, shouting "Long live the President!" went over the bridge with him to the eastern bank, where the troops were waiting to conduct him on to Philadelphia. The whole city came out to meet him, and as he passed through dense lines of cheering men the bells of every church rang out a merry peal, and every face, says one who saw them, seemed to say, " Long, long, long live George Washington!"

That night he slept at Philadelphia, was addressed by the Executive Council of State, by the Mayor and Aldermen, by the judges of the Supreme Court, the faculty of the University of Pennsylvania, and the members of the Society of the Cincinnati, and early the next morning set out with a troop of horse for Trenton. On the bridge which spanned the Assanpink Creek, over which, twelve years before, the Hessians fled in confusion, he passed under a great dome supported by thirteen columns, and adorned with a huge sunflower, inscribed, "To thee alone," and was greeted by a little band of musicians led by a German named Pfyles. The music which they played had been composed for the occasion by Pfyles, was dedicated to Washington under the name of "The President's March," and became so popular that in the stirring times of 1798, when Hopkinson wrote the words of "Hail Columbia," he set them to the music of "The President's March" because everybody knew it. The women of Trenton had ordered the dome put up, and just beyond the bridge were waiting with their daughters, who, as he passed under the dome, began singing:

> Welcome, mighty chief, once more
> Welcome to this grateful shore:
> Now no mercenary foe
> Aims again the fatal blow—
> Aims at thee the fatal blow.
>
> Virgins fair and matrons grave,
> Those thy conquering arms did save,
> Build for thee triumphal bowers.
> Strew ye fair his way with flowers—
> Strew your Hero's way with flowers.

As the last lines were sung the bevy of little girls came forward, strewing the road with flowers as they sang. Washington was greatly moved, thanked the children on the spot, and before he rode out of town the next morning wrote a few words to their mothers.

From Trenton he passed across New Jersey, escorted from county to county by the State militia, to Elizabethtown, where a committee, with a barge provided by Congress, was ready to carry him to New York. Rowed by thirteen of the harbor pilots, the barge sped on through the Kill van Kull toward New York Bay, followed by a train of boats bearing the few officers of the old Confederation necessity still kept in their places. In one was the Board of Treasury; in another, the Secretary of War; the Secretary of Foreign Affairs was in a third.

About the entrance to the Kill was gathered a navy of river craft gay with flags and brightly dressed women, and noisy with cheering men. As the barges of the President and his party passed by, snows and shallops, trackscouts and row-boats, with one accord took place in line, and the procession, stretching out for more than a mile, swept on toward New York, past the Spanish war ship Galveston, which saluted with thirteen guns; past the ship North Carolina, which answered the Spaniard's salute, while over the water to those on shore came the blare of conchs and trumpets, the sound of song and music, and the stirring notes of "Stony Point." As the little fleet came round the head of Governor's Island the shouts were taken up by the crowd that lined the shore or stood in a dense mass about the spot which, bright with flags and bunting, marked the landing-place at Murray's Wharf. There Washington was met by Governor Clinton and the members of Congress, and escorted by all the troops in the city to the house made ready for his use. That night the revelry was louder than ever, for scarcely a tavern but had a song or an ode written for the occasion by some frequenter who passed for a poet. Of the few that have come down to us, one was sung to the air of "God save the King":

> Hail, thou auspicious day!
> For let America
> Thy praise resound.
> Joy to our native land!
> Let ev'ry heart expand,
> For Washington's at hand,
> With glory crowned.
>
> Thrice beloved Columbia, hail!
> Behold before the gale
> Your chief advance.

> The matchless Hero's nigh;
> Applaud him to the sky,
> Who gave you liberty,
>   With gen'rous France.
>
> Thrice welcome to this shore,
> Our leader now no more,
>   But ruler thou.
> O truly good and great,
> Long live to glad our state,
> Where countless honors wait
>   To deck thy brow!

The friends to the new Government had hoped for a speedy inauguration. But Federal Hall was still unfinished, and the ceremony of taking the oath was put off one week. This week was spent by the President in receiving and returning the calls of congressmen, and in riding about the streets and noting the great change which had taken place since he saw the city last. Five years before, some of the same men who so lately welcomed him as President had gone out to the Bull's Head Tavern to welcome him as General, and after a few days had escorted him to the same wharf at which he so recently landed, and had there, with hearts full of love and gratitude, waved farewell as he was rowed over the bay on his journey to Congress at Annapolis. Then the city was a scene of desolation. Her commerce was gone; her docks were empty; two terrible fires had burned down nearly a thousand of her houses. During the seven years of British occupation many of her streets and buildings had been suffered to fall into decay, many of her churches had been desecrated and turned into riding-schools and stables, and thousands of her citizens had been living in exile up the

Hudson or in New Jersey. But no sooner were the British driven out than her citizens returned, and with an energy that seemed marvellous began to repair and more than repair the damage done by fire and war. The streets were better paved and better lighted; the houses every year became more grand and pretentious, and the limits of the city extended by steady encroachments on the rivers and bay. Public opinion had already doomed Fort George, which stood just below the Bowling Green, and in a few months workmen were levelling the ramparts to make way for a house for the President. One traveller described the city as a miniature London. Another puts down in his journal some remarks on the markets, where fish were sold both dead and alive; on the fine houses he saw on Dock Street and Queen Street and Hanover Square; on the goodness of the footways, so wide that three persons could walk abreast; on the pavements, over which no dray drawn by more than one horse was ever allowed to pass; and on the sights which he saw on Broadway. The buildings along it were new and poor, but the street was long, wide, and unpaved, and therefore a favorite drive. There every morning and afternoon "the gentry" rode in their coaches and phaetons, and "the common people" in open chairs. It was fashionable to be seen, toward sunset, walking on the mall that surrounded the fort, or to go over to Brooklyn and stroll about the earthworks while an oyster supper was being made ready at the inn.

In these amusements the President-elect took no part, but waited with solemn gravity for the inauguration. At nine on the morning of that day the people repaired by thousands to the churches to offer up prayers for his Divine guidance. At ten Congress met.

In the Senate all was confusion, for, the moment the business of the day began, Mr. Adams had propounded a question of etiquette. The House, he said, would soon attend them, and the President would surely deliver a speech. What should be done? How would the Senate behave? Would it stand or sit while the President spoke? Members who had been in London and had seen a Parliament opened were for following the custom of England, which was, Mr. Lee declared, for the Commons to stand. Mr. Izard declared the Commons stood because there were not benches enough in the room for them to sit. A third was in the midst of a strong protest against aping the follies of royal governments, when Mr. Adams announced that the clerk of the House was at the door. A new question of etiquette at once arose, for the Vice-President was at a loss how to receive him. The sentiment of the admirers of England was that the clerk should never be admitted within the bar, but that the sergeant-at-arms, with the mace upon his shoulder, should march solemnly down to the door and receive the message. This, unhappily, could not be done, for the Senate had neither a mace nor a sergeant. What should be done was still unsettled when the Speaker, with the House of Representatives at his heels, came hurrying into the Chamber. All business was instantly stopped, and the three senators, who ought to have attended the President long before, set off for his house. As Washington could not leave till they arrived, the procession, which had been forming since sunrise, was greatly delayed, and for an hour and ten minutes the senators and representatives chafed and scolded. At last the shouting in the streets made known that the President was come. A few minutes later he entered the room, and both Houses were formally presented. This ceremony over, Mr. Adams informed him that it was time to take the oath of office. He rose and, followed by the members of Congress, went out on the balcony of Federal Hall. Before him were the windows, the house-tops, the streets, crowded with citizens of every rank, brought thither from every kind of occupation by the novelty of the scene. Behind him were gathered many of the ablest and the most illustrious citizens the country had then produced. Among the senators stood John Langdon, of New Hampshire, once President of his State, and long a delegate to the Continental Congress; Oliver Ellsworth, soon to become a Chief-Justice of the Supreme Court; William Paterson, ten times Attorney-General of New Jersey; Richard Henry Lee and Richard Bassett and George Read, men whose names appear alike at the foot of the Declaration of Independence and at the foot of the Constitution of the United States; William Johnson, a scholar and a judge, and one of the few Americans whose learning had obtained recognition abroad; while conspicuous even in that goodly company was the noble brow and thoughtful face of Robert Morris, the financier of the Revolution.

The representatives as a body were men of lesser note. Yet among those who that morning stood about the President were a few whose names are as illustrious as any on the roll of the Senate: there were James Madison, to whom, with James Wilson, is to be ascribed the chief part in framing and defending the Constitution; and Fisher Ames, the finest orator the House ever heard till it listened to Henry Clay; and Elbridge Gerry, the Antifederalist, who pronounced the Constitution dangerous and bad, who would not sign it in Convention, but who lived to see his worst fears dissipated, and died a Vice-President of the United States; and Roger Sherman and George Clymer, who with Gerry dated their public service to a time before the Revolution, and who in defence of that cause had staked "their lives, their fortunes, and their sacred honor," and signed the first grand charter of our liberties.

When the President, surrounded by men such as these, had taken his place before the railing of the balcony, and the shouts of welcome had died away, a scene occurred which has been well described by one who saw it. "I was on the roof," wrote Miss Eliza Quincy, "of the first house in Broad Street, which belonged to Captain Prince, the father of one of my school companions, and so near Washington that I could almost hear him speak. The windows and the roofs of the houses were crowded, and in the streets the throng was so dense that it seemed as if one might literally walk on the heads of the people. The balcony of the hall was in full view of this assembled multitude. In the centre of it was placed a table with a rich covering of red velvet, and upon this, on a crimson velvet cushion, lay a large and elegant Bible. This was all the paraphernalia for the august scene. All eyes were fixed upon the balcony, where at the appointed hour Washington entered, accompanied by the Chancellor of the State of New York, who was to administer the oath; by John Adams, Vice-President; Governor Clinton, and many other distinguished men. By the great body of the people

WASHINGTON'S INAUGURATION. 177

he had probably never been seen except as a military hero. The first in war was now to be the first in peace. His entrance on the balcony was announced by universal shouts of joy and welcome. His appearance was most solemn and dignified. Advancing to the front of the balcony, he laid his hand on his heart, bowed several times, and then retired to an arm-chair near the table. The populace appeared to understand that the scene had overcome him, and were at once hushed in profound silence. After a few moments Washington arose and came forward. Chancellor Livingston read the oath, according to the form prescribed by the Constitution, and Washington repeated it, resting his hand upon the table. Mr. Otis, the Secretary of the Senate, then took the Bible and raised it to the lips of Washington, who stooped and kissed the book. At this moment a signal was given by raising a flag upon the cupola of the hall for a general discharge of the artillery of the battery. All the bells in the city rang out a peal of joy, and the assembled multitude sent forth a universal shout. The President again bowed to the people, and then retired from a scene such as the proudest monarch never enjoyed."

Livingston was then Chancellor of the State of New York, and when the last words of the oath had been uttered he turned to the people and cried out, " Long live George Washington, President of the United States!" The cry was instantly taken up, and with the roar of cannon and the shouts of his countrymen ringing in his ears, Washington went back to the Senate Chamber to deliver his speech. What there took place is best told in the language of one who was present: " This great man was agitated and embarrassed more than ever he was by the levelled cannon or pointed musket. He trembled, and several times could scarce make out to read, though it must be supposed he had often read it before. He made a flourish with his right hand, which left rather an ungainly impression. I sincerely, for my part, wished all set ceremony in the hands of the dancing master, and that this first of men had read off his address in the plainest manner, without ever taking his eyes from the paper, for I felt hurt that he was not first in everything."

The people meanwhile went off to their favorite taverns to drink prosperity to Washington and Adams, and wait with impatience for the coming night. As the first stars began to shine, bonfires were lighted in many of the streets, and eleven candles put up in the windows of many of the houses. The front of Federal Hall was a blaze of light. There was a fine transparency in front of the theatre, and another near the Fly Market, and a third on the Bowling Green, near the fort. But the crowd was densest and stayed the longest before the figure-pieces and moving transparencies that appeared in the windows of the house of the Minister of Spain, and before the rich display of lanterns that hung round the doors and windows of the house occupied by the Minister of France.

The country over which Washington was thus made ruler was not three and a half times as large as the present State of Texas, and did not contain as many people by a million as are at present living within the State of New York. By the treaty of peace with Great Britain the boundary of the United States was defined as the St. Croix River from its mouth to its source; a meridian to the highlands parting the waters that flowed into the Atlantic from the waters that flowed into the St. Lawrence; the highlands to the northwest branch of the Connecticut River; down the river to the forty-fifth degree of north latitude; westward along this forty-fifth parallel to the middle of the St. Lawrence; up the St. Lawrence to the lakes; and up the great lakes to the most northwestern corner of the Lake of the Woods. There all geographical knowledge ended. The Mississippi had not been explored above the present city of St. Paul. Where its source was no man knew; but supposing it to be somewhere in British America, the northern boundary was to be finished by a line due west from the Lake of the Woods to the Mississippi. Thence the line ran down the middle of the Mississippi to the thirty-first parallel, eastward along this parallel to the Appalachicola, down the Appalachicola to the Flint, and then along the northern boundary of the present State of Florida to the sea.

Around their limits lay the possessions of two great powers with whom our relations were far from friendly. Spanish territory surrounded us on the south and west; yet there was no treaty of any kind with Spain. The possessions of Great Britain bounded us on the north and east; yet the only treaty with England was that of independence made in 1783, and, claiming this treaty to have been violated because the States did not repeal the laws forbidding the recovery of debts due her subjects, she held and fortified the ports on Lake Champlain, at Oswegatchie, at Oswego, at Niagara, at Detroit, on the island of Michilimackinac, in what is now Michigan, and continued to hold them for thirteen years. Spain would make no treaty unless it was distinctly agreed that the citizens of the United States should not navigate the Mississippi River below the thirty-first degree.

Of the eight hundred and sixty-five thousand square miles contained within the boundaries of the United States, part belonged to the eleven States and part had been inherited by the new Government from the Continental Congress. Maine was still a district of Massachusetts; Vermont had as yet no recognition as a State, and was not a member of the Union. Neither was Rhode Island, nor North Carolina, nor what is now Tennessee. Over these regions, therefore, the laws of Congress and the authority of Washington did not extend. Pennsylvania did not own all her frontage on Lake Erie. Kentucky was still a part of Virginia. What is now Alabama and Mississippi above the parallel of thirty-one degrees was claimed entirely by Georgia, and in part by the United States. The wilderness north of the Ohio and west of Pennsylvania had, save some reservations by Virginia and Connecticut, been ceded by four States to the old Congress, and passed by the name of the Territory of the United States northwest of the River Ohio.

Three fourths of the United States were uninhabited. The western frontier then ran close along the coast of Maine, crossed central New Hampshire and northern Vermont to Lake Champlain, passed round the shores of the lake, down the Hudson River, across New Jersey, and the mountains of Pennsylvania to Pittsburg, over Maryland and the tide-water region of Virginia, and along the Blue Ridge Mountains to the Altamaha River, and by it to the sea.

The area of this inhabited strip was, in round numbers, two hundred and forty thousand square miles, or one square mile for each sixteen of the inhabitants. But population was by no means so equally distributed. One fifth were in Virginia; one ninth in Pennsylvania; almost one half in the five States that lay south of the Mason and Dixon line. These were the great plantation States, and, populous as they were, they did not contain but one city of the first class. Savannah and Charleston and Wilmington and Alexandria and Richmond were smart towns and nothing more. Not one of them had a population of five thousand souls. Indeed, the inhabitants of the six great cities of the country summed up to but one hundred and thirty-one thousand.

Sparse as the population was, the rage for emigration had already seized it, and hundreds of emigrants were pouring over the mountains in three great streams. One, made up of New England men, went out through Massachusetts and were pushing rapidly up the Mohawk Valley; a second, from the Middle States, was hastening up the Potomac River to its head waters and spreading over the rich valleys of West Virginia between the Ohio and the Great Kanawha; a third had crossed the mountains of North Carolina and was hurrying down the valley of the Tennessee, there to begin that wonderful progress which is the most marvellous in the history of man.

A CENTURY OF CONSTITUTIONAL INTERPRETATION.

WHEN Major William Jackson, Secretary of the Constitutional Convention of 1787, set off to lay the signed copy of the Constitution before the Continental Congress, he bore with him a letter from Washington and a copy of three resolutions passed by the Convention. One of these resolutions expressed the wish that, when nine States had ratified the new plan of government, the Congress should name the day when government should begin under the Constitution. After much delay and much debate the first Wednesday in March, 1789, was chosen.

The first Wednesday in March fell on the fourth of the month, and on that day the Constitution under which we now live became the supreme law of the land. Though the conventions of eleven States had then ratified, but three had done so unanimously. To thousands of well-meaning men in every State the new plan was offensive because it was too costly; because it was to be a a Government of three branches instead of a Government of one; because the power of taxing was vested in Congress; because liberty of the press was not assured; because trial by jury was not provided in civil cases; because there was no provision against a standing army, and none against quartering troops on the people; because religious toleration was not secured; because it began with "We, the people," and not with "We, the States"; because it was not only a Confederation, which it ought to be, but a Government over individuals, which it ought not to be. In the conventions of eight States the men holding these views made strong efforts to have the Constitution altered to suit their wishes. In Pennsylvania, in Connecticut, in Maryland, the "amendment mongers," as the Federalists called them, failed. But in five conventions they did not fail, and in these the ratifications were voted in the firm belief that the changes asked for would be made. When Washington was inaugurated the amendments offered numbered seventy-seven. But Congress was too busy laying taxes, establishing courts, and forming departments to give any heed to the fears and dreads of a parcel of countrymen. Nor was it till the Legislature of Virginia protested that the House of Representatives found time even to hear the amendments read. The language of the protest was of no uncertain kind.

The members were reminded that the Constitution was very far from being what the people wished. Many and serious objections had been made to it. These objections were not founded on idle theories and vain speculations. They were deduced from principles established by the bitter experience of other nations. The sooner Congress recognized this fact, the sooner it would gain the confidence of the people and the longer the new Government would last. The anxiety which the people felt would suffer no delay. Whatever was done must be done at once, and as Congress was too slow to do anything at once, the Virginia Legislature asked that a convention be called to propose amendments and send them to the States. For a while it seemed as if the protest from Virginia would share the same fate as the amendments from the States. Is the Constitution, it was asked, to be patched before it is worn? Is it to be mended before it is used? Let it be at least tested. Let us correct, not what we think may be faults, but what time shows really are defects. So general was this feeling that the House would have done nothing had not Madison given notice that he intended in a few weeks to move a series of amendments which would, he hoped, do away with every objection that had been lodged against the Constitution by its most bitter enemies. His amendments were nine in number. Out of them Congress made twelve. The first, which fixed the pay of congressmen, and the second, which fixed the number of the members of the House of Representatives, were rejected by the States. Ten were ratified, and December fifteenth, 1791, they were declared to be in force.

But the framers of the amendments were doomed to disappointment. Their work did not prove to be enough. And while the States were still considering it, the "mongers" were clamoring as loudly as ever for something more. Congress had begun to exercise its powers. The exercise of its powers had produced heart-burnings and contentions and warm disputes. The question of constitutional right had been often raised, and before the Government was two years old the people were dividing into two great parties—the loose constructionists and the strict constructionists; the men who believed in implied powers and the men who believed in reserved powers; the supporters of a vigorous national government and the supporters of State rights.

It might seem, at first sight, that this diversity of opinion was but another phase of that general diversity of opinion which is to be found in all communities on all kinds of subjects—on art, on music, on dress, on religion, on etiquette. But the history of the past hundred years goes far to show that the constitutional opinions held by any set of men, at any particular time, and in any particular place, have been very largely determined by expediency. The people, the Congress, the Legislatures of the States, the political conventions, the Presidents, the Supreme Court, have each in turn interpreted the Constitution. Now the dispute has been over the powers of Congress, now over the nature of the Constitution itself, now over the manner and meaning of its ratification. Now the contending parties have tormented themselves with such questions as, Is it a compact, or an instrument of Government? Was it framed by the people, or by the States? Is there a common arbiter? May the States interpose? May the General Government coerce? May a State secede? Yet the cases are few indeed where the answers to these questions have rested on great principles and not on expediency.

The contest began in 1790 over the powers of Congress. The State debts were assumed. A national bank was started. The first excise was laid, and a round tax was put on carriages. Every one of these measures touched the interests of a section or a class. The debts of the Eastern States were larger than the debts of the Southern States. The bank stock was held by Northern men to the exclusion of Southern men.

Whiskey was the staple of western Pennsylvania. The cry of partial legislation was therefore raised, and the Legislatures of Pennsylvania, of Maryland, of Virginia, and of North Carolina denounced the assumption act as unconstitutional and infamous. The people of western Pennsylvania rose in open rebellion against the whiskey tax. A carriage owner, pleading that the carriage tax was direct and therefore unconstitutional, took his case to the Supreme Court and obtained a definition of what is a direct tax. Even the President had doubts as to the right of Congress to charter a national bank, and called for the opinions of his Cabinet. The great leader of the Federalists and the great leader of the Republicans replied, and each for himself laid down rules for constitutional interpretation.

Hamilton approved of the bank, set forth the loose construction view, and declared the powers of Congress to be of three sorts—express powers, implied powers, and resultant powers. Express powers were, he said, such as are clearly stated in the Constitution, and are well understood. The implied powers were not indeed so well understood, yet they were just as clearly delegated. Nowhere did the Constitution say Congress shall have power to tax whiskey, Congress shall have power to tax rum. Yet the existence of that power could not be doubted, nor could it be doubted that it was merely a particular power implied from the general power to lay and collect taxes, duties, imports, and excises. Resultant powers were such as resulted from the total grant of powers.

Jefferson disapproved of the bank, set forth the close construction view, and would admit but two kinds of powers—those expressly granted, and those absolutely necessary (not merely convenient) to carry out the powers expressly given.

The loose constructionists prevailed. The bank charter was signed. The whiskey insurrection came to nothing. The Supreme Court decided that a tax on carriages is not a direct tax, and the close constructionists, defeated and angry, fell back on their last resource, and before the first session of the Second Congress ended five constitutional amendments, defining the powers of Congress, appeared in the Senate. One pronounced every tax direct which was not laid on imports, excises, transfers of property, and proceedings at law. Another denied Congress the power to grant a charter of incorporation, or to set up a commercial monopoly of any kind. The third excluded from Congress every man concerned in the direction or management of a bank or moneyed corporation. The fourth went further still, and proposed to shut out from the possibility of a seat in either House any man who sat on the board of directors, or filled a clerkship, or owned a share of stock of the Bank of the United States. The fifth proposed that the judicial power of the United States should be vested not only in one Supreme Court and such inferior courts as Congress might ordain and establish, but in such State courts as the Congress should deem fit to share it.

The fifth amendment was aimed full at the Supreme Court. On the bench of that court sat John Jay, the Chief-Justice, and James Wilson, Iredell, Cushing, Rutledge, and Blair, the five associate justices. But little business had come before them, yet they had handed down two decisions which seemed to every strict constructionist to threaten the ruin of Republican government. One declared that the tax on carriages was not direct, and the other asserted the right of a citizen to sue a State. At this even the friends of loose construction took fright, and once more expediency became the cause of action. The good people of Massachusetts were at that very moment being sued by an alien and a subject of Great Britain, and the Legislature, alarmed by the decision of the court, bade its senators, and requested its representatives, to spare no pains to have the Constitution amended. The instructions were obeyed, the eleventh amendment went out to the States in 1794, and in 1798 became part of the Constitution.

With this amendment the Supreme Court drops from the constitutional discussions for a time, and the behavior of the President takes its place. In 1793 France declared war on Great Britain, and as our country was then bound to France by the treaty of alliance of 1778, and as the first Minister from the French Republic, Citizen Genet, had just landed on our shore, the day seemed not far distant when the United States would be called on to make good the promise of the treaty and defend the French West Indies. The Administration was for neutrality, and Washington issued a proclamation to that effect. This course was the only wise and safe one. But it was a Federal measure. As such it had to be opposed; and raising the cry of unconstitutionality, for want of a better reason, the Republicans denounced the President in every Democratic newspaper and in every Democratic society the land over. He had, they claimed, violated the Constitution. He had usurped the powers of Congress. To proclaim neutrality was to forbid war. To forbid war included the power to declare war, and the power to declare war had been expressly delegated to Congress. The constitutionality of the act was defended by Hamilton in his letters of "Pacificus." What could be said against it Madison said in the letters of "Helvidius."

Hardly had this dispute subsided when a new one arose. The President and the Senate had ratified the ever-memorable treaty of 1794, and the House had been called on to vote the money necessary to put the treaty in force. But the House was then in Republican hands. The Republicans were determined to defeat the treaty, and sought to do so by refusing to vote the money needed. This the Federalists resisted as unconstitutional. The treaty-making power was, they held, confined to the President and the Senate. The duty of the House was to vote the money and be still. A great debate followed, in which the right of the House to share in making treaties, the place of treaties with respect to the Constitution and the laws, the proper subjects of treaties, were examined with a keenness which makes the debate profitable reading at the present day.

Offensive as the English treaty was at home, it was doubly so abroad. The French Directory suspended the old treaty of amity and commerce, recalled their Minister, sent the American Minister out of France, insulted the X. Y. Z. commissioners, and brought on the quasi-war of 1798 and 1799. Never since the days of the Stamp Act had the country been so enraged. Numbers of Republicans quit their seats in Congress and hastened home, and the Federalists, thus left in control, passed the Alien Enemy Act, the Alien Friends Act, the Naturalization Act, and the Sedition Bill, and opened a new era in our constitutional history. From 1789 to 1798 the discussions had been confined to the text of the Constitution. The Supreme Court had defined the meaning of certain phrases. Congress had wrangled over the exercise of certain powers. States had declared certain acts unconstitutional. Madison, Hamilton, and Jefferson had laid down rules for a correct interpretation. But now a new step was taken, and in the resolutions of 1798 and 1799 the very nature of the Constitution was defined by the Legislatures of Kentucky and Virginia. The substance of the Kentucky resolutions is that the Constitution is a compact; that to this compact each State has assented as a State; and that, as in all other cases of compact among parties having no common judge, each party has an equal right to judge for itself as well of infractions as of the mode and measure of redress. The substance of the Virginia resolutions is the same, save that in them the right of judging and interposing is given, not to a single State, but to "the States," by which is to be understood another Federal Convention.

This definition made, they declared the alien and sedition laws void and of no force, and called on the co-States for an expression of opinion. Delaware and Rhode Island, and Massachusetts and New York, and Connecticut and New Hampshire, and Vermont alone replied. Each one of the seven declared that no State Legislature ought to judge of the constitutionality of laws made by the General Government, and each gave that power solely to the Supreme Court. Such was their opinion in 1799; but the time was soon to come when four of the seven would abandon this doctrine, and when they in turn would defy the authority of

Congress, pronounce some of its acts unconstitutional, and declare others null and void. To these answers both Virginia and Kentucky made reply, and in the reply of Kentucky was laid down the statement that when the General Government is guilty of a deliberate, palpable, and dangerous infraction of the Constitution a nullification of its acts by the sovereign State aggrieved is the rightful remedy.

At this time the new century opened. The Presidential election of 1800 was held, and Adams was defeated. The two parties changed places, and with the change of place came a change of opinions. To the minds of all true Republicans the experience of ten years had shown four serious defects in the Constitution; the manner of electing the President was bad; the Senate was too independent a body; the Supreme Court was breaking down State rights; the powers of Congress were not well defined. These defects were thought to be most serious, and became during the next ten years the cause of a new batch of proposed amendments.

The most prolific source of such was the contested election of 1801. Twelve times the proposition to change the constitutional provision for electing President and Vice-President came before House and Senate. Some recommended that a separate ballot for President and Vice-President should be cast by the electors. Some were for choosing the electors by the district system; some for declaring no man eligible to the Presidency for more than four years in any term of eight; some that a person who has been twice successively elected shall not be eligible for a third term till four years have passed, and then only for one term more. From 1800 to 1804 the tables of the House and Senate were never free from such propositions. Then, after four years of reflection, the twelfth amendment went out to the States and was adopted; and the next session the whole matter was up again for amendment.

The attack on the judiciary began with the repeal of the Judiciary Law passed by the Federalists in 1801. Under this act sixteen new judgeships were created and filled by men who, the Constitution declared, should hold their places during good behavior. But the Republicans, asserting that abolishing the office was not by any means removing the man, repealed the law and swept the "midnight judges" out of place. This done, they took one step more and impeached the Federal judges Pickering and Chase. Pickering, a raving lunatic, was removed. Chase, the most hated Federalist alive, was not removed. He had escaped, in the opinions of the Republicans, because the Constitution required judges to be impeached, and because, on his impeachment, Federal senators from Republican States voted for acquittal. But his enemies hoped to reach him and others in time, and promptly brought in three constitutional amendments. Again and again it was proposed that judges of the Supreme and all other courts of the United States should be removed by the President on the joint address of both Houses. The Legislatures of Kentucky and Pennsylvania and Vermont asked that the judges of the Supreme Court and all other courts of the United States should hold office for a term of years, and in this Massachusetts joined. Another proposition, made by Pennsylvania, was that in cases of impeachment a majority vote be enough to convict. Another plan gave power to each State Legislature to recall any senator elected by it at any time. The Legislature of Pennsylvania, recalling the Sedition Law so fearlessly administered by Chase, proposed that the judicial power of the United States should not be construed to extend to controversies between a State and the citizens of another State, between citizens of different States, between citizens of the same State claiming lands under grants of different States, and between a State and the citizens thereof and foreign States, citizens, or subjects.

It would have been well for Pennsylvania could the amendment have passed; for in 1809 her Governor became engaged in a bitter contest with the Supreme Court, her troops were drawn up around the home of the Rittenhouse heirs to prevent the marshal serving a mandamus: and a committee of her Legislature formally resolve that in a Government such as that of the United States, where there are powers granted to the General Government and rights reserved to the States, conflicts must arise from a collision of powers; that no provision is made by the Constitution for determining such disputes by an impartial tribunal; and that to suffer the Supreme Court to decide on State rights is simply to destroy the Federal part of our Government. The Court triumphed. But the Legislature was not discouraged, and it framed an amendment to the Constitution providing for the creation of an impartial tribunal to decide such disputes, and called for an expression of opinions by the co-States. Virginia answered, and in 1810 asserted what in 1798 and 1799 she had denied— that there was a common arbiter, and that the common arbiter was the Supreme Court of the United States.

But Pennsylvania was still unconvinced, and in 1811 her Legislature plainly affirmed the Virginia and Kentucky doctrine of 1798.

But the Republican States were not the only ones with constitutional grievances. The Federal States found grievances in the purchase of Louisiana and in the long embargo. There is not in the Constitution an express grant of power to buy land from foreign countries. Up to 1803 a Republican would therefore have flatly denied that such a purchase could legally be made. But the Republicans were now in power. The purchase was most desirable, and they proceeded to defend it by arguments drawn from the "general welfare clause," from the treaty-making power, from the war power; and they voted money to buy Louisiana.

The last of men to oppose such a purchase should have been the Federalists. But they were then in opposition, and became in turn most strict constructionists. They declared the treaty with France unconstitutional because the treaty-making power gave no right to acquire soil; because the ports in Louisiana were to be more favored than ports elsewhere; because the President and the Senate had regulated trade with France and Spain, a right the Constitution expressly declared to belong to Congress; and because from this territory new States were to be admitted into the Union. New England looked with dread on the admission of such new States, and to keep down their votes in the House of Representatives Massachusetts proposed a constitutional amendment, asking that henceforth representation and direct taxes be apportioned according to the number of free inhabitants. The resolution was read, was ordered to lie for consideration, and for eleven years seemed to be forgotten. It was a protest, and was not intended to be anything more. Seventeen States then formed the Union. The assent of thirteen was therefore necessary to amend the Constitution. But as eight States tolerated slavery, no amendment could pass without the assent of at least four slave States; and to suppose that four slave States would consent to cut down their representation at the request of Massachusetts was never seriously thought of for a moment. It was in truth but a protest, and the first of a series of protests which during eleven years continued to come from the Federal States of New England.

The next expounding of the Constitution grew out of the embargo and the exercise of the war powers of Congress during the war of 1812. No express power to lay an embargo can be found in the Constitution. But the Republicans had cast away much of their doctrine of strict construction, deduced the right from the power to regulate commerce, passed the laws of 1807 and 1808, and heard their constitutional right so to do denied by the very men who in 1794 had been instrumental in passing an embargo. To explain this was easy. The Federal embargo of 1794 was laid, it was said, for a short time, and was a regulation of commerce. The Republican embargo of 1807 was for an unlimited time, and was a destruction of commerce. Congress had power to regulate commerce, therefore the Federal embargo of 1794 was constitutional. Congress had no power to destroy commerce, therefore the Republican embargo of 1807 was not constitutional. This interpretation the Legislature of every Federal State, and the people of every Federal county and town, accepted and asserted, and piled the table of the Tenth Congress high with addresses and memorials all declaring that the embargo acts were oppressive, unconstitutional, null, and void. But the only reply to such remonstrance was an act, to them more infamous still—the "Force Act" of 1809.

Since the days of the Alien and Sedition laws power so vast had never been bestowed on the President. Indeed, what the Alien and Sedition acts were to Virginia and Kentucky in 1798 that was the Force Act to New England in 1809. With one voice the Federalists denounced it, and with one consent asserted the doctrine of State interposition. The people of Boston voted it repugnant to the true intent and meaning of the Constitution, and petitioned the Legislature to interfere and save the people from the ruinous consequences of the system. From Portland came a call to adopt such measures as in 1776 were used "to dash in pieces the shackles of tyranny." The people of Hallowell declared that when those delegated to make and execute laws transcend the powers given them by a fair construction of the instrument whence their powers come, such a law is null; they voted the Force Act such a law, and petitioned the Legislature to interfere and stop the career of usurpation. The New Haven meeting described the act as repugnant to the Constitution, oppressive, and a violation of the constitutional guarantees that "excessive bail shall not be required, nor excessive fine imposed," nor "the right of the people to be secure in their persons, houses, papers, and effects" violated. Delaware pronounced the act "an invasion of the liberty of the people and the constitutional sovereignty of the States."

A committee of the Legislature of Massachusetts, to which the petitions were referred, reported that the embargo acts were oppressive, unjust, unconstitutional, and not legally binding on the citizens of the State. They too recommended interposition, but interposition in the form of an act to protect the citizens against unreasonable, arbitrary, and unconstitutional searches of their dwellings. And now the Republicans gave way, and in 1809 the embargo was lifted.

The third decade of our history under the Constitution covers the war of 1812. A week before the war was formally declared General Dearborn, by order of the President, issued a call on the States for militia. In most of the States the call was promptly obeyed. But in Massachusetts, Connecticut, and Rhode Island the troops were flatly refused. There were, in the opinions of the Governors, but three purposes for which the militia of a State could be called out by a President, and these three were: to repel invasion, to execute the laws, to suppress insurrection. But the laws were everywhere executed. There were no insurrections to put down. No enemy had invaded the soil. The call was therefore unconstitutional. This interpretation was approved in Massachusetts by the judges, in Rhode Island by the Council, and in Connecticut by the Assembly, which now in turn put forth a definition of the Constitution and the rights of the States under it. In this she declares that the State of Connecticut is a free, sovereign, and independent State; that the United States are a confederacy of States; that we are a confederated and not a consolidated republic; and that the same Constitution which delegates powers to the General Government forbids the exercise of powers not delegated, and reserves them to the States respectively.

Two years now passed by, and New England was again aflame. The cause was the refusal of the Government to defend the coast, and the desperate efforts of the two secretaries to get troops and sailors for the war. The need of men for the army and the navy brought before Congress the conscript plan of the Secretary of War, the impressment plan of the Secretary of the Navy, the bill to enlist minors without the consent of their parents or guardians; and Connecticut bade her Governor, if they passed, call the Legislature together that steps might be taken to preserve the rights and liberties of the people and the freedom and sovereignty of the State. The refusal of the General Government to defend the coast of New England drew from the Legislature of Massachusetts the call for the Hartford Convention. To it came delegates from the States of Massachusetts, Rhode Island, and Connecticut, chosen by the legislatures, and delegates from two counties in New Hampshire and one in Vermont, chosen by conventions of the people. Their duty was to devise and suggest for adoption, by the respective States, such measures as they might deem expedient, and if necessary provide for calling a convention of all the States to revise the Constitution.

They deemed it expedient to propose seven amendments to the Constitution. They would have had representatives and direct taxes apportioned according to the number of free persons. They would have had no new States admitted into the Union without consent of two thirds of both Houses of Congress; no embargo laid for more than sixty days; no President ever re-elected, and no two consecutive Presidents from the same State. They would have cut off naturalized citizens from seats in Congress and civil offices under the authority of the United States. They would have made a two-thirds' vote of both Houses necessary to lay a commercial restriction or to pass a declaration of offensive war.

These in time were duly laid before Congress, where they were buried under a host of other amendments. The old proposition to remove judges by joint address of both Houses had come up three times; to elect the President by district system, six times. There, too, were others designed to shorten the term of senators; to give Congress and the States concurrent power to train the militia; to prevent increase of pay of congressmen till after one election had intervened; to declare that if any citizen of the United States shall accept, or receive, or retain, or claim any title of nobility or of honor, or shall, without leave of Congress, accept any present, any pension, any office, any emolument of any kind, from emperor, king, prince, or foreign power, he shall cease to be a citizen of the United States and be incapable of holding office. Strange as it may seem, this last proposition passed each House, was approved by the President, went out to the States, and may be found in copies of the Constitution printed in Madison's term, as article thirteenth of the amendments. When the House in 1817 called on the President for an explanation, it came out that twelve States had ratified, that thirteen would have put it in force, and, supposing the thirteen would surely be obtained, the amendment had been inserted by the Secretary of State in the copies of the Constitution ordered printed by Congress.

More curious still was an amendment providing for the abolition of the Vice-Presidency, the yearly election of representatives, the triennial election of senators, and the choice of President by lot. The senators were to be parted into three classes, one of which was to go out each year. These retiring senators, called up in alphabetical order, were, in the presence of the House of Representatives, to draw each a ball from a box. One ball was colored, the rest were white; and the man fortunate enough to draw the colored ball was to be President for a twelvemonth.

Mingled with these were a few propositions which began to show the first results of the war. Congress was to have power to lay a duty of ten per cent. on exports, build roads and canals in any State with the consent of the State, and establish a national bank with branches. From the President was to be taken all power to approve or disapprove bills. To Congress was to be given power to appoint heads of all departments, fill all vacancies in the judiciary, and appoint all office-holders under the Government of the United States.

In nothing is the spread of the loose-construction idea so well shown as in the feeling of the Republicans toward the National Bank. In 1791 they denounced it. In 1811 they refused to recharter it. But now in 1816 they reprinted the arguments of Hamilton to prove the constitutionality of a bank, and passed the charter of the second bank, which Madison, the opposer of banks, signed, and which the Supreme Court, in 1819, declared constitutional. But while the question of constitutionality thus disappeared, the ancient hatred remained. It was still to the popular mind a "moneyed

CENTURY OF CONSTITUTIONAL INTERPRETATION. 201

monopoly," an "engine of aristocracy," a great monster "trampling on the vitals of the people."

The charter of the bank marked, for a time, the limit of broad construction. This limit reached, a reaction followed, and with the opening of the fourth decade began a new contest over State rights. Ohio had taxed two branches of the Bank of the United States, and when the bank resisted had sent her officers to break open the vaults and carry off the tax money by force. The bank entered suit against the officers in the Circuit Court of the United States and won it, and Ohio in her turn affirmed her belief in State rights and nullification. She protested against the decision of the Court as a violation of that amendment of the Constitution which declares that a State may not be sued. She protested against the doctrine that "the political rights of the separate States that compose the American Union, and their powers as sovereign States, may be settled and determined by the Supreme Court." She "approved the resolutions of Kentucky and Virginia," and called on each State for an expression of opinion. None replied. But eight soon followed her example. The first was Kentucky; and from her in 1822 came a constitutional amendment proposing that in all suits to which a State was a party an appeal should lie to the Senate.

New York came next. In 1824 the United States set up a claim to the right to require boats navigating canals to take out licenses and pay tonnage duty, and a resolution appeared in the New York Assembly declaring that the State must interfere in defence of her citizens. The Federal courts in 1822 declared unconstitutional the South Carolina acts according to which any free negro sailor who came into the ports of the State could be imprisoned until he sailed again. Governor Wilson, when stating this decision to the Legislature, called on the members to preserve the sovereignty and independence of their State, and told them it would be better "to form a rampart with our bodies on the confines of our territory" than to be "the slaves of a great consolidated government." The Legislature replied that the law of self-preservation was above all laws, all treaties, all constitutions, and would never be shared with any other power.

In 1824 Congress passed the "Woollen Bill," and Virginia, North Carolina, South Carolina, Georgia, Alabama, and Mississippi made haste to declare that the tariff, and the internal improvements for which they believed the tariff laid, were not authorized by the plain construction, true intent, and meaning of the Constitution. Each defined the Constitution as a compact into which each State had entered as a sovereign State. Each asserted that no common arbiter was known, and that each State therefore had the right to construe the compact for itself. Each then proceeded to construe it, and declared that the power to lay important duties was given for the purpose of revenue and revenue only, and that every other use of it was a palpable usurpation of power not given by the Constitution.

To these resolutions Congress gave no heed, and in 1828 passed the "tariff of abominations." Then the indignation of the South burst forth. On the day the news reached Charleston and Savannah, every British ship in the harbors pulled down its flag to half-mast. For months not a public dinner was given in the South but the diners drank destruction to the American system and prosperity to State rights. In scores of towns the sky was reddened by burning effigies of Henry Clay.

In the midst of this commotion Senator Foote, of Connecticut, moved that the Committee on Public Lands be instructed to inquire whether it be expedient to limit for a while the sale of lands to such as had already been offered and were then subject to entry; and so brought on the Webster-Hayne debate. There was nothing in the motion of a constitutional nature, but the tariff, and the acts of South Carolina on the tariff, were the topics of the hour and could not be kept from the discussion. During three days the Senate and the crowd that packed the chamber heard the Constitution expounded as it was never expounded before. The Virginia doctrine of 1798 pronounced the Constitution a compact between sovereign States, denied that any common arbiter existed, and asserted the right of interposition by "the States." But the Carolina doctrine as now set forth by Hayne was the Kentucky doctrine of 1798, and asserted the right of nullification by a single State; and asserted that right, not as a revolutionary right existing on the ground of extreme necessity, but as a sovereign right existing under the Constitution.

Thus set forth, nullification became a favorite doctrine, and in 1830 was adopted by Massachusetts, and in 1831 and in 1832 by Maine. William, King of the Netherlands, had rendered his decision on the disputed Northeast boundary, and had traced out a line which, had it been accepted, would have deprived both Maine and Massachusetts of large tracts of land. But Massachusetts notified the General Government that it would be well not to accept the decision, as any act purporting to carry it out would be "wholly null and void, and in no way obligatory" on their Government or people. Maine declared she would never consent to give up an acre of her territory on the recommendation of any foreign power. The decision of William was not accepted, and no chance was given the States to carry out their threats. But the hour was at hand when another State, for another reason, was to make the test.

The "Southern movement" of 1828 and 1829, the burning effigies, the toasts, the remonstrances, the resolutions, the boycotts, had all been lost upon the tariff-men. The threat of nullification, the threat of interposition, the threat of resistance, had been made by so many States, in so many parts of the Union, that they had lost all terrors. Virginia and Kentucky, and Pennsylvania, and Ohio, and New York, and North Carolina, and South Carolina, and Mississippi, and Alabama, and Georgia, and Massachusetts, and Maine had each made them, and it was well known that more than one State had made them never intending to carry them out. The tariff-men therefore, quite undismayed, laid the great tariff of 1832. But the threat of one State was not idle; and November nineteenth, 1832, a Convention of South Carolina delegates declared the tariff laws no longer binding on her people.

And now the States were called on to make good their threats, and one by one proved wanting. A year before, the Legislature of Maine had declared, "Maine is not bound by the Constitution to submit to the decision which is or shall be made under the Convention." But she now declared nullification to be "neither a safe, peaceable, nor constitutional remedy." Massachusetts had declared that any law to carry out the decision of the King of the Netherlands would be "wholly null and void." But she now declared that while she would resist a law she would not nullify. The Legislature of Ohio in 1820 had expressly adopted the Virginia and Kentucky resolutions of 1798 and 1800. But there, too, opinions had changed; and Ohio now declared that the doctrine that a State has power to nullify a law of the General Government is revolutionary and "calculated to overthrow the great temple of American liberty."

But it is needless to recall the long resolutions passed by the States; the proclamation of Jackson; the great debate in the Senate between Webster, Calhoun, and Clay; the offer of Virginia to mediate; the call of Georgia for a Southern Convention; the Force Act passed by Congress; or the compromise measures which persuaded South Carolina to repeal her ordinance of November, 1832. It is enough to know that each party held to its principles while it gave up its particular acts. The tariff of 1832 was altered, but the constitutionality of the protective tariff was not given up. The ordinance of nullification was repealed, but the right to nullify and secede was not disavowed. Then was the time to have secured such a disavowal. The States had committed themselves against the doctrine and could not have refused a constitutional amendment forbidding it. But no such amendment was offered.

Of the amendments that were offered in the House and Senate, one proposed to give Congress power to build roads and canals; another, to carry on internal improvements for national purposes; a third, that money used for building roads and digging canals should be apportioned according to population. A fourth related to the bank; for the charter of the second National Bank, in 1816, again brought up the question of constitutionality, and Pennsylvania, Ohio, and Indiana demanded that an amendment be added forbidding the charter of any bank except for the District of Columbia. But the amendment which was always present, which was rejected and tabled and postponed, sent to special committees, to the Judiciary Committee, to the Committee of the Whole, passed in one House and rejected in another, yet never for a session absent from the journals, related to the manner of electing the President. The extension of the franchise in some of the States, and the rapid growth of what Benton called the "demos krateo" in all the States, had greatly strengthened the belief that the people, and the people alone, should choose the President. From 1820 to 1825, therefore, the old amendment for a choice of electors by districts was urged over and over again.

For twenty years the Presidents had been natives of Virginia, and for twenty-four years ex-Secretaries of State. But against these a revolt now took place. They also became the cause of proposed constitutional amendments. No man was to be eligible to the Presidency who had been a congressman within two years, or held any office under the Government within five years of the day of election. The States were to be arranged in four classes and a President to be taken out of each class in rotation.

With such idle schemes Congress went on amusing itself till the memorable election of 1824. Then the Electoral College a second time failed to make a choice, and a second time a President was chosen by the House of Representatives. This time the man of the people was beaten, the will of the people was said to have been defied, and senators, representatives, and State legislatures joined in one demand that the college of electors be swept away.

Hardly had the election been decided in the House when Mr. McDuffie, of South Carolina, proposed that the election of President should never be made by Congress; that there should be a direct vote of the people by districts, and that the man who carried a majority of the districts should be President. Buchanan was for giving the choice in contested elections to the State legislatures. Hayne was against all intervention of Congress. Dickerson was against a third term, and the Senate sent his amendment to the House. Phelps was for going back to the old custom abolished by the twelfth amendment. Sloane was for a *per capita* election throughout the United States. Benton, from the Senate committee, reported in favor of a popular vote in districts; the abolition of the Electoral College; a majority of districts necessary to a choice, and when no majority a re-election as before; if no choice then, a choice by the Congress. So vital had the question become, that in the four years of Mr. Adams's Presidency thirty-three amendments concerning it were offered in the House and Senate. Then, wearied with it all, a member urged giving Congress power, after 1830, to propose amendments every ten years and no oftener. But the manner of election was not changed. Jackson was chosen in the old way; the dread which the Democrats had of the Electoral College ended, and the dispute over the manner of electing was changed to a dispute over the length of term. Jackson, in his message to Congress, asked for a definite limit, and more amendments followed. Some would give a President no more than two terms; some, one term of four years; others, one term of five. Again nothing was done, and again the President returned to the subject in his message in December, 1836. The select committee reported on it and were discharged, and the proposition came up regularly each session, only to be thrust aside by others more pressing.

On March fourth, 1829, Jackson began what his enemies have called his "reign," and the amendments offered during his terms were prompted more by the bitter hatred the Whigs felt toward him than by any public necessity. He removed men from office by hundreds; and the Whigs retaliated by offering an amendment that all tenure of office not otherwise provided for by the Constitution should be regulated by Congress. He demanded that Duane should withdraw the deposits from the Bank of the United States. Duane refused, was removed, and for this the Whigs retaliated with an amendment that the Secretary of the Treasury should be chosen annually by the joint vote of House and Senate and should nominate, and by and with the advice of the Senate appoint, all officers whose duty it was to disburse the revenues. Jackson gave five members of Congress places in the Cabinet. Three more he sent to foreign courts. Four more he made comfortable with collectorships, appraiserships, and district attorneyships, and to stop him the Whigs proposed a third amendment. By it senators and representatives were not to be eligible to any office in the gift of President or Secretary of the Treasury during the term for which they were elected to sit in Congress, nor for two years thereafter. But the great constitutional question was the right to abolish slavery.

The Missouri Compromise had stirred up Benjamin Lundy, Benjamin Lundy had stirred up Garrison, and Garrison in turn had roused the antislavery feeling of the North. Hundreds of antislavery societies had sprung into existence, and from these petitions, signed, it is said, by thirty-four thousand names, praying for the abolition of slavery in the District of Columbia, came pouring in. Once more the interests of a section were attacked. Once more expediency produced the charge of unconstitutionality. Congress had no power to abolish slavery anywhere. To ask it to abolish slavery was to ask it to do an unconstitutional act, and petitions making such requests were themselves unconstitutional and ought not to be received. A motion that the House of Representatives would not receive any petition for the abolition of slavery in the District of Columbia was sent to a committee. From that committee, in May, 1836, came a report that Congress had no power to interfere with slavery in any of the States; that it ought not to interfere with it in the District of Columbia; and that all "petitions, memorials, resolutions, or papers, relating in any way or to any extent whatever to the subject of slavery or the abolition of slavery, shall, without being either printed or referred, be laid upon the table, and that no further action whatever shall be had thereon."

Thus was the Constitution violated. Thus was the famous "gag rule" enacted. Thus was begun the glorious contest waged by John Quincy Adams in behalf of the right of petition. Thus was slavery brought up for settlement under the Constitution.

On March fourth, 1837, Andrew Jackson quit office and Martin Van Buren began what the Whigs called "Jackson's Appendix," and during four years the amendments offered were Whig amendments, setting forth old Whig principles. The President was to have one term. Congressmen were to be ineligible to offices in the gift of the President for two years after the close of the term for which they were elected to serve in Congress. Judges of the Supreme Court were to serve for seven years and no longer. With these came up from time to time other amendments expressive of the moral sense of the community. The collector of the port of New York went off a defaulter for one million five hundred thousand dollars; Congressman Cilley was murdered in a duel.

Shocked at such enormities, the whole community cried out for reform, and two constitutional amendments promptly appeared in Congress. Embezzlers were to be forever disfranchised. Duellists were to be forever shut out from office-holding under the Government of the United States.

But all of these were overshadowed by the great constitutional question of the hour—the right of Congress to abolish slavery in the District of Columbia. In the two years which had elapsed since the "gag rule" was passed a great moral awakening had begun. Slavery, as well as duellists and embezzlers, was growing hateful, and the antislavery movement had entered the political field to stay. The Legislature of Massachusetts pronounced the "gag rule" unconstitutional, and asserted that Congress had power to abolish slavery in the District of Columbia. So did Vermont. Connecticut repealed the "black code." From a few hundred in 1835, the antislavery societies rose to two thousand in 1837. The abolition petitions which reached Congress in the early months of 1838 are said to have borne signatures traced by three hundred thousand hands. Then was it that Calhoun brought in five resolutions defining the powers of Congress and the States over slavery. Then was it that Mr. Clay moved eight more on slavery, the slave-trade, and the petitions. Then was it that Mr. Atherton moved yet another five, drawn up by the Democratic caucus, declaring that the Government of the United States was a Government of limited powers and had no jurisdiction over slavery in the States; that petitions to abolish slavery in the District and the Territories were part of a plan indirectly to destroy slavery in the State; that as Congress could not do indirectly what it could not do directly, these petitions were against the true intent and spirit of the Constitution, and that they ought, when presented, to be laid on the table without being debated, printed, or referred. One by one they were adopted, and hardly were they adopted when a member moved an explanation.

The States were not associated on principles of unlimited submission. The Federal Government was a Government of limited and specific powers derived from the people of the States, and the House of Representatives in adopting the "gag rule" had but fulfilled its constitutional duty and in no way infringed the right of petition or the freedom of debate. Then was it that John Quincy Adams moved the first antislavery constitutional amendment. Save Florida, no slave State should ever again be admitted into the Union. On July fourth, 1842, hereditary slavery was to cease and all negroes born after that day to be forever free. On July fourth, 1845, there was to be an end made to slavery and the slave-trade in the District of Columbia.

A week later the first half-century under the Constitution ended. The second half opened with a lull in constitutional discussion. During two years not an amendment was offered. There began a new threshing of the old straw. The term of the judges, the term of the President, the manner of electing him, the exclusion of congressmen from office, were repeatedly made the subjects of proposed amendments. There was a long debate on the constitutionality of the protective tariff. There was a renewal by Massachusetts of the old demand that representation and direct taxes be apportioned according to the number of free inhabitants, and of the old question of the constitutionality of a bank.

The great Whig victory of 1840 turned over the administration of affairs to the loose-construction party. But the death of Harrison in 1841 gave it back again to the strict constructionists; for such Tyler had always been and such he always remained. Still the Whigs were not dismayed, and one by one brought forward their promised reforms. They repealed the Sub-Treasury Act, and Tyler signed the bill. But he vetoed, as unconstitutional, the bill to establish "The Fiscal Bank of the United States," and the bill to establish a "Fiscal Corporation."

For this, Whig voters burned him in effigy all over the Union. For this, the Whig caucus read him out of the party, and in an earnest address to the people called for a lessening of the executive power by limiting the veto, by restricting the President to a single term, and by giving the appointment of Secretary of the Treasury to Congress. The people gave the address small heed; but the great Whig leader did, and in December, 1841, moved three constitutional amendments. Henceforth a majority vote was to be enough to pass a bill over the veto; henceforth the Treasurer and the Secretary of the Treasury were to be appointed by Congress, and no congressman given any office during the term for which he had been elected. Clay defended his amendments with all the eloquence and skill of which he was master. Calhoun attacked them with more than common zeal, and the Senate laid them on the table. But the end was not yet. The last reduction provided by the compromise tariff was to take place June thirtieth, 1842. The Whigs passed a bill suspending this reduction till August first, 1842, and Tyler sent it back with his "I forbid." Unable to override the veto, the Whigs passed a new tariff act, and this also Tyler sent back with his "I forbid."

The House took up the message which accompanied this veto—the "ditto veto," as it was nicknamed by the Whigs—and sent it to a Committee of Thirteen. John Quincy Adams was the chairman, and wrote a report which ended with another call for the constitutional amendment proposed by Clay, for a limitation of the veto. The report accomplished nothing; but the question at issue was by no means dead, and appeared in both the Whig and Democratic platforms of 1844.

The custom of laying constitutional "planks" in a party platform was brought in by the National Republicans in 1832. Those were the days when nullification was rife, when the Supreme Court was defied, when the outlay of public money on internal improvements was still thought unconstitutional. But such was not Republican doctrine; and in their platform, the first ever framed by a national convention, they boldly declared for internal improvements, and pronounced the Supreme Court the only tribunal for deciding all questions arising under the Constitution and the laws.

As this was the first, so for eight years it was the last party platform. Then, in the campaign of 1840, the Democrats imitated the Republicans of 1832, framed their first party platform and in it laid down the party views on the Constitution. The Federal Government was declared to be one of limited powers. These powers were derived solely from the Constitution and were to be construed strictly. Such a construction gave to Congress no power to make internal improvements, to assume State debts, to charter a bank, nor to meddle with the domestic institutions of the States. In these principles neither time nor experience wrought any changes, and for twenty years they were regularly reaffirmed by every Democratic convention. Four years later the men who nominated Clay drew up three resolutions, which must be considered as the first Whig platform, and in them demanded one term for the President and a reform of executive usurpations, which every true Whig understood to mean the constitutional amendments supported by John Quincy Adams and Henry Clay.

But the election was contested on very different grounds. It was under the cries of "The reannexation of Texas and the reoccupation of Oregon," "The whole

CENTURY OF CONSTITUTIONAL INTERPRETATION. 215

of Oregon, or none," "Fifty-four forty or fight," that the Democrats entered the campaign. It was under such cries as "Texas or disunion," "Give us Texas or divide the spoons," that they won it. The treaty of annexation had failed in the Senate on constitutional grounds. Some denied the right to acquire foreign soil in any manner. Some objected to annexing it by treaty: to remove their scruples annexation by joint rule was proposed, only to be resisted by those who claimed that annexation by treaty was the only constitutional method of procedure. A compromise followed, and Tyler was left to submit to Texas the joint rule or open negotiations for a new treaty, as he saw fit. He submitted the joint rule and gave the country Texas. Then came the war. The war gave us new territory; the new territory had to be governed, and the attempt to set up territorial governments in California, New Mexico, and Utah brought up the question whether those governments should be slave or free.

On the one hand were the Free-soilers, holding two definite theories of the status of slavery under the Constitution. Slavery in the State was, they held, a purely domestic institution. State laws created it. State laws protected it, and these laws the Federal Government could not repeal. For slavery in the States, therefore, the Federal Government was not to blame. But for the existence of slavery in the Territories the Federal Government was to blame; for over the Territories the States had no authority and the Congress all authority. But the Constitution expressly denied to Congress power to deprive any man of life, liberty, or property without due process of law. Congress had, therefore, no more power to make a slave than to make a king;

no more power to set up slavery than to set up monarchy. The Congress must prohibit slavery in the Territories, in the District of Columbia, and wherever else its authority was supreme.

On the other hand were the Democrats, resisting the Wilmot proviso, resisting the exclusion of slavery from the Territories; demanding the fulfilment by the North of the constitutional obligation to return fugitive slaves; asserting the doctrines of popular sovereignty and non-interference, and threatening disunion if every demand were not conceded. Non-interference meant the constitutional right of every slave-holder to take his slaves to any State or any Territory and be secure in their possession, and the constitutional duty of Congress to do nothing tending directly or indirectly to hurt slavery even "in its incipient stages." Popular sovereignty meant the right of the people in a Territory to determine for themselves when they framed their State Constitution whether they would or would not have slavery.

By 1850 these two doctrines had become so well defined that an attempt was made to fasten them on the Constitution. One amendment proposed that the Constitution should never be amended so as to abolish slavery without consent of each State in which slavery existed. By another resolution the Committee on the Judiciary were to frame an amendment setting forth that the people of each separate community, whether they do or do not reside in the Territories, have a right to make their own domestic laws and to establish their own domestic government.

Again the proposed amendments were thrown aside; but the doctrine of popular sovereignty triumphed. By the compromise of 1850 it was applied in the organization of Utah and New Mexico, and in them slavery was established. By the act of May twenty-second, 1854, it was again applied in the organization of Kansas and Nebraska, and in Kansas slavery was desperately resisted. When that dreadful war was over, Clay was dead; Webster was dead; the old Whig party was dead; the Free-soil party had given place to the Republican party; the Dred Scott decision had been made, and the Democratic party was rent into two sectional factions, holding two very different views on "sovereignty." The Southern wing, led by Breckinridge and Lane, still held to the old form of "popular sovereignty," and still declared that when the settlers in a Territory, having an adequate population, form a State Constitution, the right of sovereignty begins; that they then have the right to recognize or prohibit slavery, as they see fit, and must then be admitted as a State with their Constitution free or pro-slavery, as they wish; still held that the government of a Territory is provisional and temporary, and that while it lasts all citizens of the United States have equal rights to settle in the Territories without their rights or property being impaired by congressional action. The Northern wing, led by Douglas, proclaimed the doctrine of "squatter sovereignty," the right of the people while still in the territorial condition to determine through their territorial legislatures whether they would or would not have slavery.

The Republicans, on the other hand, asserted the normal condition of the Territories to be that of freedom, and denied the authority of Congress, of the territorial legislatures, of territorial constitutional conventions, and of any individual to give legal existence to slavery in the Territories. In 1860 this doctrine triumphed, and the Southern States at once began to carry out the threats so often made, and one by one seceded.

Then came up for final settlement two questions, many times discussed in vague or general language: May a State secede? May the Federal Government coerce? The answer of Buchanan to these questions is given in his message to Congress in December, 1860. He admitted, as all men must admit, that revolution is a "rightful remedy" for tyranny and oppression. He denied that secession was a constitutional remedy for anything. But he asserted that the Constitution gave no power to coerce a State when it claimed to have seceded. He admitted that the Constitution did give the power to enforce the laws of the Union on the people of a so-called seceded State; but he asserted that he was powerless to do so because he could not comply with the terms of the law of 1795, which provided for putting that power into effect. Having laid down these principles, he fell back on the old remedy and urged an "explanatory constitutional amendment." This amendment was to declare, not that secession was unconstitutional, not that the General Government might coerce, but that the right of property in slaves was recognized in every State where it then existed or might exist; that this right should be protected in the Territories so long as they remained Territories; and that all State laws hindering the return of fugitive slaves were unconstitutional, null, and void.

The hint was taken, and men of all parties made haste to lay before Congress a vast mass of propositions and amendments. One was for urging the States to call a constitutional convention. Jefferson Davis was for declaring by amendment that property in slaves stood upon the same footing as other kinds of property and should never be impaired by act of Congress. Andrew Johnson had a long list of six more. Mr. Crittenden, a senator from Kentucky, offered seven. From the House Committee on the State of the Union came seven. From the Peace Conference came seven. All were compromises. The slave States had complained that they were not given equal rights in the Territories. They were now given rights; and the public domain was parted by the old Missouri Compromise line of 36° 30′. In the Territories north of the line there was to be no slavery; in the Territories south of the line slavery was to be protected. The slave States had demanded "popular sovereignty." They were now given popular sovereignty, and the Territories both north and south of 36° 30′ were to be suffered, when they formed State constitutions, to set up or prohibit slavery. The free States had complained of the acquisition of territory for the purpose of spreading slavery. The Federal Government was now forbidden to acquire any territory in any way, save by discovery, without the consent of a majority of the senators from the States where slavery was not allowed and of a majority of the senators from the States where slavery was allowed. The free States had demanded the abolition of slavery in the District of Columbia; but this was refused, and in future neither the Constitution nor any amendment was to be so construed as to give Congress power to meddle with slavery in the States, nor to abolish it in the District without the consent of Maryland. The free States had demanded that the slave-trade between the States be stopped, and this was granted. The slave States had demanded a better enforcement of the fugitive-slave law: this too was granted, and the States were to have power to pass laws to enforce the delivery of fugitive slaves to legal claimants. All these amendments, and all the provisions of the Constitution touching slavery, were never to be changed without the consent of each State. But the day for compromise was gone. Congress would not accept them, and March second, 1861, sent out to the States a short amendment in their stead, providing that Congress should never abolish nor meddle with slavery in the States. Maryland and Ohio alone ratified it. The war made it useless, and in February, 1864, it was recalled, to be followed in February, 1865, by an amendment which the States did accept and which abolished slavery in the United States forever. Then began the days of reconstruction, and when March thirtieth, 1870, came, two more amendments had been added to the Constitution.

With these the amending stopped; but the rage for amendment went on burning with tenfold fury. State sovereignty was gone; Federal sovereignty was established. The national Government, not the State Government, was now looked up to as the righter of wrongs, the corrector of abuses, the preserver of morals; and individuals, societies, sects, made haste to lay their grievances before Congress and ask to have them removed by constitutional amendment. The change which the war has produced in this respect is most marked and curious. During the twenty-eight years which have passed since 1861, three hundred and seventy-seven amendments

CENTURY OF CONSTITUTIONAL INTERPRETATION. 221

have been offered. Many of these, it is true, have in one form or another tormented Congress for ninety years; but among them are others which indicate nothing so plainly as the belief that the Government is now a great national Government and that its duty is to provide in the broadest sense for "the general welfare" of the people. To Congress, therefore, have come repeated calls for constitutional amendments, forbidding special legislation; forbidding the manufacture and sale of spirituous liquors; forbidding bigamy and polygamy; forbidding the repeal of the pension laws; giving Congress power to pass uniform marriage and divorce laws, and power to limit the hours of labor; giving women the right to vote; giving the States power to tax corporations; and for amendments abolishing and prohibiting the convict-labor system and acknowledging the existence of a God.

A CENTURY'S STRUGGLE FOR SILVER.

WHEN the articles of Confederation went into force in the month of March, 1781, the Continental Congress, for the first time in its existence, was given power to coin money and regulate the value thereof. The need of such regulation was great; for there was at that day no national coinage; no uniform circulating medium, no legal tender, no common money of account. In the towns and cities along the seaboard the currency was composed of paper bills put out by the States and confined in circulation to the limits of the States wherein they were printed; of loan-office certificates, indents, and continental notes issued by authority of Congress, and passing at different rates of discount at different places; and, to some extent, of specie made up of the coins of England, France, Portugal, and Spain.

Back from the seaboard, and especially along the frontier, debts were generally paid in produce or lumber; barter was the chief medium of exchange; and, if any standard of value existed, it was a bushel of wheat or a gallon of whiskey; a bundle of skins, or a hundred-weight of tobacco. The money of account used by the Congress was the Spanish milled dollar and its fractions. The money of account used by the States, the merchants, and the people was the pound and its fractions. But neither the pound nor the dollar had a common value the country over, for each expressed a very different value in New England and in New York; in Pennsylvania and in the South. To make matters worse, not a doubloon nor a moidore, not a guinea nor a crown, not a joe, not a sixpence, not a gold or silver coin of any denomination passed current by tale; for all had been so clipped or plugged that no one would take them save by weight.

To cure the evils produced by so disordered a currency, and replace it gradually by a national and uniform circulating medium, was no easy matter, and was not accomplished in fifty years. The work, however, was begun in 1782 by the Continental Congress calling on its Superintendent of Finance to report a table of rates at which foreign coins should be received at the post-offices and the Treasury, for as Congress could not lay a tax of any kind no Federal custom-houses existed. Robert Morris was Secretary of Finance, and, instead of merely reporting a table of rates, he took occasion to lay before Congress some wholesome advice on the subject of a national currency. He told it that credit could not be established, that business could not flourish, that industrial enterprises could not be securely carried on till a uniform currency existed; that what was wanted was not a table of the relative values of foreign coins, but a standard of our own by which in future to estimate them; in a word, a national coinage.

Having heard the report, Congress took no action. But the idea was not abandoned, and by 1786 matters had gone so far that a unit had been chosen, the names and denomination of many of our present coins selected, and an ordinance passed establishing a mint and regulating the alloy of coin. The ordinance, however, was never put into force. The balance of trade was heavily against the States. To settle this balance the foreign coins were gathered up and shipped to London, and the people, stripped of every kind of circulating medium, forced a majority of the States to again put forth paper money, and brought on that dreadful era of force acts and tender laws, depreciated paper and token money, which marked the closing years of the Confederation. Abandoning all attempts, under these circumstances, to coin the precious metals, the Board of Treasury, acting under an ordinance of Congress, contracted for the manufacture of a few copper cents, which, bearing date 1787, are now to be found in the cabinets of collectors under the name of " Fugios."

With the establishment of government under the Constitution, Congress once more returned to the subject of a national coinage, and in 1791, after listening to the famous report of Hamilton, ordered that a mint be established, and that Washington secure such artists and such machines as might be necessary. One year later another act specified the officers of the mint, established the unit, fixed the standard of fineness, and named the coins that were to be struck. Gold, silver, and copper, the law provided, were to be coined without charge for all comers in the order of their arrival; the gold into eagles, half-eagles, and quarter-eagles; the silver into dollars, half dollars, quarter dollars, dimes, and half dimes; the copper into cents and half cents.

Having thus provided for a bimetallic currency, the law further ordered that the ratio between the two metals should be fifteen to one, or that fifteen pounds weight of pure silver should have the same legal value as one pound of pure gold. The unit was the silver dollar, and into it were to go 371¼ grains of pure, or 416 grains of standard silver.

Though the law was passed in April, such haste was made to carry it out that by October a site had been procured in Philadelphia, a mint (the first public building erected by the Federal Government) had been put up, and the coinage of silver half dimes had begun. Some cents and half cents were struck in 1793; but the serious work of coinage did not begin till October, 1794. The Treasury having no authority to purchase bullion, the mint was forced to depend on individuals and the Treasury for a supply of bullion or foreign coins. This supply proved trivial and irregular. As neither gold nor silver was mined in the country, no private interest existed eager to avail itself of the free coinage offered by the mint. As foreign coin still circulated freely from hand to hand, and were still a legal tender for Government dues, merchants were under no inducement to turn them in for recoinage. The Secretary of the Treasury, it is true, was in duty bound to send every piece of foreign coin received on payment of dues to the mint to be recoined before it again passed into circulation. But each succeeding Secretary so flatly refused to obey the law that ten years after the establishment of the mint not a dollar had been coined on account of the Government.

The chief supplies were the banks. Indeed, it was from one of them—the Bank of Maryland—that the first deposit of silver was received in July, 1794. It consisted of French coin worth $80,715, and from the same dollars and half dollars were struck and returned to the Treasury in October. In coining them the director deliberately and wilfully disobeyed the law. Believing that the prescribed standard would debase the coin and cause it to turn black when used, he had recommended that a change be made, and that for every nine parts pure silver there should be one part alloy. Confident that his recommendation would be approved, he had ordered the dollars to be made in accordance with the new standard, and was not a little chagrined when, a year later, Congress having given no heed to his suggestion, he was forced to coin according to the old law. Meantime every depositor whose silver had been used had suffered a loss. Each did, it is true, receive back all his silver; but he received less dollars than he was legally entitled to. One such sufferer applied to Congress for relief; but his claim was disallowed. When the first silver coin was delivered at the Treasury in 1794, the President, as the law required, issued his proclamation, declaring that on the fifteenth day of October, 1797, all silver coins of foreign mints, the Spanish milled dollar alone excepted, should cease to be legal tender. Some half-eagles made from gold bullion, deposited by a Boston merchant, having been sent to the Treasury in July, 1795, a like proclamation was issued concerning foreign gold coin, and the day seemed near when the people of the United States would have a national coinage of their own.

But when the prescribed time expired, eagles and dollars, dimes and half dimes, were almost as scarce as if no mint existed. The reason is plain. The Administration was trying to do what no power has ever yet succeeded in doing—it was trying to put in circulation, side by side, a sound and an unsound currency. The foreign coins—old, worn, clipped, and light of weight—

drove out the new American dollars and eagles, which, sound and of full weight, were of far more value as a commodity in foreign markets than as a circulating medium at home. They were therefore exported in such numbers that enough could not be had to pay the dues of] merchants at the Custom-House, and in 1798 the law was suspended, and foreign coins remained a legal tender till 1802. But the exportation of our coin still went on, and when 1802 came the country was as far as ever from enjoying a metallic currency of its own. Popular sentiment meantime turned strongly against the mint. It was denounced as another of the many costly and useless pieces of political machinery saddled on the people by the Federalist party. "This mint," it was said in 1800, "has been seven years in existence, yet the entire output of coins, gold, silver, and copper, is short of $2,600,000, while the cost of making them has exceeded $200,000. To coin ten dollars entails an outlay of one dollar, and when the ten are coined half of them are instantly gathered up and shipped to London as bullion. For the few pieces which remain locked up in the vaults of banks we pay, accordingly, twenty per cent of their value for the privilege of trying to have a national coinage. The game is not worth the candle. The burden is too great to be borne." In the House of Representatives the popular feeling was so strongly reflected that in 1800 a committee reported in favor of abolishing the mint, and in 1802 a bill was passed closing it. To this, however, the Senate would not agree, and for twenty-six years the mint was continued by a long series of acts running from one to five years. Not till 1828 was it permanently established.

That the evils of an unsound currency and the absence of a national coinage was so little felt in the time of Jefferson is to be ascribed to the credit currency supplied by the banks then rapidly springing up all over the country. Each gave to the people of its neighborhood a paper currency which was in no danger of exportation, which passed readily from hand to hand, and was far more portable than specie, while the Bank of the United States furnished what came very near to being a uniform circulating medium. With branches in every important city in the country ready to redeem its notes in specie; with every tax collector, every customs collector ready to take them in payment of Government dues, the five millions of bills the bank put out were accepted in all parts of the country as readily as the national bank notes of the present day. But when, in 1811, Congress refused to recharter the bank, scores of State institutions sprang up to take its place. The country was flooded with paper money far exceeding in amount the specie in the country. Redemption was not possible, and in the troubled days of the war every bank along the seaboard, out of New England, from Albany to Savannah suspended specie payments. Exchange was destroyed. The Federal Treasury, unable to move its money from the place of collection to the place of expenditure, was reduced to bankruptcy, and the days of barter and token money returned. Firmly convinced that a credit currency which neither rested on nor was redeemable in specie was worse than none, the people cried out for a national bank, and in 1816 the second Bank of the United States was chartered for the sole purpose of "regulating the currency." But specie must be had on which to rest its paper, and to bring back specie certain foreign coins were, in 1816, once more made legal tender, and remained so—the gold till 1819, the silver till 1827.

Food distress in Europe changed the balance of trade in favor of the United States, specie came back in great quantity, and some relief was given to the banks and the Treasury. But the people gained nothing, for the dearth of small change went on. Without the slightest authority by law the director of the mint had coined no silver dollars since 1804, no quarter dollars since 1808, and no dimes since 1810 save a few in 1811 and 1814, and no half dimes since 1806. Two dollar bank bills torn in two and four pieces, tickets of 1, 2, 3, 6¼, 10, 12½, 18¾, 25, 37½ and 50 cents in value and issued by individuals, by stage companies, by mayors of cities, by corporations of every sort, constituted the money with which the people transacted the business of the market-place and the shop. To make matters worse, the Bank of England in 1819 resumed specie payments after a suspension of twenty-six years, and the tide of specie again turned strongly toward London. First went our gold pieces, which were so undervalued that $4.56 in coin contained as much gold as an English sovereign. Next went our silver, driven out by the debased and worn products of the French and Spanish mints. Gold now disappeared not only from sight, but from the vaults of the banks, and from 1819 to 1834 the circulating medium of our country became a credit currency based on foreign coins. The mint, indeed, continued year by year to turn out its coin, and during these years $25,000,000 in round numbers in silver and $4,500,000 in gold pieces were struck. But nine tenths of them were sent away or melted into bullion.

This state of affairs called forth much discussion, many reports, many plans of relief, but no legislation. At one time the House of Representatives thought seriously of prohibiting the exportation of specie. At another it was proposed to cut down the weight of the monetary unit and make American coin worth more for use at home than for shipment abroad. Session after session, however, went by and nothing was done till 1834. The promoters of a new industry then came forward and turned discussion into action. The United States had become a gold-producing country, and though the amount mined (about $678,000 in 1832 and $868,000 in 1833) seems small in these days, it was enough to call for legislation. Such a yield, it was feared, would lower the price. To keep up the price a market must be found, and this market it was the duty of the Federal Government to provide by putting gold coin into circulation. The time was most favorable. The long struggle waged by Jackson with the Bank of the United States was practically over, for his triumphant re-election in 1832 made the end of the bank certain.

Millions of dollars in bills which for twenty years had been the real circulating medium of the country were soon to be called in. The place of this paper must be supplied, and over the kind of money that should replace it a lively contest now took place. On the one side were the friends of the State banks, the paper-money men, the inflationists, as they would be called in our day. On the other side were the enemies of the old bank, the friends of Jackson, the hard-money men, the advocates of a national coinage, the producers of gold. Led on by

Thomas Benton, they won and placed on the statute-book the Gold Coin Act of 1834. The wish and purpose of "Old Bullion," as his admirers delighted to call him, was to stop the importation of gold coin; to restore gold and silver money of foreign nations to its former circulation within the United States; and to make the revenue laws of the United States instrumental in establishing gold and silver as the common currency of the country. The law of 1834 was intended to accomplish the first of these ends, and to accomplish it by reducing the weight of the eagle, half-eagle, and quarter-eagle, and so raising the ratio between gold and silver to 1 to 16·002. Just what this act was expected to do was well expressed by the Washington Globe, the organ of the Administration. "A great stream of gold," said the Globe, "will flow up the Mississippi River from New Orleans, and diffuse itself all over the great West. Nearly all the gold coinage of the New World will come to the United States. This will fill the West with doubloons and half-joes, and in eight or nine months from this time every substantial citizen will have a long silken purse with fine open network through the interstices of which yellow gold will shine and glisten. Every substantial man and every substantial man's wife and daughter will travel on gold." Unhappily, this fond expectation was not realized. The mint, indeed, went hard to work and in six years turned out nearly $18,000,000 of what the people called "Benton mint-drops," and "Jackson yellow-boys." But the ratio proved a false one; silver had been underrated, and in its turn took flight. Then began, in 1840, that excess of exports over imports of silver which from that day to this has never been interrupted save in 1843, in 1846, and in 1861. When the fifties were reached matters had become so bad that it was scarcely possible to keep the fractional silver coins in circulation. Debased as they were, they had far more value as bullion than as change, and they, too, left us, and by 1853 silver was practically demonetized by the working of the law of 1834 and the discovery of gold in California.

In 1853, therefore, came the second great change in our currency laws, by which the weight of fractional coins was lessened materially and their free coinage stopped. Henceforth halves and quarters, dimes and half dimes were made solely on Government account and sold for gold in sums of $100. This sufficed for twenty years, when new legislation became necessary. The act was passed in 1873, when not a coin had been in circulation for eleven years, and was rather a codification of existing laws than new legislation. All the provisions of sixty-odd acts relating to the mint, to its branches, to the Assay Office, to the coinage, passed since 1792 were arranged, classified, simplified, stripped of all inconsistencies, and embodied in one statute. As to the coinage, three changes were made. The bronze two-cent piece, authorized in 1864 but never popular; the three-cent silver piece (not the three-cent nickel), authorized in 1851 and so little known that few persons now living could describe it from memory; the half dime and the dollar, were dropped from the list of coins. The silver dollar may be said never to have been in circulation. From the day the first specimens came from the mint the dollars were the rarest of our coins, for they were shipped year after year to London and to the West Indies. Finding that none of them remained at home, Jefferson ordered that no more should be struck, and in March, 1804, their coinage ceased for thirty-five years.* In 1839 they began to be made again; but the Gold Coinage Act of 1834 slowly demonetized silver; the premium on the dollar rose to $1.03 in gold, and Congress, seeing that the mint was a mere machine for turning silver into a convenient form for exportation, sanctioned the request that the coinage of dollars be discontinued. At the same time a great innovation was made, and a new coin ordered, not for circulation, but for shipment.

Want of a mint in China had left that empire dependent on the coins of foreign nations, and of such coins none found so ready a circulation as the dollars of Mexico and Spain. It was in such pieces that millions and millions were remitted by American merchants engaged in the China trade, a purchase which seemed quite unnecessary now that the mines of Colorado and Nevada were producing more silver than the country could well consume. The act of 1873, therefore, provided that any owner of bullion might deposit it at any mint and, after paying all charges, receive either bars or " trade dollars " weighing 420 grains troy. By a piece of carelessness on the part of Congress these new coins were made a legal tender in sums not greater than five dollars. But as each one cost much more than a dollar to make, none were used as money in our country till after 1876. In that year the legal-tender quality

---

* Three hundred and twenty-one were numbered in 1805 and 1,000 in 1836.

was taken away. The cost of manufacturing, however, was then less than a dollar, the country was about to return to specie payments, the people seemed willing to take the dollars at their face value, and owners of mines found it most profitable to hurry their silver to the mint to be turned into trade dollars. Such was the rush that in 1877 more than 13,000,000 of them were struck. This was twice as large as the output of any previous year, and would undoubtedly have been greatly surpassed in the next twelve months had not the act of February twenty-eighth, 1878, forbidden further coinage. A few hundreds were, it is true, issued each year till 1883, when 35,965,924 trade dollars had gone from the mint. Four fifths of them were either exported or used in the arts. One fifth (7,689,036), after passing about as token money, till no postmaster would take them in payment of stamps, till no bank would receive them on deposit, till no car conductor would accept them for fares, till no shopkeeper would take them save at a discount of ten per cent, they were at last rejected by the people, were purchased by syndicates and redeemed by the Government in 1887 at one hundred cents on the dollar.

The five years during which the trade-dollar act remained on the statute-books were years full of the most unforeseen and startling events. Abroad, Germany, aided by the payment of the French indemnity, changed her currency from silver to gold. Nation after nation ceased to coin silver, and even in India and in China the demand for it fell off. At home, meantime, the production of the mines went on steadily increasing, doubling, trebling, quadrupling, and pulling down the market value from $1.30 to $1.12 an ounce.

The silver States cried out for relief; Congress responded, and by the same act which stopped the coinage of the "trade" dollar provided the producers of silver with a market. Under the new law the Secretary was commanded to buy each month not less than two nor more than four million dollars' worth of silver and have it coined into standard silver dollars, to be a legal tender for any amount. Then began our silver era and our first serious struggle for bimetallism. Year by year from twenty-seven to thirty-eight millions of " cart-wheel dollars " were struck, till at the close of twelve years more than 350,000,000 had been manufactured. That the people would willingly handle so vast a quantity of so heavy and clumsy a coin was never expected. For convenience, therefore, the law provided for the deposit of the dollars (when made) in the vaults of the Treasury, and the issue in place of them of silver certificates which should be receivable for customs, taxes, and all public dues, and when so received might be reissued. Under the workings of the law some 60,000,000 of the silver dollars were sent out into circulation. Of the remainder, a part is held for the redemption of the silver certificates which now form so large a portion of the paper currency in the pockets of our people, while a part lies idle in the Treasury.

Great as was the consumption of silver in this way, it still proved of small avail. The yield of the mines went on increasing. The price went on falling, and in 1890 another and more stringent remedy was tried. By the act of July fourteenth, 1890—the ever-famous "Sherman Act"—the Secretary is compelled to buy each month 4,500,000 ounces of silver, or so much thereof as may be offered at less than $1.29 per ounce, and pay for it in Treasury notes to be redeemed on demand in gold or silver as the Secretary shall judge fit. Notes so issued are legal tender at their face value for all debts public and private, unless otherwise expressly stipulated in the contract, and, when redeemed, may be again reissued.

The present year completes the century since the mint was fairly established and began the work of making coin. A review of that century makes clear to us that the first great currency question with which the country had to deal was whether there should be a national coinage, or a legalizing and rerating of the debased foreign coin of pre-revolutionary days. The chartering of the Banks of the United States and the rise of State banks settled this question and gave the country a paper currency based on foreign coin. The winding up of the second United States Bank and beginning of gold mining brought up in 1834 the second great currency question, which was, Shall the money of the country be hard or soft, metallic or paper? The Gold Coin Act of 1834 was the attempt to settle this, and brought on the first bimetallic discussion ever held in Congress. The attempt was a failure. A false ratio and the unexpected discovery of gold in California demonetized silver, and the fractional silver coin act of 1853 marked the second effort to preserve and remonetize silver. Once more the effort proved vain and the acts of 1873, 1878, and 1890 followed.

IS SOUND FINANCE POSSIBLE UNDER POPULAR GOVERNMENT?

WHENEVER the times become hard, whenever business is depressed, money difficult to earn, and the country brought face to face with serious financial troubles, a feeling of despondency is sure to set in. Under the baleful influences of such periods of distress as that through which we are now passing men of sense and judgment lose faith in the success of Democratic institutions and the wisdom of majority rule. It is easy enough, they say, for the great mass of our fellow-citizens to form a fairly correct judgment on a question of pure politics. Even if they fail to form a correct judgment, even if they do adopt wrong standards, pursue wrong methods, and put bad men in power, it is still possible for the community to be prosperous and happy, though misgoverned. But when the question to be dealt with is so intricate and complex as to be beyond the comprehension of the great mass of men, is it safe to leave it to be decided by majority rule? In the light of our past history the answer is, Yes.

Of all the people of the earth we are the most practical and the least theoretical. Experience, not theory, has ever been our guide. Nowhere else do theories of finance, theories of political economy, of government, of social organization, count for so little. Nowhere else does that wisdom gained by daily contact with the affairs of life count for so much. The very Constitution under which we live is a signal illustration of this. It was quite as much a business as a political necessity, and bears all over it the marks of a bitter experience. The dreadful state of trade, foreign and interstate, the disorders of the currency, the lack of a uniform circulating medium, the hopelessness of trying to support a Government which could not tax—these were the considerations which outweighed all others and moved our ancestors to frame and adopt the Constitution. Any student of politics could have told them, and many did, that it was idle to expect that thirteen petty republics could regulate a common foreign trade as successfully as one central government. But not till the experiment had been made and failed were the people ready to bestow on Congress *sole* power to regulate trade with foreign countries, between the States, and with the Indians. Any student of finance could have told them that thirteen kinds of paper money issued on no security and maintained by tender laws and force acts could never become the circulating medium of a great people. But not until they had tried it, not until they had brought themselves to the brink of ruin by the experiment, were our ancestors willing to declare that no State shall coin money, emit bills of credit, or make anything but gold and silver coin a tender in payment of debts.

The financial crisis which extorted these concessions from the people of the several States was the worst this country ever went through, and it was fully believed that the like of it would never return. By the words "bills of credit" was meant what we now call paper money, and, under the injunction that neither Congress nor the States should issue them, it seemed certain that the days of fiat money were over in the United States. That the States in time would find an instrument and authorize it to do what they could not legally do themselves was not thought possible, for State banking had but just begun. On the day the Constitution became the supreme law of the land there were but three banks in the entire country. But, fostered and cherished by the amazing prosperity which sprang up under the new Government, they increased and multiplied and spread over the States till, when 1812 came, two hundred and eight State banks were doing business. Each had power to issue notes to the amount of three times its capital, and each exceeded its power. Even in the East the circulating medium was not specie, but paper, for without it the needs of trade could not have been met. A mania for banks swept over the country, and the days of paper money, of bills of credit, returned again. The behavior of the people during this time is most instructive, and to those who put not their trust in the people it ought to be most consoling, if not convincing. Affairs on the seaboard were bad enough; but it was in the wild West of those days that the crisis was severest and the remedies applied most radical.

The dull times which followed the opening of our second struggle with Great Britain, and, above all, the hard times which came after the close of the war, were the immediate causes of an immense immigration from the seaboard to the Mississippi Valley. That the arrival of these new-comers should be attended by speculation in land, in town sites, in everything of which they stood in need, was inevitable. But they came just at the time when the West was passing through a commercial revolution. The steamboat had appeared on the Mississippi and the Ohio, and no event in modern times has surpassed that in importance. The West, in the opinion of its people, was no longer dependent for its supply of foreign goods on Baltimore, Philadelphia, and New York. New Orleans was to be the great port of entry. To it were to come all the products of the West Indies, all the manufactures of Europe, the cotton fabrics, the woollen cloth, the hardware, the crockery—everything which for a generation past had been carried at great cost over the mountains—and once at New Orleans, they were to be transported by steamboat to St. Louis, to Louisville, to Cincinnati, and even to Pittsburg. The prospect of sudden commercial development, joined to the arrival of hundreds of thousands of new settlers, brought on an era of the wildest speculation, in which the whole community was eager to join. One great obstacle barred the way: money was scarce. The new-comers brought none. The old settlers had but little, and that little consisted of cut money, or Spanish dollars cut into quarters and eighths to serve as small change, some foreign coin, and the paper notes of such banking institutions as the State and Territorial legislatures had chartered, or as had sprung up and were issuing money without a legal right to do so.

This currency, which had never at any time been more than sufficient for the needs of the West, was now in the new order of things totally inadequate to

IS SOUND FINANCE POSSIBLE. 241

the wants of the people. The cry for money, above all for cheap money, for money that could be borrowed in large sums on the wildest security, went up from every part of the Mississippi Valley, and was heard. For several years no Legislature ever met but new banks were established and a flood of paper money issued, which the people made haste to borrow, invest, and lose. Ohio chartered twenty; Indiana, three; Illinois, two; Tennessee, twelve; Missouri, two, and actually issued loan certificates and, in defiance of the Federal Constitution, made her paper legal tender. Kentucky in 1818 chartered forty-six. The history of these Kentucky banks is unquestionably the most striking chapter in the annals of fiat money. The honest purpose and the high hopes with which they were created; the eagerness and universality with which their notes were borrowed and circulated; the load of debt entailed; the fury of the people when the day of reckoning came; the wicked and unjust method of relief; and the final triumph of good sense and majority rule—all combine to make it a lesson full of instruction at this moment.

There were then doing business in the State the Bank of Kentucky, with branches wherever occasion really required them, and, since 1817, two branches (or offices of discount and deposit) of the new Bank of the United States. As the branches of the United States Bank issued drafts, but no bills, and as the Bank of Kentucky was compelled to redeem its notes in specie, neither institution could begin to supply even a small part of the circulating medium demanded. It was for the purpose of supplying such a medium, therefore, that the forty-six banks were chartered. Thirty-five of them actually went into operation and were known in the hour of their popularity as ".the Independent Banks," but in the time of their adversity as "the Litter." The nominal capital of them all was not far from eight millions of dollars. The actual capital was little or nothing, for the very same specie went from bank to bank, remaining in each one just long enough for the letter of the law to be complied with. To have made their notes redeemable in specie would have been such an idle farce that it was not attempted, so Bank of Kentucky notes were substituted. It mattered little what they were redeemable in, for the people were glad to get them, and the branches of the United States Bank willingly took them in payment of drafts on the Eastern cities. As the notes of the Independent Banks were thus exchangeable for United States branch drafts, which in turn were exchangeable for specie or European products in Baltimore, or Philadelphia, or New York, the effect was the same as if Kentucky paper had been made current money at the seaboard. They were greatly in demand, were issued in large quantities, and were passing freely from hand to hand, when suddenly the Bank of the United States at Philadelphia sent forth an imperative order to its western branches to stop all loans and hurry a great sum of specie eastward. They at once responded, and in a moment the whole West was bankrupt. Bank after bank suspended specie payment, and among them was that of Kentucky. Well it might, for the amount of debts owed by the people of Kentucky to the two branches of the United States Bank was two million seven hundred thousand dollars. Public opinion forced it to resume almost immediately. But the harm was done, and the community, almost as one man, rose against the Bank of the United States. Resolutions were introduced in the Legislature asking the president of the bank to withdraw the branches from the State, and when nothing came of this a tax of five thousand dollars a month was laid on each of them. The banks, it may well be supposed, refused to pay, and in February, 1819, before the first instalment was due, application was made in the District Court of the United States for an injunction to stop the execution of the law, which did not, it was claimed, impose a tax, but inflicted pains and penalties, as it was on its very face intended to drive the two branches out of the State. The Court refused to consider the question of constitutionality of the law, because the famous case of McCulloch against Maryland was still pending in the Supreme Court, but granted a temporary injunction till the meeting of the Circuit Court in May.

This afforded some satisfaction; but no relief. Indeed, as the autumn of 1819 came, matters grew worse. The crops were abundant; flour, hemp, and tobacco were plentiful. But no market existed, and the people, realizing that the means of settling their debts were as remote as ever, resorted in desperation to county meetings and took into consideration their financial situation. The address adopted at one of these gatherings sets forth that the scarcity of money, the pressure of the banks on individuals and of individuals on those indebted to them, the difficulty of raising even moderate sums by enormous sacrifices of property, the usurious rates of interest demanded, and the general embarrassment of the business world, were hastening a general suspension of specie and the utter destruction of social order and happiness. Taken together, these causes, threatened to bring suddenly into the market, at forced sales at auction, a large part of the most valuable property in the State. The numerous sales, with few bidders, would surely shift this property from the many to the few, entail misery on the husbandman, and leave a heart-broken, dispirited population in a desolate land. Neither justice nor humanity should permit such ruin if a peaceable remedy could be found, and it could be found if the banks would suspend specie payment, stop their calls, issue more bills, and if the Legislature would meet and decide how much paper each bank could issue and what sort of security the borrower should give for it.

At some of the meetings the question was flatly put whether the banks should not be encouraged to suspend. Sometimes the decision was in the negative; but generally the will of the majority was that they should. No popular encouragement to stop payment was needed, and the Independent Banks, after seeing their notes steadily depreciate to a discount of twenty, thirty, forty per cent, were brought to such a pass that seventeen suspended, and by so doing lost their charters. The Bank of Kentucky followed, and the whole State was in confusion. Ten millions of dollars were owed the banks by the people, and from this load of debt the Legislature now attempted to rid the community by legislation.

The law chartering the litter of independent banks was repealed. The senators and representatives of the State at Washington were called on to do their best to have the branches of the United States Bank removed from Kentucky; and a stay law passed which suspended all sales under executions, decrees, and replevins for sixty days after the passage of the law if the defendant gave bonds that the goods levied on would be produced at the end of that time. The acting Governor refused to sign it. He did not believe, he said, that a law should delay or deny justice. But the Legislature passed the act over his veto, gave permission for the introduction of a bill to declare void all sales made under any execution issued in favor of the Bank of the United States or its branches, and, just before the expiration of the sixty-day stay law, passed a replevin act of a most shameful character. Thenceforth, when any execution issued, on any bond, judgment, or decree, from any court or justice of the peace, the plaintiff had the privilege of writing on the bill the words, " Notes of the Bank of Kentucky or its branches will be accepted in discharge of this execution." If he made this indorsement the defendant could replevy but for one year. Should the defendant fail to replevy, the property was to be sold on credit for one year for what it would bring. Should the plaintiff refuse to make the indorsement, the defendant might replevy for two years.

This indorsement and replevin act put off the day of reckoning, and for the time being saved the debtor from the clutches of the law. But the debts of the people, now far more than ten millions of dollars, still remained, and to liquidate them the Legislature in 1821 put in operation a new paper-money machine which it called the Bank of the Commonwealth. It was the State treasury turned into a paper-money mill pure and simple. There were no stockholders, no stock, no capital, no redemption of notes. A president and board of directors chosen annually by the Legislature managed its affairs. Its funds were all money paid in for land warrants, all revenue from the sale of land which the State owned west of the Tennessee River, the stock owned by the State in the Bank of Kentucky, and such unexpended balance as, at the end of the year, might be found in the State treasury. Its notes were to issue to the amount of three millions of dollars, were to be apportioned among the countries on the basis of taxable property, and were to be loaned on mortgage security to those and to those only who, in the words of the law, needed them "for the purpose of paying his, her, or their just debts," or intended to buy the products of Kentucky for shipment from the State. That the bank might never be under the necessity of suspending, the notes were not redeemable in specie, and that nothing might be wanting to make them as fine specimens of fiat money as ever existed, they were made legal tender for all debts due by or to the State.

That the people would take the new money was never doubted, for their debts were heavy and the paper gave them an easy means of liquidation. But that the Bank of Kentucky would refuse the new issue was certain. It was therefore reorganized, its old directors were turned out and men who favored the Bank of the Commonwealth put in, and the Bank of Kentucky almost immediately suspended.

Meantime the constitutionality of the indorsement and replevin act had been tested in the courts. That it was a flat violation of the Federal Constitution is undoubted. "No State," says that instrument, "shall make anything but gold and silver coin a legal tender in payment of debts, nor pass any law impairing the obligations of contracts." It was not long, therefore, before a test case reached the Bourbon Circuit Court of Kentucky, where the question of constitutionality was raised and decided in the negative. The Legislature happening to be in session, a member moved for the appointment of a committee to inquire into the decision of the judge who had "grossly transcended his judicial authority and disregarded the constitutional powers of the Legislature of this Commonwealth." The committee, when it reported, said that in its opinion the judge had committed a high crime and misdemeanor, and ought to be removed from office. That the judicial department had power to defeat the general policy of the State, deliberately adopted by the Legislature, was something the committee could not admit. Such a doctrine was incompatible with the constitutional powers of the Legislature, subversive of the best interests of the people, and well calculated to disturb the public peace and shake public confidence in the whole relief system which had been called for by the condition and necessities of the people. An address to the Governor asking him to remove the judge from office was accordingly brought in; but though it secured a great majority of the House it failed to pass for want of two thirds. But the end was not yet. A year later a case involving the question of the constitutionality of the relief laws reached the Court of Appeals, a body composed of three judges who held office during good behavior. Two agreed that the indorsement and replevin laws were binding on all transactions occurring after their passage, but null and void as to anything which had transpired before that time. The third went further and declared the laws were unconstitutional and would not be applied by the Court in any case.

As the news of this decision swept through the State (though it applied only to contracts made before the passage of the law), excitement and alarm went with it. The Legislature was not then in session; but the moment it met, John Adair, the Governor, sent in a most excited message. He accused the Court of showing an open disregard for the ancient distinction between right and remedy, with striking at the sovereignty of the State and the right of the people to govern themselves, and committed its decision to the Legislature's most solemn consideration. The Senate was eager to destroy the Court, and was prevented only by a tie vote from calling a State convention to amend the Constitution and change the judiciary. The House by a large majority declared the decision of the Court of Appeals to be erroneous; voted that the indorsement and replevin laws were constitutional and valid; and resolved to do something in support of them. But they did nothing, for an election was at hand and the matter went down to the people, to whom an earnest appeal was made to choose men who would vote for an address of removal. The people responded in part and sent back a Legislature of which only a majority were relief men, and again removal of the judges by the Governor was defeated. Nevertheless, a majority could do much, and, following the example set them by Congress in the early months of Jefferson's administration, it repealed the act creating the Court of Appeals, and legislated all the judges out of office. A new court was then established by another act, and on the bench were placed men who would see to it that the relief laws were sustained and administered in accordance with their plain intent and meaning. But the judges of the old court firmly refused to submit, denied the constitutionality of the repeal of the judiciary act, and continued to hold sittings and to deliver judgments.

There were thus two courts in the State, and two parties ranged around them. The "new court party" protested that liberty, republicanism, democratic institutions, State rights, self-government, were all at stake. The "old court party" admitted that liberty, republicanism, and self-government were indeed at stake. The question, said its leaders, is, Can right and justice be secured under all circumstances in a land where the will of the people rules? Is it possible for an independent judiciary to protect the rights of a minority against the will of an interested, excited, and ill-disposed majority? The answer of the people was, Yes; and when the Legislature met in 1825 the House was in the hands of the old court party, and voted to abolish the new court. The Senate which held over was in the control of the new court party, and refused to agree. Once more the question went down to the people, and in the elections of 1826 the contest was again between the old court party and the new. This time the triumph was a signal one. The friends of the old court carried both House and Senate; the replevin law was repealed, the "new court" was abolished, the old court was reinstated, and justice once more done to debtor and creditor alike.

The history of Ohio during these trying times affords another instance of the final triumph of majority rule after a period during which it seemed impossible to bring the community to a sense of right and justice. In that great State the people had entered with enthusiasm on the manufacture of money, had chartered their banks and were in the full enjoyment of a cheap and plentiful paper currency, when they heard with dismay that the Bank of the United States, that regulator of the currency, was about to open branches at Chillicothe and Cincinnati. In the hope of shutting out what, in the language of its enemies, was called "the hydra-headed foreign shaving shop," the Legislature threatened to impose a heavy tax. But the threat was disregarded; the banks came, and in 1819 an annual tax of fifty thousand dollars was laid on each of them, and the auditor commanded to issue his warrant on a certain day for the collection of it. Should the banks refuse, the agent was to seize any specie, bank-notes, goods and chattels found in the banking house, and, if necessary, break open every vault, room, closet, drawer, and box, search them, and carry away their contents. The demand for payment of the tax was made in the office at Chillicothe, at the close of a business day in September, 1819. As was expected, the money was refused; whereupon the agent, forcing his way into the vaults, broke open the boxes, carried off more than the amount of the tax, and deposited the money in the State treasury at Columbus.

For this act the auditor, his agents, and the State treasurer were sued by the bank, and while the suits were still pending the Legislature assembled and began an investigation. The times were now hard indeed. All the fine visions of the speculators, the paper-money men, the bank men, had vanished. Bankruptcy and debt were everywhere. Stay laws, replevin laws, indorsement laws, relief laws of every sort, were the order of the day. Nothing was so hateful now as a bank, and, above all, the Bank of the United States. The Supreme Court had decided that a State could not tax it. But Ohio adopted and affirmed the Virginia and Kentucky resolutions of 1798 and 1800; hurled a defiance at the Supreme Court, told it that acquiescence was not the necessary consequence of its decisions, and passed "an act to withdraw from the Bank of the United States the protection of the laws of this State in certain cases." If the bank gave notice to the Governor of its willingness to stop the suits against the State officers, and to submit to a four-per-cent tax on its dividends, or leave the State, the Governor might suspend the law by proclamation. If it did not, then every jailer was forbidden to receive into his custody any person committed at the suit of the bank, or for any injury done to it. Every judicial officer was prohibited to take acknowledgment of conveyances when the bank was a party, and every recorder from receiving and entering them. Notaries public were prevented from protesting bills or notes held by the bank and made payable to it; and justices of the peace, judges, and grand juries could no longer take cognizance of any wrong committed on the property of the bank, though it were burglary, robbery, or arson. The bank would not discontinue the suits nor leave the State, so the law went into effect, and in September, 1820, the Bank of the United States became an outlaw in Ohio.

Here again, as in Kentucky, extreme measures produced their inevitable result. A reaction set in. The good sense of the plain people prevailed over the folly of the legislators, and the law was erased from the statute-book. Both in Kentucky and Ohio the cases were extreme; yet they are striking illustrations of the fact that in this country all questions of great importance are finally settled not by Presidents, nor by Congresses, nor by the legislatures of the States, but by the hard common sense of the people, who in their own good time and way have heretofore adjusted all difficulties wisely.

FRANKLIN IN FRANCE.

THOSE who have never seen the Franklin alcove in the Boston Public Library, nor examined the catalogue of Frankliniana so carefully prepared by Mr. Lindsay Swift, can have no conception of the vast mass of literature of which Benjamin Franklin is the subject. Cooper and Mrs. Stowe alone excepted, our country has produced no writer whose works have been so generally translated and read abroad. For some of his shorter pieces a strange infatuation seems to exist, and one, Father Abraham's Address, may be read in French, in German, in Spanish, in Italian, in Bohemian, in Gaelic, and in modern Greek. Since the April day, 1790, when he expired at Philadelphia, no period of ten years has passed by without an edition of his autobiography or a new life of him appearing in some of the languages of civilized men.

It has always seemed to us that the period of Franklin's life about which least is generally known is that which covers his residence in France. Every school-boy knows the history of his early years; of the whistle for which he paid too much; of the quarrel that drove him from Boston; of the memorable Sunday walk through the streets of Philadelphia. Yet it would trouble men of wide reading to give even a tolerable account of his claims to be considered a statesman, or of his famous mission to the Court of Louis XVI.

The story of that mission goes back to November, 1775, when a stranger, lame and speaking but little English, appeared in Philadelphia. He put up at a tavern, and sent word to Congress that he had something of weight to tell. No heed was paid to him. But he persisted, and sent again and again, till John Jay, Benjamin Franklin, and Thomas Jefferson were despatched to speak with him. They met him in one of the rooms in the Carpenter's Hall, were assured of the warm sympathy of France, and were told that money, arms, and ammunition should all be theirs. When asked for his name and credentials, the stranger drew a hand across his throat, said he knew how to take care of his head, bowed himself out, and was never seen again.

The committee, however, were much impressed, and Congress, acting on their report, named another to correspond secretly with the friends of America in Great Britain, Ireland, and France. This new committee was active; letters were written to Dumas and Arthur Lee abroad, and Story, Penet, and Silas Deane were sent out with letters from home. But it was long before any word came back. Three months went by, and lengthened to six months, to eight months, without a line from one of them. Then came the letter of Dubourg to Franklin, full of assurances of the most comforting kind, and straightway Franklin, Deane, and Jefferson were chosen commissioners to France. Jefferson would not go, and, in an evil hour, Arthur Lee was elected in his stead.

The choice was made on the twenty-sixth of September, 1776. On the twenty-sixth of October Franklin set out alone, for Lee and Deane were already in France. The weather was tempestuous; the sea was boisterous and crowded with English cruisers. More than once the captain was forced to beat to quarters. But the voyage, most happily, was short, and on the third of December he landed at Auroy, on the coast of Brittany, and hastened with his two grandsons to Nantes. Then began such an ovation as has never since been given to any citizen of the United States. The writings of Rousseau, of Voltaire, of Montesquieu, had done their work, and the moment the report of "the shot heard round the world" reached France, the nation rose as one man, and took sides with liberty. At Versailles, at Paris, in the coffee-rooms, at the watering-places, in the remotest province of France, the struggle in America became the topic of the hour. The Courrier d'Avignon and the Mercure de France gave long accounts of the tea tax, of the fight at Lexington, of the enthusiasm of the women for the cause. The people of Paris drew comparisons between the full accounts of American affairs in the Mercure and the meagre accounts in the official Gazette of France, and abused the ministry for its conduct. Vergennes was called a fool, a dolt, a tool of England, because he did not openly support the "insurgents."

That this state of public feeling had all to do with the extraordinary reception given to Franklin does not admit of doubt. Had he come among a people indifferent, or but lukewarm in his cause, his reputation in the world of philosophy and of letters would have profited him nothing. But he came among a people deeply interested in his cause, and he was from the hour of his arrival at Nantes an object of boundless curiosity. "The arrival of Dr. Franklin at Nantes," a lieutenant of police wrote to Vergennes, "is creating a great sensation." Yet it was as nothing to that he created at Paris. Statesmen, churchmen, men of letters, merchants, nobles, and great ladies crowded his rooms, and welcomed him as no foreigner had ever been welcomed before. His name and his cause were on every lip, till Vergennes forbade the crowds in the coffee-houses to discuss "*des insurgens.*"

Meanwhile, the commissioners sent a note to Vergennes, asked an audience, and took up their abode at Passy, then a pleasant town on the outskirts of Paris. For a whole year the King could not be persuaded to receive them as commissioners. Franklin did not, in consequence, go to court, and was rarely seen at Paris. But he was far from idle. Day after day he was beset by all manner of suitors. Women of rank, great soldiers, courtiers high in favor, came to him in crowds. Some wanted a trifle for themselves. Some had been teased by others to tease him for a contract, a commission, a letter to Congress. Strangers on whom he had never before laid eyes had the effrontery to bring and introduce others as unknown as themselves. So incessant did this become that he never accepted an invitation to dine, never was introduced to a man of note, never heard a carriage roll into his court, nor opened a letter written in a strange hand, without feeling sure he was to be asked for something. One beggar, Dom Bernard Benedictus, sent word to the commissioners that if they would pay his gambling debts he would pray for the success of the American cause. The most persistent of all, however, were the gentlemen of the sword. To these must be added the merchants hungry for American tobacco and ship-owners longing for a chance to fit out privateers. Had their request for commissions been granted, they would have come to naught, for the French King was not disposed to openly befriend America. Indeed, it was hardly possible for an American armed ship to get leave to stay two days in a French port. Lambert Wickes was twice driven from L'Orient. At St. Malo the authorities attempted to seize his cannon and unhang his rudder. Gustavus Conyngham and his crew were flung into prison. The behavior of Wickes in returning to a port from which he had just been sent was a most impudent act, and a shameful abuse of the patience of France, and had she not been hostile to England, had she been really neutral, she would have shut her ports, as Portugal did, and Wickes would never have entered L'Orient a second time.

But the behavior of Conyngham was bolder and more impudent still. One day in March, 1777, William Hodge, a Philadelphia merchant, came to Paris, and struck an acquaintance with Silas Deane. Deane was daft on the subject of privateers, and the two soon had on foot a privateering venture of the boldest kind. A lugger was bought at Dover with Government money, was taken to Dunkirk, and there hastily and secretly fitted out by Mr. Hodge. When all was ready, Conyngham, with a Continental commission as captain in his pocket, was put in command and duly instructed what to do. He was to cruise in the Channel, and spare no pains to capture the Harwich packet-boat that plied between England and Holland. So well did he obey his instructions that he was soon back in Dunkirk harbor, with the Prince of Orange as his prize. The whole of England was in a *furor*. Insurance rose; merchants made haste to put their goods on board of French ships, and felt for a time as if the whole coast were in a state of blockade. The English minister complained most vigorously to Vergennes, and Vergennes acted with rigor. The packet-boat was seized and restored, and Conyngham and his crew were flung into prison.

This misadventure did not dishearten Deane and Hodge in the least. It taught them a little wisdom, and while Conyngham languished in jail they bought a swift cutter, armed her with twenty-two swivels and fourteen six-pounders, and applied to Vergennes for his release. The commissioners assured the Minister that Conyngham should sail at once for the United States, and Hodge gave bonds for his doing so. But he was scarcely at sea before he began to make prize of everything he met, and even threatened to lay in ashes the thriving town of Lynn. And now Vergennes made another show of harshness, and Hodge was soon in the Bastile.

But the time for such harshness was nearly over. Every day the cause of liberty grew more popular. Indeed, it is impossible to take up any of the Mémoires, Œuvres Choisies, Correspondance, Lettres Inédites, of the time without meeting unmistakable evidence of the popularity of the American rebels. Songs, catches, pamphlets, caricatures, nicknames, and street phrases all betray it. Lafayette enlists, and the whole court is thrown into excitement. The Hessians are taken at Trenton, and the booksellers cannot supply the demand for maps of America. Burgoyne surrenders, and the joy of Paris is as great as if the victory had been won by the French. "We talk of nothing but America here," wrote Madame du Deffand to Horace Walpole. "When shall we arm in favor of the insurgents?" became the question asked all over France. The answer was, "At once." News of the famous surrender was carried to Vergennes on December fourth, 1777. On the sixteenth the commissioners were told that the King would recognize the independence of America and make a treaty at once and on February sixth, 1778, a day long celebrated in the United States, the Treaty of Alliance and the Treaty of Amity were duly signed. In March the commissioners were received at Versailles. April thirteenth a French fleet commanded by D'Estaing sailed from Toulon.

In the same ship with D'Estaing went Silas Deane, for he had been recalled by Congress, and John Adams had been sent in his stead. Adams landed at Bordeaux, and met with a welcome that amazed him. The merchants, eager for free-trade with America, lit up their city in his honor, and he read in one of the gardens the illuminated inscription—"God save the Congress, Liberty, and Adams." At Paris the Courrier d'Avignon told the people that he was the brother "of the famous Adams, whose eloquence had been as deadly to the English as that of Demosthenes was to Philip," and ministers, courtiers, and men of letters hastened to pay their respects. At Passy, as he sat at the table of Madame Brillon, there was a fine demonstration in his honor.

But he found at Passy what amazed him still more.

He found the little company of Americans torn by senseless disputes and distracted by causeless jealousy. That company had, since the arrival of Franklin, been much increased. To it had been added Ralph Izard, Minister to the Duke of Tuscany; William Lee, Envoy to the courts of Vienna and Berlin; and William Carmichael, who for a time had served as secretary to Deane. Had Congress searched the country through, it could not have found six men less likely to live at peace than Franklin, Deane, Izard, Carmichael, and the two Lees. When, therefore, Adams arrived, he found that each of the six had fallen out with the other five. Deane could not abide Arthur Lee, Franklin had quarrelled with Ralph Izard, both of the Lees had quarrelled with Franklin, while William Carmichael was at sword's points with nearly all. Happily, these feuds were soon to end. Though the six could agree in little else, they all agreed in urging Congress to abolish the commission, and make one man Minister to France, and acting on this advice Izard was recalled, Arthur Lee was deprived of his commissionership, Adams was left without an appointment, and Dr. Franklin made sole Minister to the court of France.

Nor were the business affairs of the commissioners in a much better state than their private affairs. Carelessness, negligence, disorder, prevailed. Method and order Franklin could not acquire even in his youth. But he was now in his seventy-third year; had been out of business for more than thirty years, and, as a consequence of age and leisure, had grown more careless and unmethodical than ever. Men who came to see him were astonished to behold the weightiest papers scattered in profusion about the room. Some who knew him well ventured to protest, and reminded him that the French were eager to know his business, that he might in his own household have many spies, and even went so far as to suggest that his grandson should spend half an hour a day in putting his papers to rights. To these his answer was always the same. He knew that he was in all probability surrounded by spies; but it was his practice never to be concerned in any business he was not willing to have everybody know, and the disorder went on. All the commercial affairs, all treaty matters, all money matters, all the diplomatic affairs of the United States abroad, were in the hands of the commissioners. They made loans, bought ships, paid salaries, exchanged prisoners. Yet not a note-book, not a letter-book, not an account-book of any kind, had been kept.

Such a shameful disregard of the first principles of business alarmed Adams, who turned himself into a drudge, introduced something like order into the office of the commission, and in a long letter to Samuel Adams drew a pretty just character of Franklin as a man of business:

" The other (Franklin) you know personally, and that he loves his ease, hates to offend, and seldom gives any opinion till obliged to do it. I know also, and it is necessary that you should be informed, that he is overwhelmed with a correspondence from all quarters, most of them upon trifling subjects and in a more trifling style, with unmeaning visits from multitudes of people, chiefly from the vanity of having it to say that they have seen him. There is another thing which I am obliged to mention. There are so many private families, ladies and gentlemen, that he visits so often—and they are so fond of him that he can not well avoid it— and so much intercourse with the Academicians, that all these things together keep his mind in a constant state of dissipation. If, indeed, you take out of his hands the public treasury, and the direction of the frigates and Continental vessels that are sent here, and all commercial affairs and intrust them to persons to be appointed by Congress, at Nantes and Bordeaux, I should think it would be best to have him here alone with such a secretary as you can confide in. But if he is left here alone even with such a secretary, and all maritime and commercial as well as political affairs are left in his hands, I am persuaded that France and America will both have reason to repent it. He is not only so indolent that business will be neglected, but you know that although he has as determined a soul as any man, yet it is his constant policy never to say 'Yes' or 'No' decidedly but when he cannot well avoid it." . . .

The fears of Mr. Adams were as unfounded as his criticism was just. Franklin was indolent, was fond of society, was unable to say Yes and No. But he was, at the same time, the most original character produced in America during the eighteenth century, and he accomplished a work in France no other American could possibly have done. On the March day, 1778, when, in buckleless shoes, wigless, and in the plainest clothes, he made his way through a crowd of painted beauties and powdered fops to the presence of the King, his position in France completely changed. On that day he ceased to be a solicitor of favor. On that day he became the recognized representative of the United States, and more than ever the centre of attraction at Paris. Mr. Lee and Mr. Deane were mere ciphers. What they thought, or did, or said, was, to the French people and the French court, of no consequence whatever. No paper ever mentioned their names. No great man ever darkened their doorways. The ear of Vergennes was never open to them till a letter from Franklin had prepared the way. This position Franklin reached in a way Mr. Adams could not understand. That a man who flung his papers all over the floor, kept no accounts, copied no letters, hated business, dined out six nights a week, and would not send away even a pestering fellow with an angry " No ! " could really be serving his country well was to Mr. Adams an absurdity. Mr. Adams would have lived at Paris, ignored the people, deluged the Ministers with notes, and have been well snubbed before he had been six months in France. Franklin went to Passy, lived secluded, gave the Ministry no trouble whatever, and by his tact, his shrewdness, his worldly wisdom, his wit, his skill in the management of men, made himself the most popular man in France, and by his popularity overcame a reluctant Minister and yet more reluctant King. This done, the rest of his work was easy. He had but to keep the good-will and love of the French people, and he kept them completely. Hardly was the ink of the treaty dry when canes, hats, snuffboxes, all became "*à la* Franklin." His face appeared on rings, on snuffboxes, in the window of every print-shop, and over the mantle-piece of every man of fashion. " 'Tis the fashion nowadays," sneered one of his haters, " to have an engraving of Franklin over one's mantle-piece, as it was formerly to have a jumping-jack." Of such portraits more than two hundred are believed to be in existence. A bust of him was set up in the Royal Library. Medallions of him were plentiful at Versailles, and a large store of such terracotta medallions, as fresh as on the day when they were first baked, was found in an old warehouse at Bordeaux in 1885.

It was rare that Franklin came to Paris, yet when he did he was instantly recognized by the people. His brown suit, his fur cap, his powderless hair, his spectacles, and his walking-stick betrayed him at once to men who had never laid eyes on him before. Crowds followed him in his walks and gathered about him in the public places. When he entered the theatre, the courts of justice, the popular resorts, he was greeted with shouts of applause. His good sayings were spread all over France, with countless other *anecdotes américaines*. Poets wrote him sonnets. Noble dames addressed him in verse. Women of fashion crowned his head with flowers. Grave Academicians shouted with delight to see him hug Voltaire. His friend, the Abbé Morellet, well described him in the lines—

> Notre Benjamin
> En politique il est grand,
> A table est joyeaux et franc.

The absurdity of the famous kissing scene at the Academy of Science is outdone by the absurdity of another scene, some months later, at a meeting of the masonic lodge of the Nine Sisters. Voltaire was then dead, and the business of the meeting was a eulogy of the old philosopher. In the hall of the lodge sat Madame Denis, niece to Voltaire; the Madame de Villette, at whose house he died; Greuze, who painted the beauties and gallants of the court of Louis; Franklin, and a host of famous men. That nothing might be wanting to give solemnity to the occasion, a deep gloom pervaded the hall, and a huge sepulchral pyramid reminded the audience for what purpose they were gathered. The astronomer Lalande addressed Madame Denis. La Dixmerie read a long eulogy, and, as he stopped from time to time to take breath, the audience were kept awake by selections from the operas of Castor and Roland, played by an orchestra which Piccini led.

The eulogy ended, soft music, a blaze of light, and claps of stage thunder followed ; the pyramid vanished, and in its place stood a huge picture of the apotheosis of Voltaire. The painter represented him as rising from the tomb. Envy, tugging at his shroud, strove to hold him back, but was driven off by Minerva, while Benevolence and Truth introduced him to Corneille, Racine, Molière, who hovered near. As the beholders sit in dumb admiration, Lalande, Greuze, and Madame de Villette seize each a crown and place them on the heads of Franklin, La Dixmerie, and Gauget, who in turn hasten to lay them at the feet of the picture of Voltaire.

Popularity so extraordinary was not, however, unmingled with contempt. One writer of memoirs describes him as " one of the great charlatans of the eighteenth century." Another cannot abide his table manners, and despises him for putting butter in his eggs and eating them from a glass. A third denounces him in a long poem. The author of a " History of a French Louse " exhausts the French language in a disgusting description of him.

Of all this Franklin knew nothing, and went on with the business of his office, which was, in his opinion, to keep the cause of his country before the eyes of the people of France. His homely sayings, his *bon mots*, his republican simplicity of dress and manner, did much to accomplish this end. But he left no expedient whatever untried, and taking up his pen he wrote a dialogue between Great Britain, France, Spain, Holland, Saxony, and America; a catechism relative to the English national debt; and persuaded Dubourg to make a translation of the constitutions of the thirteen States. Vergennes objected to their publication. The Government would not give a license. But the book came out, and the cause of America was more popular than ever. The constitutions were described as a code that marked an epoch in the history of philosophy; as a code that richly deserved to be well known; and the men who framed them were pronounced superior to Solon and Lycurgus.

In the midst of this discussion Lafayette returned, and the enthusiasm for America flamed higher still. Crowds beset him wherever he went. Magistrates overwhelmed him with honors. Great ladies insisted on kissing him. The King honored him with a reception at court, and the Queen bestowed on him a regiment of dragoons. The Ministers even consulted him on American affairs; and soon learned with pleasure that he had brought a commission creating Franklin sole Minister of the United States to the court of France. With it came such an injunction as a mother, when going out for an afternoon, might lay on a family of unruly boys. The American agents in Europe were bidden to behave themselves and quarrel no more; but the injunction was not obeyed, and in a little while the feud between the two Lees, Ralph Izard, and Franklin was hotter than ever before.

As for Arthur Lee, to the last hour of his stay in France he spared no pains to insult Franklin, thwart him, embarrass his affairs, and invariably met with success. But no success was more complete than that which attended the quarrel of John Paul Jones and Landais. Jones had come over from the United States in the little ship Ranger, and had set his heart on having command of a fine vessel which the commissioners were building at Amsterdam. But the commissioners put 'm off, and sent him on his ever-memorable cruise. First he appeared before Whitehaven, and threatened to burn the shipping. Then he stood over to the Scotch shore, harried the lands of the Earl of Selkirk, and carried away his plate. The next day he fell in with the Drake, an English ship of twenty guns, engaged and took her, and came back with his prize to Brest. Emboldened by victory, Jones again besought the commissioners, who now began in earnest to intercede with the French court. In June he was promised the ship. But it was one thing to promise and another thing to do, and in place of the ship came excuses, delay, and new promises. To keep up the semblance of good faith, the French Minister of Marine requested Jones to give up the command of the Ranger and wait in France for something better. This he did, and at once the gossips fell upon him and declared that he had been driven from the American service. Thereupon the commissioners came to his relief with a certificate stating that he had not. In the midst of his troubles, a copy of Father Abraham's address, which in France bears the title " La Science du Bonhomme Richard," fell in his way, and he read that piece of homely wisdom, " If you would have your business done, go ; if not, send." So well did this seem to apply to him that he determined to act on it, and, utterly ignoring the Minister of Marine, he wrote direct to the King, and soon had command of the Duc de Duras. That the letter ever reached the King is very uncertain; but Jones firmly believed it did, and, in honor of the source whence he got his advice, he changed the name of the Duc de Duras to Le Bonhomme Richard.

Jones now set sail with all the speed he could, and with him went the Alliance, commanded by the crazy Pierre Landais, the Pallas, the Vengeance, and the Cerf. Scarcely was he out of sight of land when new troubles began. The Cerf and the Vengeance left him, and Landais showed signs of insubordination. But Jones cruised along, threatened Leith, and, when off Scarborough, fell in with the Baltic fleet of merchantmen convoyed by the Countess of Scarborough and the Serapis. While the Bonhomme Richard engaged the Serapis, the Pallas engaged the Countess. But Landais, made more crazy than ever by excitement, suffered the fleet to escape, while he sailed round and round the fighters, firing alike on friend and foe. Out of this grew a bitter quarrel between Jones and Landais. For a time it seemed that the scandal of the affair would be further increased by a duel. But they appealed to Franklin, who removed Landais from the Alliance, and put Jones in command. It was a sorry day for him when he did, for the Frenchman now turned upon him, and enjoys the distinction of being one of the few men who ever got decidedly the better of Franklin in a dispute. Again and again Landais entreated to be restored to command. Franklin as often refused. Then, storming with rage, the Frenchman hurried to L'Orient, where he met that black-hearted traitor Arthur Lee, whom the Alliance was to carry home. What Landais could not think of to embarrass Franklin, Lee did, and between the two a most shameful piece of business was concocted. They stirred up a mutiny of the crew. They persuaded one hundred and fifty of them to sign a paper that they would not lift the anchor till their prize money was paid, and their lawful captain, Pierre Landais, restored; and one day, while Jones was ashore, Landais boarded the Alliance and took command. Franklin now applied to the French Government, and orders went down to L'Orient to blow the Alliance out of the water if she made an attempt to sail. But she did sail, and with Landais in command.

This was in July, 1780, and from that time on the story of Franklin's mission has but little interest till negotiations were begun for a peace. Concerning the signing of that famous document an idle story has long been current, and is still believed. Narrators of this tale declare that when the commissioners were all assembled, and were about to affix their names to the treaty, Franklin excused himself and left the room, and that, when he came back, he was dressed in an old and almost threadbare suit of brown. Nothing was said by the commissioners. But their looks betrayed astonishment, and Franklin told them that the clothes he then had on were those he wore when Wedderburne so shamefully abused him before the Privy Council. The story is pure fable. It has not a scrap of truth to rest on. The incident never occurred. Franklin never asserted it, and it was during his lifetime denied, and flatly denied, by one of the officials who was present at the signing.

Another incident in his life that is commonly misunderstood is the famous Strahan letter; the letter, we mean, ending, "You are now my enemy, and I am yours." We know of no collection of his works and letters in which this document is not treated as a piece of spirited and sober writing. Yet it certainly was no more than a jest. Had this not been so, all friendship, all correspondence between the two would have ended the day the letter was received. But no such falling out took place, and they went on exchanging letters long after the war had seriously begun.

With the signing of the treaty the labors of Franklin in France may be said to have ended. He continued, indeed, to act as Minister till the summer of 1785, when Jefferson succeeded him. But old age was upon him, his infirmities were many, and his time was chiefly given to his friends and his pen. The work which he did in France is, we believe, generally unknown, because it has never yet been fairly set forth. Borrowing money, fitting out ships, buying clothing, powder, and guns, settling disputes, writing despatches, was the least important and the least creditable part of what he accomplished. When he landed in France, in 1776, neither the King, nor the Ministers, nor the mass of the nobility had any heart in the American cause. His sole support was public opinion, the most fickle and treacherous of all support. Yet he never for a moment lost it. By his tact, his knowledge of men and the ways of men, he turned it from the wild enthusiasm of a day into downright admiration for the American people.

HOW THE BRITISH LEFT NEW YORK.

IN March, 1776, the British army, or, as it was then commonly called, the Ministerial army, sailed from Boston, where for months past it had been closely besieged by Washington and the Continentals. Then, and for a few months thereafter, no English force was on our soil. But that the respite was only for the time being, and that the enemy would surely return and attack some other seaport, was the belief of everybody. In the opinion of Washington, New York city was almost certain to be the place. Its splendid harbor, its geographical position, the easy connection which the Hudson and Lakes George and Champlain afforded with Montreal and Quebec, all tended to mark it out as a city so desirable for the enemy to possess and hold as a base of operations, both by land and sea, that when, in January, 1776, a rumor was current of the intention of Sir Henry Clinton to lead an expedition against the city Washington made haste to send General Charles Lee, with such troops as could be gathered in Connecticut, to put the city in a state of defence. And it was well he did, for on the very day Lee entered New York by land Clinton, with his contingent, appeared off Sandy Hook.

Convinced that the expedition of Clinton would

now be followed by a much greater one under Howe, Washington, as soon as the British were out of sight at Boston, began to prepare for the transfer of the army to New York. Lee was replaced by Putnam, who, in April, was himself superseded by the commander-in-chief under whom the work of defence which had been started by Lee was hurried on with all possible speed, and in a little while the water-fronts of the East and North Rivers, the islands in the upper bay, the Narrows, and the heights of Brooklyn were bristling with redoubts and earthworks. Another long line of defences ran over the hills in what is at present the heart of Brooklyn, and was intended to cut off the approach of the enemy from the lower bay by way of Long Island.

For the defence of these works Washington had gathered some seventeen thousand troops, of whom ten thousand were ready for the field, when, on the twenty-ninth of June, the long-expected British fleet, amounting all told to one hundred and thirty ships, came in sight off Sandy Hook. No attempt to prevent a nearer approach was made, and without any opposition the soldiers were landed and went into camp on Staten Island, where they remained unmolested until August twenty-second. By that time, new arrivals having raised their number to twenty-five thousand, and all offers of peace having failed, Howe determined to begin the attack, and on August twenty-second sent fifteen thousand men across the Narrows to the beach at Gravesend. But it was not till August twenty-seventh that the battle was fought and the Americans driven within their lines on the hills of Brooklyn. By a little vigorous action Howe might easily have dislodged them, but he chose to begin a regular siege, and thus suffered Washington, on the night of August twenty-ninth, to withdraw his army from Brooklyn to New York.

Unfavorable winds had so far kept the fleet down the bay, but on September third a twenty-gun ship and some boats came up and anchored in the Wallabout. More ships and transports joined them on the fourteenth, and next morning the little fleet moved up the East River to the foot of what is now Thirty-fourth Street, where the British landed, and, driving the Americans across the island and up to Harlem Heights, took the city.

Thenceforth, to the end of the war, New York was in British hands. Thousands of the inhabitants had fled on the approach of the enemy, and thousands more went off after the battle of Long Island, so that not more than nine hundred took the oath of allegiance in 1776. But the place of those who went into exile was gradually supplied by men and women loyal to the Crown, who, as the war progressed, were driven from their homes in various parts of the country and sought a refuge in New York. There they were assigned quarters in the deserted houses of the old inhabitants, and became, to all intents and purposes, a new population. It is easy to imagine with what feelings these people beheld the happy termination of the war, and realized that they must soon give up not only their old homes and property which had been confiscated by the States, but must even quit their country. As early as November, 1782, seven officers of the King's Rangers called public attention to the island of St. John. They had been there, the officers said, and knew it to be the very spot for a great city. The harbor was safe and spacious, the climate was delightful, and the idea that in Canada men were starving and freezing was entirely erroneous. Game abounded all over the island, while in the river were the finest shell-fish to be found along the whole coast from New York to Labrador.

To refugees not knowing where to turn for an abiding place these assurances were most comforting, and, with the approach of spring, numbers set off for the island. Other companies were preparing to follow, when news of peace reached this country, and the exodus became general.

The provisional treaty had been signed at London in November, 1782, and, although no time was lost in sending tidings of the event to the United States, it was late in March, 1783, when a ship bearing the treaty reached Philadelphia, and April before the town major of New York proclaimed the news that the war was over from the steps of what was then the City Hall.

By the seventh article of the treaty his Britannic Majesty bound himself to withdraw his troops and forces with all convenient speed. When the time came to put this provision into execution only two places on our coast were in possession of the King—the mouth of the Penobscot River in Maine and the mouth of the Hudson in New Jersey and New York. How soon the British left the Penobscot was a matter of small concern. But the evacuation of New York was eagerly expected both by the old Whig inhabitants eager to get in and by the Tory refugees eager to get out. To depart was far from easy, as the shipping was not plentiful, and the Tories within the lines numbered some thirty thousand souls.

The British commandant announced that none but refugees should be transferred by the King, and defined a refugee as a loyal subject of the Crown who had lived for twelve months past within the limits of the British army. The first step, therefore, required of each man desirous of transportation at Government expense was to prove residence. Having thus established his claim to be considered a refugee, he must have the house he occupied by consent of the commander of the army inspected and pronounced in good repair, pay his rent for the same at the vestry office, satisfy all his creditors, and make out a list of the articles he wished to take with him. When he had proved to the satisfaction of the commissioners that each article on the inventory was really his own, his name was entered in a book in the office of the adjutant-general, and in time he and his family were assigned berths in some ship or transport.

The first fleet sailed early in April and bore away, it is said, nine thousand refugees. All over the country this piece of news was heard with delight, and many Whigs, believing the evacuation of the city to be near at hand, quit the farms and villages where they had dwelt for seven years and hurried to New York to take possession of their old homes again. Such as were willing and able to pay a quarter's rent in advance and ask no questions were soon in possession of their houses and shops; but such as paid no rent found their claims unheeded, or were forced once more to take refuge with the farmers without the lines. These filled the Whig newspapers with their lamentations and with accounts of the evil doings of the Tories.

The city, they asserted, was in a dreadful condition. Every place of worship except the Episcopal church, the Moravian church, and the Methodist meeting-house was desecrated and used for secular purposes. One was a riding-school, another was a storehouse, a third was a barracks. The plain duty of Sir Guy Carleton was to have these buildings repaired and cleaned, the pews put back, and the galleries rebuilt before he left the city. He ought also to stop the insults daily offered to the American flag and suppress the nightly raids of the Tories. Peace existed. The United States was an independent power, yet no ship captain dared to enter New York Bay with an American flag at his mast-head. All within the lines was supposed to be under British rule, yet from towns along the lines came stories of bands of Tories harrying the country. They would come, it was said, from Long Island and New York in the night, skulk about all day, and at night begin their work of burning barns and haystacks, beating men, and extorting money.

But there were in the city thousands of men who did not come within the definition of refugees, or if they did, desired to go to places other than those to which the King would send them. These formed companies of their own and went off as fast as ships could be chartered. Some one who wished to go to Port Roseway, or St. John, to Halifax, to Annapolis, to Cumberland, to the Bermudas, or to Fort Frontenac, would pass around a paper stating the fact and asking for signatures. All who signed bound themselves to depart at the summons of the leader. Such a summons generally consisted of a notice in the Gazette that a ship to carry a certain company would be ready on such a day at such a dock. But as the time of departure drew near, the hearts of many seem to have failed them.

The notices then began to contain warnings to be prompt. Now a leader would assume a threatening tone and after reminding his company that it was unreasonable to expect that his ship would lie at her wharf for no other reason than to oblige indolent people, would bid them be on board by noon of a certain day or their places would be given to men from the army. Another hoped his shipmates would not forget to drink to their wives and sweethearts that night, as he expected them, one and all, to be on board the next morning to turn the windlass and have a pleasant sail to Staten Island.

All through the summer the press for passage went on, till the sloops and packets were not numerous enough to carry off half the refugees who wished to go. In one day as many as 5,539 names were registered at the office of the adjutant-general. During the year the records show that 29,244 persons—men, women, children, and servants—went off never to return. In general their place of destination was Nova Scotia. River St. John was a favorite place, but thousands made their abode at Port Roseway, at Annapolis Royal, at Fort Cumberland, or at Halifax.

Each company that departed was the cause of renewed rejoicing to the Whigs. The mortality from independence fever, as they nicknamed the eagerness of the Tories to leave, was said to be rapidly depopulating the city. Nova Scotia they called Nova Scarcity, and described it as a land where there was nine months winter and three months cold weather. When it was known that one ship had foundered and gone down off Sandy Hook with all on board not a word of sympathy was uttered.

A letter from New York in the autumn declares there was no subject of conversation but the evacuation and no business but thieving. Houses left vacant by those who had gone were, it seems, plundered by men and women. Hardly a neighborhood but some foot passenger was stopped and robbed in the streets. Alarmed and enraged, the Whigs who had returned obtained consent of Sir Guy Carleton, and, forming themselves into a night watch, walked the streets, and in a week had fifteen offenders in jail. No disturbances of importance took place. A mob, one day in October, excited by the appearance of an American flag at the mast-head of a vessel, boarded her, tore it down, and carried it in triumph about the streets. On another occasion the inspector of markets pulled the bell off the Fly Market and carried it home, declaring that the rebels should never have the use of it. But Carleton interfered, satisfied the complaints of the ship captain, and made the inspector replace the bell.

At last, on November twelfth, Sir Guy Carleton notified Washington that the outposts north of McGowan's Pass (now near the northeastern entrance to Central Park) and at Hempstead, Long Island, would be withdrawn on November twenty-first; that Brooklyn and New York would be evacuated on the twenty-second, and Paulus Hook (now Jersey City) and Staten Island as soon as possible. But a week later the order was changed, and Washington informed that New York would be evacuated November twenty-fifth at noon, and that Staten Island would be retained until transports could be secured to carry away the sixty-five hundred troops remaining.

On November nineteenth, accordingly, Washington and Knox and Governor Clinton and their staffs came down to Day's Tavern, a public house near what is at present One Hundred and Twenty-fifth Street and Eighth Avenue. A small detachment of troops had already gone on to McGowan's Pass where, on the twenty-fourth, orders were issued to the soldiers to be ready to march at eight next day.

Meanwhile the returned Whigs in the city had gathered at the famous tavern of Mr. Cape, a site now covered by the Boreel Building, and after framing resolutions asking everybody, Whig or Tory, who had lived in the city during the war to leave, and pledging themselves to maintain order, chose a committee to select a badge for Evacuation Day. The committee selected a cockade of black and white ribbon to be worn on the left breast and a sprig of laurel in the hat, and enjoined all true Whigs to appear thus decorated at the Bull's Head Tavern on the morning of the twenty-second, the day first appointed by Carleton.

Change of date made a slight change of plan. Citizens on horseback were now requested to assemble at the Bowling Green, and citizens on foot at the Tea Water Pump. After General Knox with the troops had taken possession of the city the citizens were to go back with him and meet Washington and Clinton at the Bull's Head.

The programme was fully carried out. Early on the twenty-fifth the troops broke camp at McGowan's Pass, marched down the old Post Road to the Bowery, and down the Bowery to the barricade, halted there till the last British guard was withdrawn, and then went on through Chatham Street and Pearl Street and Wall Street to Broadway, and drew up in front of Mr. Cape's tavern. Then a detachment went off to old Fort George to raise the Stars and Stripes, only to find the staff soaped and the halyards missing. A sailor was found, however, who climbed the pole by nailing on cleats as he went, and having reeved it, had his pockets filled with "bits" and pennies by the crowd. The flag was then raised and saluted with thirteen guns. The military ceremony over, the civic procession began, and the General and Governor, repairing to the Bull's Head, were escorted to their lodgings by a grateful people.

Though the city was evacuated on the twenty-fifth, it was not until December third that the British flag was drawn down at Staten Island, and not till December fifth did Admiral Digby with the last of the fleet sail down the lower bay and put to sea.

THE STRUGGLE FOR TERRITORY.

THE story of the claims of European nations to so much of the territory of North America as now lies within the limits of the United States goes back to the time when Henry of Portugal was urging forward those voyages of exploration along the coast of Africa which led to the discovery of the Cape of Good Hope and a new route to India. That no other people might rob him of the fruit of his labors he procured a series of Papal Bulls granting to him all the lands his subjects should discover from Cape Non to India. The right of the Pope to thus dispose of heathen lands and heathen people was not at that day even doubted, and Prince Henry was left in the undisturbed enjoyment of his monopoly till Columbus, sailing westward, discovered the Antilles. Then Spain in turn applied for a Papal Bull, and Alexander VI drew a north and south line one hundred leagues west of the Azores and confirmed Spain in the possession of every country her navigators might find to the west of it. In this for a time Portugal refused to concur. But on the sixth of June, 1494, a treaty was made with Spain, the line drawn by Alexander was then moved to three hundred and seventy leagues west of Cape de Verd, and the earliest title of Europeans to America was established.

Thus made secure in the possession of her discoveries, the subjects of Spain pushed boldly out into the Caribbean Sea and the Gulf of Mexico. It was under the flag of Spain that one hardy mariner discovered and named Florida; that another explored the peninsula from Key West to Pensacola; that a third went round the northern shore of the gulf to Mexico and became the first of Europeans to behold the Mississippi. It was under her flag that Ayllon sailed along the coast of Georgia and South Carolina; that De Soto marched across the country from Tampa Bay to the Mississippi, and Coronado from the Gulf of California to Kansas.

During all these years the validity of the Spanish claims was never once seriously disputed. Cabot was indeed commissioned to discover "countries which were before that time unknown to Christian princes." But his discoveries were so plainly within the grant to Spain that Henry VII never for a moment thought of asserting sovereignty over them. Verrazzano in 1524 did indeed carry the French flag along the coast from Georgia to Newfoundland, and Cartier and De Roche at a later day explored the Gulf and River St. Lawrence, and even took possession of the country in the name of France. But at both these times a bloody war was raging between France and Spain, and the invasion and seizure of Spanish territory in the New World was as proper an act for a Catholic king as the invasion and seizure of Spanish territory in the Old World, and the attempted settlements were in no sense a questioning of her title.

Her title, indeed, was undisputed till Elizabeth was on the throne of England, till Protestantism was firmly established, and till Sir Humphrey Gilbert and Sir Walter Raleigh set forth to "discover and search such remote heathen and barbarous lands, not actually *possessed* of any Christian prince, as to them shall seem good." Then was set up the Protestant doctrine that the Pope could not dispose of heathen lands, and that all such countries belong to the prince whose subjects not merely discover but occupy them. The dispute thus begun as to the ownership of America raged with violence for nearly a century more, till by the treaty of 1670 Spain "agreed that the King of Great Britain and his subjects should remain in possession of what they then possessed in America," and the Protestant principle of discovery and occupation as the basis of title was finally established.

By that time the British were in possession of the whole Atlantic coast from Maine to Georgia; had already marked out the bounds of Massachusetts and Connecticut, Rhode Island and New York, New Jersey, Maryland, Virginia, and the Carolinas, and had already begun that movement westward which in another half century brought them to the foot of the Alleghanies.

While the English were thus engaged on the Atlantic slope the French were equally busy exploring that part of our country which lies between the Mississippi and the Blue Ridge, the Great Lakes and the Gulf. Far back in the sixteenth century Cartier explored the St. Lawrence, and led out a colony to settle on its banks. But the attempt failed, the colonists perished, and for sixty years the Indians seldom saw a white man among them. At last, in 1608, Samuel Champlain repeated the attempt, led a band of hardy adventurers to the Isle of Orleans, and hard by, on the high bluffs which look down on the river and the island, marked out the city of Quebec. The colonists found themselves far from home, in a cheerless climate, in a vast wilderness, and in the midst of tribes of red men who beheld the little hamlet with no friendly eye. So much depended on the good-will of the Indians that Champlain left nothing undone to gain it. He made them presents, joined them in an alliance, and went with them on the war-path to the shores of that beautiful sheet of water which still bears his name. There a great battle was fought. The arms and the courage of the French prevailed, and a victory full of consequences to the white men was won. For three generations after the battle every Algonkin was the steady friend, and every Iroquois the implacable enemy, of the French; and to this more than to anything else is to be ascribed the exploration and settlement of the Northwest. The Iroquois were powerful through all New York. The Algonkins ruled along the St. Lawrence and the chain of lakes. When, therefore, the French missionaries began their search for proselytes and furs they shunned the Iroquois and travelled westward among the tribes of the Algonkin nations.

Le Caron, a Franciscan, went first, and for ten years toiled among the Indians on the Niagara and the shores of Lake Huron. Brebeuf and Daniel went next, reached Sault Ste. Marie, and founded at St. Ignatius, St. Louis, and St. Joseph, villages of Christian Huron. But the Iroquois overwhelmed them, destroyed the villages, and burned the missionaries at the stake. Mesnard went yet farther to the west, saw the waters of Lake Superior, paddled in a canoe along its southern shores, built a church at St. Theresa Bay, and disappeared forever at the portage of Keweenaw. Long afterward his breviary and his cassock were found among the Sioux. Allouez followed him, explored both shores of the lake, and at the western end met the Sioux and heard for the first time of the great river the Indians called the Messipi. But all the glory of its exploration belongs to Marquette.

He set out, in May, 1673, from Mackinaw, with six companions, in two birch canoes, paddled down the lake to Green Bay, entered Fox River, and dragging the boats through its boiling rapids, came to a village where lived the Miamis and the Kickapoos. There Allouez had preached and taught. But beyond it no white man had ever gone. The Indians would have dissuaded them, told them of warriors who would cut off their heads, of monsters who would swallow their canoes, and of a demon who shut the way and drowned in the waters that seethed about him all who came within his reach. But the zeal of Marquette burned fiercely, and on the tenth of June, 1673, he led his little band, with two Indian guides, over the swamps and marshes that separated the village from a river which the guides assured him flowed into the Messipi. This westward-flowing river he called the Ouisconsin, and there the guides left him, as he says, "alone, amid that unknown country, in the hands of God."

With prayers to the mother of Jesus, the little band shoved their canoes boldly out upon the river, and for seven days floated slowly downward toward the Mississippi. The stillness of the Ouisconsin River, now crowded with villages and towns, seemed oppressive. Never before had they seen such buffalo, such deer, such stags. The sand-bars that stopped their way, the innumerable islands covered with vines and groves, and bordered with pleasant slopes, the paroquets that screamed in the trees, the "wingless swans" that strutted on the banks, the great fish that they feared would dash their canoes to pieces, filled them with indescribable awe. At last, on the seventeenth of June, they floated out on the bosom of the Mississippi, and turned their canoes to the south. Four days they followed the bends and twists of the river, and on the twenty-first of the month saw in the mud of the western bank footprints, and a path that disappeared in a meadow. Leaving the canoes with their companions on the river, Marquette and Joliet took the path through the meadows to a cluster of Indian villages, on the shore of what is now believed to be the River Des Moines. There they feasted, spent the night, and went back next morning to their followers, and, while the savages crowded the banks of the Mississippi, resumed their journey. They floated down the stream, past the rocks whereon were painted the monsters of which they had heard so much, past the mouth of the Missouri, past the Ohio, and stopped not far from the mouth of the Arkansas, where the voyage ended, and whence the party went slowly back to the lakes.

Taking up the work where Marquette left it, La Salle, in 1682, explored the Mississippi to its mouth, and standing on the shores of the Mexican Gulf, with a clod of earth in one hand and his sword in the other, formally took possession of the country for the King of France, and named it Louisiana. Two years later, when seeking the mouth of the Mississippi by sea, he reached the bay of Matagorda, and founded Fort St. Louis on the coast of Texas. By the custom of nations, the discovery and exploration of the Mississippi gave to France all the country that river drained. The discovery of the Texas coast gave to her all the country drained by the rivers of that coast, while the establishment of Fort St. Louis carried her claim to the coast southward to a point midway between Fort St. Louis and the nearest Spanish post. The nearest Spanish post was in the Province of Paduco. On the rude maps of the eighteenth century Louisiana, therefore, extends from the Rio Grande to the Mobile, from the Gulf of Mexico to the country beyond the source of the Mississippi River, and from the Smoky Mountains to the unknown regions of the West. To the claim of discovery and the claim of exploration was soon added a third—that of settlement; and, before the first quarter of the eighteenth century ended, Biloxi had been founded, and Mobile; the forts Rosalie, Toulouse and Tombigbee, Natchitoches and Assumption, Chartres and Cahokia erected, and the streets and ramparts of New Orleans marked out by De la Tour.

Thus firmly in possession of the Mississippi on the south and holding the St. Lawrence and the lakes on the north, the French began to overrun the country; built Fort Lake Pepin, Fort Vincent, Niagara, Detroit, Toronto, Ticonderoga, and Crown Point; strengthened their settlements on the Mississippi and the Illinois; took formal possession of the valley of the Ohio; built Presqu' Isle and Le Bœuf, and Venango, and, when the second quarter of the century ended, at the gateway of the Ohio River, came face to face with the English.

The conflict which followed has come down in history as the French and Indian War. It ought to have been called the war for possession, for when it was over, French power in America was gone. By the treaty of November third, 1762, France gave to England Nova Scotia, Acadia, Cape Breton, Canada, all the islands and all the coasts of the Gulf and River St. Lawrence, and divided her possessions in what is now our country into two parts. The line of partition ran down the Mississippi River from its source to the River Iberville, through the Iberville to Lake Maurepas, and along the north shore of Lakes Maurepas and Pontchartrain to the Gulf of Mexico. All to the east she gave to England; all to the west she gave to Spain.

The French cession to Spain was in the nature of compensation, for she too had taken part in the war, had been forced to surrender Havana to the English, and to get it back had given Florida in exchange. As indemnity for the loss of Florida, France made over to Spain the Island of Orleans and all the region west of the Mississippi.

Thus were the French expelled from North America. Thus were the possessions of Spain enlarged. Thus was our country divided between two contestants, and the first stage in the struggle for possession closed. But the first was scarcely over when the second began. In less than twelve years after the signing of the Treaty of Paris the Revolution opened, the hereditary enemies of England joined us, and in a little while Great Britain, France, Spain, and the United States were all four contending for the possession of the Mississippi Valley. The United States, standing by the ancient colonial charters, demanded as her boundary the St. John River, the Quebec line from the highlands of Maine to Lake Nipissing, a right line to the source of the Mississippi, the Mississippi to thirty-one degrees, eastward along that parallel to the Appalachicola, down the Appalachicola to the Flint, eastward to the head waters of the St. Mary's, and down the St. Mary's to the sea. But of such boundaries Spain would hear nothing. Her policy had always been to shut out rival powers from the waters of the Gulf. She had therefore gone into the war for the sole purpose of recovering Florida, and had succeeded beyond her expectations. Galvez, who governed Louisiana, had led an expedition into West Florida and had captured the British posts at Baton Rouge and Natchez, at Pensacola and Mobile. Her commandant at St. Louis had, in the dead of winter, penetrated into the heart of the Northwest, had seized the English post of Fort St. Joseph, had taken formal possession of the country it controlled, had displayed the Spanish standard, and had carried off the English colors as a title deed. That Spain would abandon the fruits of her victories without a struggle was not to be expected, and when the Commissioners met at Paris to frame a treaty of peace the struggle began.

To the claim for territory set up by the United States, the Spanish Ambassador replied that the country beyond the mountains had never belonged to the States while colonies; that it had never even been claimed by them; that previous to the Treaty of Paris it had belonged to France, and that after the treaty it remained a distinct part of the dominion of Great Britain, because by a proclamation in 1763 King George had drawn a line around the headwaters of the rivers flowing into the Atlantic, had set apart the country between it and the Mississippi River for the Indians, and had forbidden his subjects to settle there; and that now, in consequence of the conquests of Spain in West Florida, on the

Mississippi, and on the Illinois, the West belonged to Spain. He proposed, therefore, in the name of his Catholic Majesty, a western boundary for the United States, and was good enough to trace it in red ink on a copy of the rude map the Commissioners had before them. Running up the Flint River, the line followed the mountains to the waters of the Great Kanawha, passed down the Kanawha to the Ohio, skirted Pennsylvania, and passed along the south shore of the lakes to the Mississippi. The claim was both extravagant and absurd. But, extravagant as it was, the French Minister of Foreign Affairs, to the amazement of the American Commissioners, was far from disapproving it. This made it serious for the instructions given to Dr. Franklin, Mr. Adams and Mr. Jay were to undertake nothing in the negotiations for peace without the knowledge and concurrence of France. Vergennes admitted that the conquests of Spain did not justify her in claiming the whole eastern slope of the Mississippi Valley. But he asserted, and asserted positively, that the claim of the United States derived no support from anything in their colonial history, and proposed a compromise. The United States should be bounded on the west by the Chattahoochee, the mountains, and a line midway through the present State of Ohio. All west of this line and north of the Ohio River was to be left with England. What is now comprised in Kentucky, in Tennessee, in Alabama, and Mississippi, north of thirty-one degrees, was to be Indian Territory under the protection of Spain and the United States.

Widely as these two propositions differed, in some respects they agreed entirely in this: that the United States should own no territory beyond the mountains.

But the American Commissioners, determined that she should, broke through their instructions, and, without the knowledge of France, signed the preliminary treaty of peace in November, 1782. When the treaty, duly signed and sealed, was laid before the French Minister, he was astonished and deeply mortified.

He stormed, he raged, he bitterly reproached Franklin and his associates for the course they had taken. Nay, even Congress and the Secretary for Foreign Affairs were for a time disposed to blame the commissioner. But the deed was done, the West was saved; and when the definitive treaty was signed, in September, 1783, the western limit of the United States was irrevocably fixed at the Mississippi. The southern boundary was the thirty-first degree of latitude from the Mississippi to the Appalachicola, down that river to the Flint, eastward to the St. Mary's River, and by it to the sea. But a secret article declared that if Great Britain, when she made peace with Spain, recovered West Florida, the south boundary of the United States should be the line from the mouth of the Yazoo River due east to the Appalachicola—a line which since 1764 had been the north boundary of West Florida. Great Britain did not recover West Florida. Indeed, by a treaty signed the same day on which she signed that with the United States she ceded West Florida to Spain. As no boundary was given, Spain claimed it with the boundary it had when the Revolution opened—that is, with the line from the mouth of the Yazoo River. When, therefore, his Catholic Majesty heard of the secret article, he promptly informed Congress that no treaty between the United States and England could settle the boundary between the United States and Spain; that West Florida, with the bounds it had in 1775, was his; and that until such time as the two Governments should agree on the limits of Louisiana and the Floridas he would assert his territorial claims and maintain his jurisdiction over the river. The threat was no idle one. The posts which she had taken from England during the war, and which lay within the limits of the United States, she held and fortified, and for twelve years the Spanish flag waved over Baton Rouge and Natchez. She built new forts; she made treaties with the Indians, and suffered no American ships to enter or go out of the Mississippi. Then began yet another phase of the struggle for the possession of the valley.

On the November day, 1782, when peace was made with Great Britain the population of the United States did not amount to three millions of souls, and had but just begun to push through the mountains into West Virginia and Kentucky and Tennessee. Few in number, scattered along the banks of the Ohio and the streams flowing into the Ohio, joined to the East by no ties, commercial or political—nay, parted from it by the mountains and the lack of decent means of communication—having no channel by which to reach the markets of the world save the Mississippi River, they seemed destined by Nature to become some day an independent people.

Nor could the Confederation, while it lasted, do anything to hinder such a separation. A few statesmen of the Virginia school were far-sighted enough to see the vast importance of protecting American interests in the Mississippi Valley. But the East was ready enough to sacrifice the interests of the West; and in 1786, when Spain demanded as the price of a treaty of commerce an agreement that the citizens of the United States should not navigate the Mississippi for twenty-five years, John Jay, the Secretary for Foreign Affairs to Congress, readily consented. This price, however, was never paid. The protests of Virginia and the solemn threats of the people of Kentucky forced Congress to pause, and we had no commercial relation, no definition of bounds, no treaty with Spain, till 1796.

Long before that time, however, the movement of our population westward began, and the people came pouring over the mountains in three great streams. With the increase of population came an increase of discontent. The prohibition of the navigation of the Mississippi grew every year more and more galling till, when the French Revolution opened the markets of the West Indies to neutrals, and produced an immense demand for flour, pork, and bacon—the staples of the West—it became unbearable, and the old spirit of discontent grew rapidly to a spirit of revolution which every bold, daring, and reckless man labored hard to fan into open insurrection. At one time it seemed not unlikely that the people of the valley would separate from the States and form a union with the Spaniards. At another time it seemed quite probable that they would leave the Union, drive out the Spaniards, seize Florida and Louisiana, and form a new republic in the Mississippi Valley. Now it was George Rogers Clark organizing an expedition to seize Natchez, Baton Rouge, New Orleans. Now it was the French Minister Genet sending out agents to stir up hatred of the Spaniards in the West and enlist troops to attack them. Now it was Senator William Blount, of Tennessee, expelled from the Senate of the United States for trying to induce

Great Britain to send a fleet to close the Mississippi while he led an army down the river from Canada and attacked Louisiana. Now it was James Wilkinson intriguing with the Spanish Intendant and, under threats of leading an army from Kentucky, obtaining commercial concessions for himself. Rascality, corruption, intrigue were on every hand. Spanish agents constantly travelled on various errands up and down the Ohio; American speculators as constantly visited New Orleans.

It was a due sense of the dangers which thus threatened the two Governments, but chiefly a fear of English conquest, that in 1796 induced Spain to make her first treaty with the United States. By that treaty she accepted thirty-one degrees from the Mississippi to the Appalachicola as the south boundary of the United States, and withdrew her troops from the posts she had so long held on the east bank of the river. But as she still owned both banks of the Mississippi below thirty-one degrees, she would not open it for navigation. She would merely suffer citizens of the United States for three years to come to deposit merchandise at New Orleans, and, after paying enormous storage duty, reship them when they pleased.

Meagre as these concessions were, they served to alarm the two foremost men in France—Napoleon Bonaparte and Talleyrand, at that time Minister for Foreign Affairs to the Directory. No sooner did he hear of the treaty than he wrote to the French Minister resident in Spain a letter in which is fully portrayed the policy of France toward America for many years to come.

"The court of Madrid," said Talleyrand, "ever blind to its own interests and never docile to the lessons of experience, has again quite recently adopted a measure which cannot fail to produce the worst effects upon its political existence and on the preservation of its colonies. The United States have been put in possession of the forts situated along the Mississippi which the Spaniards had occupied as posts essential to arrest the progress of the Americans in those countries." The Americans, he then went on to say, were determined to rule America. This ambition could only be stopped "by shutting them up within the limits which Nature seems to have traced for them." As Spain could not do this, she would do well to cede Florida and Louisiana to France, in order that the Republic might do it for her.

The rupture between the United States and France followed immediately, and Talleyrand fell from power on July twentieth, 1799. But in October Napoleon returned from Egypt, and November ninth, or, as the day was called in the French calendar, eighteenth Brumaire, executed the famous *coup d'état*. Talleyrand was almost immediately recalled, the old policy of shutting up America within the limits assigned to her by Nature was resumed, and in July, 1800, instructions were sent to the French Minister at Madrid to begin the negotiations which ended in the treaty of retrocession. He was to demand from Spain the provinces of Louisiana, East Florida, West Florida, and six seventy-four-gun frigates. He was to offer in return a piece of European territory for the young Duke and Duchess of Palma. The Duchess of Palma was the daughter of Charles IV of Spain; the Duke was his nephew. The offer was most tempting, and, backed up by the wishes of the Queen and her daughter, it was accepted, a bargain was struck, and October first, 1800, the secret treaty was signed at San Ildefonso. By that treaty Spain pledged herself to retrocede the province of Louisiana as she had received it from France. France in turn pledged herself to add the duchy of Tuscany to the dukedom of Palma, make of them the kingdom of Etruria, and place on this new throne the daughter and son-in-law of the King of Spain.

To make good the promise was to Napoleon an easy matter. The battle of Hohenlinden humbled Austria. The treaty which followed that battle deprived the Grand Duke of Tuscany of his duchy, and the young King and Queen of Etruria were soon on their way to Italy. But a year sped by before Napoleon began to think seriously of occupying Louisiana. Then he commanded an expedition to be made ready to sail in the last week of September, 1801. But one delay followed another. The First Consul failed to display his usual energy, and when the King of Spain on the fifteenth of October signed the order for the delivery of Louisiana to France, neither ships nor troops were ready. It was November before Leclerc weighed anchor and made for a land he was destined never to reach. His orders bade him stop on the way at San Domingo, destroy the little negro republic ruled by Toussaint L'Ouverture and reduce that former possession of France to its old allegiance. Happily for us, that work was never done. The attempt to reduce the negroes to subjection consumed one fine army of seventeen thousand men. Yellow fever, more terrible than war, swept away a second while engaged in the task of holding the negroes in subjection, and the West was saved.

The treaty of San Ildefonso was supposed to be

secret. But the news that by it Louisiana had been ceded to France reached this country in 1802, and the Spanish Intendant at New Orleans, acting on his own authority, in the hope, perhaps, of winning the favor of Napoleon, proclaimed the right of deposit at New Orleans suspended, and shut the Mississippi in October, 1802. In a fortnight the whole West was in a furor and clamoring loudly for war. To see a people so weak, so impotent, as the Spanish in possession of the mouth of the river was one thing. But to see such a nation as France ruled by such a man as Napoleon in possession was another and a very different thing. Prevented it must be at all hazards, and, without waiting for the consent of Congress, Jefferson bade Livingston, our Minister at Paris, offer to purchase the Island of Orleans. "There is," he wrote, "on the globe one single spot the possessor of which is our natural and habitual enemy. It is New Orleans, through which must pass to market the produce of three eighths of that territory which from its fertility will yield more than half of our whole produce and contains more than half of our whole population."

The Federalists, when Congress met, took up the cry, and Jefferson despatched Monroe to join Livingston in the attempt to buy the Spanish possessions east of the Mississippi.

While these things were happening in the United States, events of yet greater importance were happening in Europe. The heroic struggles of five hundred thousand Haytian negroes who would not be enslaved, the fifty thousand soldiers whose lives had been sacrificed, the millions of francs that had been squandered, not in subjugating but in desolating San Domingo, had destroyed Napoleon's dream of empire in the New World. From the day news of Leclerc's death reached him all idea of a colonial system vanished. To abandon San Domingo and Louisiana outright would have been to confess defeat. Napoleon, therefore, in his characteristic way, began to cast about him for an excuse, and found it in that quarrel with England which broke the peace of Amiens and again involved Europe in war.

Fortunately for us, at the very moment his determination to abandon his colonies was reached, Livingston appeared before his minister with an offer to buy the Island of Orleans, and was met with the counter proposition to buy all Louisiana. No instructions authorized Livingston to go so far. But time was short; Napoleon was imperious; England, it was feared, would in case of war seize Louisiana, and to save it both Livingston and Monroe broke through their instructions, and in 1803 signed the treaty and the two Conventions which secured us Louisiana. The price was in round numbers fifteen millions of dollars.

Jefferson was greatly puzzled when these three documents reached his hand. He had offered to buy an island for a dockyard and a place of deposit. He was offered a magnificent domain. He had been authorized to expend two millions of dollars; the sum demanded was fifteen. As a strict constructionist he could not, and for a while he did not, consider the purchase of foreign territory as a constitutional act. But, when he thought of the evils that would follow if Louisiana remained with France, and of the blessings that would follow if Louisiana came to the United States, his common sense got the better of his narrow political scruples, and he soon found a way of escape.

He would accept the treaty, summon Congress, urge the House and Senate to perfect the purchase, and trust to the Constitution being mended so as to make the purchase legal. The six months allowed for deliberation would expire on the thirtieth day of October. The Congress was therefore summoned to meet on October seventeenth.

Nothing so finely illustrates the low state to which the once prosperous Federalists were fallen as the turbulent and factious opposition they now made to the acquisition of Louisiana. Some were worried lest the East should become depopulated, lest a great emigration should set in, lest old men and young men, abandoning homes and occupations, should cross the Mississippi and perhaps found there a republic of their own. Some feared that mere extent of territory would rend the Republic apart; that no common ties of interest could ever bind together under one government men who fought Indians and trapped bears around the head waters of the Missouri, and men who built ships and caught fish in the harbors of the Atlantic coast. Some affected the language of patriots and lamented the enormous increase the purchase would make in the national debt. This, indeed, became a favorite theme, and soon Federal writers and printers all over the land were vying with each other in attempts to show the people what an exceedingly great sum of money fifteen millions of dollars was.

Fifteen millions of dollars! they would exclaim. The sale of a wilderness has not usually commanded a price so high. Ferdinand Gorges received but twelve hundred and fifty pounds sterling for the Province of Maine. William Penn gave for the wilderness that now bears his name but a trifle over five thousand pounds. Fifteen millions of dollars! A breath will suffice to pronounce the words. A few strokes of the pen will express the sum on paper. But not one man in a thousand has any conception of the magnitude of the amount. Weigh it, and there will be four hundred and thirty-three tons of solid silver. Load it into wagons, and there will be eight hundred and sixty-six of them. Place the wagons in a line, giving two rods to each, and they will cover a distance of five and one third miles. Hire a laborer to shovel it into the carts, and though he load sixteen each day, he will not finish the work in two months. Stack it up dollar on dollar, and, supposing nine to make an inch, the pile will be more than three miles high. It would load twenty-five sloops; it would pay an army of twenty-five thousand men forty shillings a week each for twenty-five years; it would, divided among the population of the country, give three dollars for each man, woman, and child. All the gold and all the silver coin in the Union would, if collected, fall vastly short of such a sum.

Statistics, most happily, were of no avail. The mass of the people approved of the purchase, the Senate ratified the treaty and the Conventions, and on December twentieth, 1803, Louisiana was taken possession of by the United States.

In the treaty of purchase no boundary was given. When the United States took possession in December, 1803, the eastern boundary was the Mississippi from its source to the thirty-first parallel; but where the source of the Mississippi was no man knew, and what was the boundary below thirty-one degrees was long in dispute. Americans claimed as far eastward as the Perdido River, but Spain would acknowledge no claim east of the Mississippi and south of the thirty-first parallel save the Island of Orleans. The south boundary was, of course, the Gulf of Mexico; but whether it extended along the Gulf to the Sabine or the Rio Grande was not settled. The mountains, wherever they might be, were believed to bound it on the west, and the possessions of Great Britain, wherever they might be, were known to bound it on the north.

Want of definite boundaries on the southeast and on the southwest now involved us in a serious dispute with Spain, which war abroad and at home and a suspension of all diplomatic relations with Spain from 1808 to 1815, prolonged till 1819, when a treaty was made which secured Florida at a cost in round numbers of five million dollars, and for the first time drew a boundary line on the southwest. Starting at the mouth of the Sabine, it passed up that river to the parallel of thirty-two degrees, thence due north to the Red River, westward along that river to the one hundredth meridian, thence due north to the Arkansas River, whose south bank it followed to the river's source in the mountains. As nobody knew where the source of the Arkansas was, the treaty provided that the line should be drawn from the source, when found, either due north or due south, as occasion might require, to the parallel of forty-two degrees north latitude, and thence westward along that parallel to the Pacific Ocean.

Just before the treaty of 1819 was made with Spain, the Convention of 1818 was concluded with Great Britain, and a northern boundary was given to Louisiana. This line of demarcation between the territory of the United States and the territory of his

Britannic Majesty was to begin at "the most northwestern point of the Lake of the Woods," run "due north or south, as the case may be," to the forty-ninth parallel of north latitude, and westward along that parallel to the summit of the Stony—or, as we know them, the Rocky—Mountains. The region which lies beyond the mountains, and is now comprised in the States of Idaho, Washington, and Oregon, was claimed by each nation. The claim of the United States rested on the discovery of the Columbia River by Captain Gray in 1792, on the exploration of the country by Lewis and Clark in 1804–1806, and on the settlement built by the Missouri Fur Company at Fort Hall in 1808, and by the Pacific Fur Company at Astoria in 1810. But, as it was still a wilderness, to dispute about it seemed so idle that "the high contracting parties" agreed that for ten years they would hold the country in joint occupancy, and that such occupancy should in no wise affect the claim of either.

And now a new claimant appeared in the Emperor of Russia who, in 1822, put forth a ukase and asserted his ownership of the whole northwestern coast from Behring Sea southward to fifty-one degrees of north latitude, and warned all foreigners not to come within three hundred miles of the coast.

Against this John Quincy Adams, then Secretary of State, protested vigorously and bade the American Minister at St. Petersburg admit no part of the Russian claims, but rest the claims of the United States on the Spanish treaty of 1819, which secured all the rights and pretensions of Spain to the coast north of forty-two degrees; on the discovery of the Columbia by Grey; on the exploration of the country by Lewis and Clark;

and on the settlement at Astoria. He might, however, agree that no citizen of the United States should land at any Russian settlement without permission of the Russian commander; that no subjects of the Emperor should land at any American settlements without consent of the American authorities; and that no American settlements should be made north and no Russian settlements should be established south of fifty-five degrees north latitude.

Meantime Great Britain had protested against the imperial ukase, and had in like manner been invited to an amicable negotiation for the adjustment of her claims. It was supposed that, as England and America held the country in joint occupation, the two nations would carry on a joint negotiation with Russia. But when it was found that the British envoy had power to discuss, but not to conclude anything, and that authority to act jointly was not likely to be given him, Henry Middleton began the negotiation on behalf of the United States alone by offering fifty-five degrees as a boundary or line of demarcation. Russia then offered 54° 40', which was accepted and incorporated in the Convention signed in April, 1824.

The discussion thus raised by Russia made it most fitting that the United States and England should come to an understanding as to their respective pretensions. Adams, therefore, instructed Benjamin Rush to bring up the matter, and to state definitely the grounds on which the United States took her stand. The Russian application of the colonial principle of exclusion was not to be admitted as lawful on any part of the northwest coast of America. Indeed, it was to be denied that such a principle could be applied by any European nation. It was true that by the Nootka Sound Convention of 1790 England had agreed that, so far as Spanish settlements extended in North and South America, Spain possessed the exclusive rights territorial, and of navigation and fishery, to a distance of ten miles from the coasts so actually occupied. But the independence of the South American nations and of Mexico has extinguished, said Adams, the exclusive colonial rights of Spain in North and South America, and the American continents henceforth will no longer be subjects of colonization. Occupied by civilized independent nations, they will be accessible to Europeans on that footing alone, and the Pacific Ocean and every part of it will remain open to the navigation of all nations in like manner with the Atlantic."

As to the boundary, Rush was to offer to stipulate that no settlements be made in future by the Russians south of fifty-five degrees, by citizens of the United States north of fifty-one degrees, or by British subjects either south of fifty-one or north of fifty-five degrees. He might, however, if England insisted on it, accept forty-nine degrees as the boundary from the Rocky Mountains to the sea. These two propositions were accordingly made by Rush, and were met the one with a declination and the other with a flat denial. Great Britain, it was answered, considered the whole of the unoccupied parts of America as open to her future settlements as heretofore, and would make no exception of the northwest coast, whether north of forty-two degrees or south of fifty-one. Yet she would, from pure goodness, from a desire to close sources of disagreement which the future might multiply and aggravate, waive her rights, and suggest a line of demarcation. This line was the parallel of forty-nine degrees from the summit of the Rocky Mountains to the northeasternmost branch of the Columbia River, and thence down the Columbia to the Pacific Ocean. Rush rejected it as promptly as England had rejected that of the United States, and tendered forty-nine degrees from the mountains to the sea. Again, England declined the offer, and the negotiations came to naught.* In 1825, however, Great Britain made an agreement with Russia by which she also accepted the line 54° 40' as the south boundary of Alaska, and as such it has remained to this day. Thus was the country between 42° and 54° 40' once more left to be contended for by Great Britain and the United States, and when the ten years of joint occupation provided for by the Convention drew to a close, the claimants being still unable to settle the ownership, joint occupation was continued indefinitely with the new condition that it could be ended by either party on one year's notice.

With this agreement the Oregon country ceased to trouble the people till in the summer of 1832 four Flat-Head Indians suddenly appeared in St. Louis, sought out General William Clark, and told him they had come from what is now the State of Washington in search of the white man's Bible. The Indians were fed and feasted, armed, blanketed, hung with ornaments, but were not given the Bible. Among those who heard this singular request was a young clerk in the office of Clark. Touched by the refusal of the Bible, he sent an account of the whole proceeding to a friend in Pittsburg, who wisely gave the letter to the

---

* Negotiations ended in July, 1824.

public. The heart of the country was deeply moved, and four missionaries, sent out by the Methodist Board of Missions and the American Board of Commissioners for Foreign Missions, were soon on their way to Oregon. It is only with one, Marcus Whitman, that we have to deal. He crossed the mountains in 1835, entered the Columbia valley, went among the Nez Percés, and brought home so strong a report to the Board of Missions that he was sent back with H. H. Spalding as a missionary to the Indians. With them went their wives, the first white women who ever passed over the Rocky Mountains into the Northwest. The party set out from the East in the early spring of 1836 for St. Louis, where they joined the annual expedition of the American Fur Company to the fur regions of Oregon. The route was up the Missouri to Council Bluffs, and along the Platte River across Nebraska. Late in May they were on the South Fork; in June they were on the Laramie, and in July entered the famous South Pass, through which, since that day, tens of thousands of emigrants have poured into Oregon. At this place the White River Mountains and the Rocky Mountains come close together, separated only by the pass, than which there is perhaps no more interesting spot to travellers in the whole Northwest. It is the great divide of the waters of the continent. The traveller who takes his stand on that high plateau has in plain sight, at his feet, within a radius of a quarter of a mile, the head waters of the three great rivers of the Northwest. Before him lies the little stream that marks the humble beginning of the Yellowstone, and on his right hand is the fountain of the North Platte, the waters of both of which rivers in time reach the Gulf of Mexico. On his left are the head waters of the Columbia, which finds its outlet in the Pacific.

It was the fourth of July when Whitman reached this spot, and, recollecting the day and the work that lay before him, he passed a short way down the Pacific slope, called on the party to dismount, raised the American flag, and, while they all kneeled around the Book it was their mission to carry to the Indians, he, with prayer and praise, took possession of the Western Continent in the name of Christ and of His Church.

In September, 1836, Whitman reached Walla Walla, and by the end of 1841 one hundred and thirty-seven emigrants had followed him from the United States. Such an inroad of Americans alarmed the English Fur Companies, who now began to hurry forward emigrants from Canada. Joint possession then began to mean the right of the people of each country to settle Oregon, with the fact clearly in view that whichever secured the greater number of settlers would end joint occupancy and hold Oregon forever.

And now occurred another of those apparently trifling incidents on which great events so often turn. Four Indians begging for a Bible brought Whitman to Oregon. A dinner at the English trading-post, Fort Walla Walla, sent him back with all possible speed to Washington. The occasion of the dinner was the arrival at the fort of the agents of the Fur Company with fifteen boats loaded with goods for the Indians on the Frazer River. Whitman was the sole representative of the United States at the feast, which was scarcely begun when a messenger entered with word that one hundred and forty English colonists had crossed the mountains, had entered Oregon, and were even then at the Columbia River. A great shout rose from the assembled company, and one of them, springing to his feet and waving his cap, cried out, "Hurrah for Oregon! The Americans are too late. We have the country now."

That moment the policy of the English Government was made plain. The traders that came up from St. Louis in the summer brought word that a treaty was soon to be made to put at rest the long-vexed question of the boundary. Knowing this, Whitman thought England was attempting to settle Oregon and then hold it by the right of prior settlement, and, thinking so, he determined that the Government at Washington should know of it without delay. Not a moment was lost. He left the table instantly, galloped to his home at the mission station, and in twenty-four hours was on his way to Washington with two companions.

A horseback ride of four thousand miles over the best of roads in the best of weather would have been a matter of no small discomfort. But he was to make it across a wilderness in the dead of winter. His route was southward across Idaho, across Utah, past Salt Lake, past the site soon to be occupied by the Mormon city, across New Mexico to Sante Fé, and on by the Santa Fé trail to St. Louis. He crossed the swollen rivers on improvised floats, encountered terrible storms on the prairie, was snow-bound for days in the gorges, was lost in a blizzard, lived on the bark of cotton-wood trees, was chased by the wolves, and once gave himself up for lost. But he pushed on, and, frozen, weak with hunger, and almost dead, reached Santa Fé January third, 1843. January seventh he was on his way to St. Louis, where, to his dismay, he learned that the

Webster-Ashburton Treaty had been concluded August ninth, 1842, ratified by the Senate August twenty-sixth, and proclaimed the law of the land November tenth. But he was not too late, for the treaty said not one word about the boundary of Oregon. Once more he pushed forward, and on March third, 1843, five months from the day he left the Columbia, he strode into the office of the Secretary of State at Washington.

He came in the very nick of time. The question then asked on every hand was, "Is Oregon worth having?" for not one man east of the Missouri had any conception of what Oregon was. The existence of a great American desert was firmly believed, and part of this desert was east of Oregon. "What," exclaimed Mr. McDuffie in his speech in the Senate, January twenty-third, 1843, "is the nature of this country? Why, as I understand it, seven hundred miles this side of the Rocky Mountains is uninhabitable, a region where rain scarcely ever falls, a barren, sandy soil, mountains totally impassable. Well, now, what are we going to do in this case? How are you going to apply steam? Have you made anything like an estimate of the cost of a railroad from here to the Columbia? Why, the wealth of the Indies would be insufficient. Of what use will this be for agricultural purposes? Why, I would not for that purpose give a pinch of snuff for the whole territory. I thank God for his mercy in placing the Rocky Mountains there."

The mission of Whitman was to dispel this ignorance; and he did so. He destroyed the American desert of Mr. McDuffie. He told the President and the Secretary just what Oregon was, and obtained from them the solemn promise that nothing should be done with regard to Oregon till he had led out a caravan of American settlers. Encouraged by the promise, he now turned west in search of emigrants, and so well did he succeed that in June a caravan of two hundred wagons moved out of Westport on the Missouri and headed for the Northwest. As the news of the success of the exposition spread over the country, a rage for emigration broke out in the West, and grew wilder and wilder each year, till in the summer of 1846 five hundred and fifty-eight wagons crossed the Missouri River for Oregon, and raised the white population of that country to several thousand souls.

Meanwhile, the people had taken the question up, and, under the popular cry, "Reannexation of Texas," "The whole of Oregon or none," "Fifty-four forty or fight," the Democrats entered the campaign of 1844 and won it. Polk was inaugurated March fourth, 1845, and in the speech he made that day from the Capitol steps he declared that the American title to the country of Oregon was clear and unquestionable. Lord John Russell, when he read this remark, called it "a blustering announcement." The Democrats, when they read Lord Russell's sneer, flung back the taunt, "Fifty-four forty or fight."

But the Administration had no intention of fighting, and on July twelfth, 1845, offered to compromise on the line of the forty-ninth parallel. England refused. Polk withdrew the offer, declared he would now have all of Oregon or none, and in December urged Congress to give the year's notice, abandon joint occupancy, and protect the American settlers taken out by Whitman. The Western Democrats cried out for instant notice. But the South deserted them, and April sixteenth, 1846, notice in very gentle and conciliatory language passed the Senate. England now offered the forty-ninth parallel, which was promptly accepted and incorporated in the treaty of 1846.

The willingness with which the Democrats abandoned the claim to "the whole of Oregon or none" was in great part due to the coming war with Mexico in consequence of the annexation of Texas.

When the treaty of 1819 was made with Spain, and the Sabine, the Red, and the Arkansas Rivers were taken as the boundary line between the possessions of the United States and Spain, Mexico, then in revolt against Spain, assumed jurisdiction over Texas, and in 1823, when Iturbide had made himself Emperor, with the title of Augustine the First, was opened to colonization by foreigners. The law, whose passage was chiefly due to the persistence of Stephen Austin, repealed the royal order of Philip II for the extermination of foreigners, promised them liberty, security of property, and civil rights, provided they professed the Roman Catholic religion, offered each farmer not less than 177 and each stock-raiser 4,428 acres of land, and released them for six years to come from the payment of taxes, duties, and tithes.

But the law had hardly been enacted when a revolution swept Iturbide from the throne and put "The United States of Mexico" in place of the empire. By the new Constitution, Texas was joined to the neighboring province of Coahuila, and under the name of "The State of Coahuila and Texas" became a member of the Republic, and in 1824 passed a colonization law of her own. Then the settlement of Texas by citizens of the United States began in earnest, and in time fourteen huge grants of land were taken by contractors pledged to bring in 5,290 families before a certain date.

For a while all went well. But about 1830 trouble began between the Texans and Mexico, grew more and more serious year by year till March second, 1836, when Texas formally declared herself a Republic. But she had no idea of independent existence, and annexation to the United States was merely a question of time. Indeed, in 1837 Texas made a formal offer of annexation. But the Legislature of eight Northern States protested, and Van Buren would hear nothing about it. Tyler, who followed him, would hear nothing against it, and in 1844 surprised the Senate with a treaty of annexation. It was rejected; but the Democrats made it a question in the campaign of 1844, and, having won the election, annexed Texas in 1845 and brought on the Mexican War. The treaty of Guadalupe Hidalgo, which closed the war, carried the boundary of the United States to the Gila River and added 522,900 square miles to the public domain. In 1853 the Gadsden purchase established the present south boundary of Arizona and New Mexico from the Rio Grande to the Gulf of California, and ended the struggle for the West. Since that day the United States has acquired but two pieces of foreign soil. One was Alaska, bought from Russia in 1867. The other was the little island of Navassa, acquired in 1891.

FOUR CENTURIES OF PROGRESS.

As we all well know, it was with no idea of finding a new continent that Columbus weighed anchor in Palos and sailed out into the "sea of darkness." That magnificent trade which for centuries past had been going on between Europe and Asia—a trade which built up first Constantinople, then Venice, and then Genoa—was hopelessly gone. The Turk had thrust himself across the great caravan routes and throttled it. The crusaders had failed to throttle the Turk, and the cry of all Europe was for a new route to the Indies. Portugal attempted to find one, and, under the special protection of the Pope, her navigators crept slowly down the African coast. As league after league of that continent was discovered, and the flag of Portugal was carried past Cape Non, past Cape Blanco, past Cape Verde, along the gold coast, and far below the River Congo, to the country of the Hottentots, yet no route eastward found, it became quite clear that even if such a passage did exist the length of it would make it hardly practicable, and the demand for a shorter route to the Indies became more imperative than ever. This Columbus undertook to satisfy. The lands both he and his followers discovered in nowise resembled what Europe knew the East to be—the land of spices and costly fabrics, of magnificent cities, of palaces and treasuries heaped with gold and precious stones. Yet thirty years passed away and Magellan made that most marvellous of voyages before Europe understood that a New World had been discovered, and that a great continent blocked the way to India. Profound disappointment followed this. Europe had no use for new land, and one hundred and fifteen years passed away before the first lasting English settlement was made within our boundary.

The first century after the landing of Columbus in the Bahamas was spent in wondering what to do with the New World. The Pope had given it to Spain, and Spain for one hundred years did her best to ruin it. With the second century a better era opens, and the period of occupation is reached at last.

Again and again attempts had been made to establish colonies and found States. But one and all came to naught till in 1607 the English landed at Jamestown. There were, it is true, at St. Augustine and at Santa Fé, and in the valley of the Gila River, small hamlets whose founding antedated that of Jamestown. But they were mere military posts or missionary stations, and formed no part of any scheme of colonization. Till the opening of the seventeenth century all such attempts had failed because they had been undertaken by private individuals, and because the men who came out as colonists were adventurers, not settlers.

But the task in which so many had failed was made possible toward the close of the sixteenth century by the pressure of economic and religious distress. The increase of population; the rise in the price of food; the rapid conversion of great quantities of arable land to pasturage; the destruction of the monasteries, which threw on the communities the tramps these houses had so long supported; the crowds of disbanded soldiers from the low countries that filled the cities—produced in time a class so distressed that emigration even to the New World was gladly welcomed by them. When, therefore, the merchants of London and of Plymouth formed their companies, in 1606, they found a class ready at hand on which to draw for settlers. What economic distress did for Virginia, religious intolerance did a few years later for Massachusetts; and by the end of the first quarter of the seventeenth century the English colonization of what is now the United States was fairly under way. Before the middle of the century the Dutch held the islands and shores of New York Bay, the banks of the Hudson and the Mohawk, while the Swedes had made a lodgment on the Delaware. But these colonies were short-lived, for the Swedes soon fell a prey to the Dutch; the Dutch in turn were overcome by the English, and when the century drew to a close the authority of Great Britain was supreme along the whole Atlantic coast from Maine to Florida. Florida and the Gulf shore as far as Pensacola were in Spanish hands. Beyond Pensacola, to the Rio Grande River, the coast belonged to France, for by that time La Salle had explored the Mississippi to its mouth, had taken formal possession in the name of his master of that noble valley which the great river drains, and had made a landing on the shores of Texas. What is now New Mexico, Arizona, and California belonged to Spain, and boasted of at least one city more than a hundred years old.

Thus, two centuries after the landing of Columbus in the Bahamas our country was still, in the main, an unbroken wilderness. At that time the English-speaking colonies were but ten in number, with a population not so great by several hundred thousand as the present population of the city of New York. These people dwelt in a fringe of towns and little hamlets which lay close to the seashore, or were at most one hundred and fifty miles from it. Of the country which lay back of this coast line, and stretched away to the Mississippi and the Great Lakes, less was then known than we now know of the heart of Africa. The French had lately discovered the Mississippi and had floated down it from the Wisconsin to the Gulf. But no white man living had seen the valley of the Ohio, or of the Susquehanna, of the Cumberland, or of the Tennessee, or, indeed, of any of the great tributaries of the Father of Waters.

Of the thin fringe of towns which skirted the coast from Maine to Carolina, not one contained as many as ten thousand souls. Almost all were surrounded by stockades or defended by block-houses, and many were at that time hard pressed by the Indians, for "King William's War," as the colonists called it, was raging. Falmouth, or, as we know it, Portland, and Maine east of the Penobscot had just been laid in ashes by the Indians, while Schenectady, the extreme outpost of English civilization in New York, had suffered the same fate a few years before. Coming along the coast southward we find York and Exeter and Dover and Portsmouth existing. Eastern Massachusetts was fairly well peopled, and was just then dreadfully tormented by the Salem witchcraft delusion. Along Cape Cod and the Sound, and up the valley of the Connecticut, were many towns whose names are familiar to us. In New York, the Hudson was occupied as high up as Albany, and the Mohawk as far up as Schenectady. In New Jersey, Amboy had been founded, and Elizabethtown and Burlington and a host of smaller towns. Pennsylvania, the youngest of the colonies, was not twelve years old. Philadelphia was but ten, Charleston was not twenty-five, Baltimore, Savannah, and New Orleans did not exist.

Life in the best of such towns as did exist would now be thought hard and unbearable. Were we to strip from our daily life such luxuries, such comforts, such conveniences—nay, such necessaries—as the progress of two hundred years has given us, and which the men of that day did not possess, we should think ourselves fast approaching the condition of the red men. Not a street in the whole land was paved, or lighted, or sewered. Every drop of water came from private wells or the town pump. Every peaceful citizen was expected to be in bed by nine at night; those found on the streets after that hour were supposed not to be peaceable, and were sure to be stopped by the watch and questioned. Nowhere was there a museum or a theatre or a show or any place of amusement. No man in the country had ever seen a newspaper, or a piece of anthracite coal, or a stove, or a friction match. Very few had ever seen a printing press, for there were but two clumsy hand presses in the entire country. Of steam machinery of every kind the world was ignorant. From the barn of the farmer would go the reaper, the thresher and binder, and every kind of improved rake and plough. In their place would be found the cradle, the scythe, the hand rake, and the flail. From the table of the humblest man would disappear many articles now of common daily food, for neither the tomato, nor the sweet potato, nor the orange were in general use. Indeed, save the sweet potato, none were eaten at all.

We should miss again that humanitarian spirit which is one of the many blessings of our time. Sympathy for the unfortunate did not exist anywhere. The debtor was cast into prison. The pauper was sold to the highest bidder. The criminal was dragged out into open day and pilloried, or flogged, or placed in the stocks. Prison discipline and hard labor were not considered remedies for crime. The culprit was not to be cured of his evil ways, but made an example of, or, if sent out again into the community, so marked that all who met him might know his character. His ear must be cut off. His forehead must be branded. He must wear a letter of bright-colored cloth sewed to his clothing. Many things which now pass for vulgarity and bad manners were then serious offences, and cursing men and scolding women were punished publicly.

But in nothing would the astonishing progress be so marked as in the daily occupations of men. Startling though the statement may seem, it is strictly true that a hundred vocations can easily be named which now give a comfortable livelihood to millions of our fellow-citizens, yet were utterly unknown in 1692. Could a man who witnessed the landing of Penn come back to life and undertake to read down the "wants" column of a great morning newspaper, he would find it utterly impossible to understand the expressions he would meet in every line. The district messenger, the telegraph operator, the "lineman," the stenographer, the typewriter, the "saleslady," the car driver, the gripman, the conductor, the brakeman, the bookkeeper, the street sweeper, the paver, the pork packer, the electrician, the elevator boy, the engineer and the fireman, and the hosts of others whose trades and occupations are so well known to us, are persons concerning whose daily life he would not be able to form the faintest conception. The great corporations, the railroads, the steamboats, the express companies, the mills and factories of every sort which cover our land and give employment to ten times as many human beings as there were then in all the colonies together, are every one of them the creatures of our time. The opportunities for making a livelihood were therefore vastly restricted, for the kinds of occupations were not only few, but the trades at best yielded poor returns. What we call "the workingman," "the laborer," "the mechanic," "the mill hand," had no existence as classes. Every farm-house was a miscellaneous factory, and the farmer a jack of all trades. He and his sons made their own shoes, beat out their own nails and spikes, hinges, and every sort of ironmongery, and made much of the furniture and all the implements used on the farm. The wife and her daughters manufactured the clothing from dressing the flax and carding the wool to cutting the cloth. Even in towns large enough to support a few artisans, each made with his own hands whatever he sold. Taking the country through, the chief occupations of the people were farming for a living and trade for making money. New Hampshire was chiefly agricultural. Massachusetts, Rhode Island, and New York chiefly commercial. The Southern colonies were wholly given up to planting.

When another century had passed and 1792 came, these conditions had greatly changed, and changed for the better. By that time the Swedes had fallen a prey to the Dutchman, the Dutchman to the Englishman, who had driven out the Frenchman, and in his turn had been expelled from the United States.

In 1792 our country touched the Mississippi, but not the Gulf of Mexico, and numbered fifteen States bound together by a Constitution just five years old. Since that day we have reached the Gulf, we have crossed the Mississippi, we have built up two-and-twenty Commonwealths on the plains beyond, we have made our Constitution sure, and given to Europe such an object lesson in "government of the people, by the people, for the people," as will not be in vain. Every art, every science, every branch of human industry has been enormously developed by us. Whatever abridges distance, whatever annihilates time, whatever alleviates human pain, whatever extirpates disease, has nowhere been so fostered as in these United States.

Scarcely had the third century of American history closed when Robert Fulton, following in the footsteps of Fitch and Rumsey, gave to the world the first successful steamboat, and opened not only the era of steam-navigation, but of American invention. Could we but stretch forth our hands and take out of the life of the world to-day every machine, every article of real necessity, every convenience, every comfort due to the ingenuity of our countrymen, we should bring back a condition of affairs which to us would be almost intolerable. We should destroy every steamboat, pull down every line of telegraph, and silence every telephone on the face of the earth. From the bed of every ocean would come innumerable cables, and from the streets and houses of every city would go ten thousand electric lights. We should take from the surgeon chloroform, discovered by Guthrie, and again inflict on the patient all the pain and suffering banished by the labors of Dr. Morton and Dr. Wells. From every house would go the sewing-machine, which has lightened the labors of millions of women and revolutionized the industries of the world. From every farm would go the reaper, which has cheapened food and made possible the great grain-fields of Russia, of the Argentine Republic, and of our own West. From every army would go the revolver, from the arts would be taken galvanized iron, and every application of India-rubber, which, till Goodyear made his discoveries, was little better than a useless gum.

As we have grown more intelligent, so we have grown more liberal, more tolerant, more humane. When this century opened there was not a blind asylum, nor a deaf and dumb asylum, nor a lunatic asylum, nor a house of refuge in all our land. We have turned our prisons from stews and brothels and seminaries of crime into reformatories of crime. We have cut down the number of crimes punished with death from fifteen to two. We have ceased to use the branding iron and the treadmill; we have abolished imprisonment for debt; we have exterminated slavery, and raised the laborer from a vassal to a man. We have covered our country with free schools and free libraries, and set up institutions for the protection not only of children but of dumb brutes. In the face of these facts it is wicked to talk of degeneration and decay.

INDEX.

Adams, John, chosen Vice-President, 160–162; inaugurated, 166, 167; sent to France, 259, 260; his sketch of Franklin, 261, 262.

Adams, John Quincy, on the Russian claims, 18–20; on the Panama mission, 26; constitutional amendment on slavery, 211, 212; report on veto power, 213.

Aix-la-Chapelle, Congress at, 8; Spanish affairs laid before, 9.

Alexander, Emperor of Russia, originates Holy Alliance, 2; establishes Duchy of Warsaw, 7; abandons liberalism, 7; sends a fleet to Spain, 8, 9; meddles in affairs of Spain, 10; at Troppau, 11.

Alexander VI, Pope, bull of, regarding America, 281.

Alexandria, reception of Washington at, 167.

Amendments, a supposed thirteenth to the United States Constitution, 89–93; States ask for constitutional amendments, 184; Virginia urges, 184, 185; Madison proposes, 184; ten declared in force, 184; attempts to amend the Constitution, 1790–'94, 187, 188; the eleventh amendment, 187, 188; regarding election of President, 191, 192, 199, 206–208, 210; twelfth amendment, 192; regarding the removal of judges, 192, 199, 212; Pennsylvania asks for a new tribunal, 193; Massachusetts asks that representation and direct taxes be apportioned according to free inhabitants, 194, 195, 212; Hartford Convention amendments, 198, 199; reputed thirteenth amendment, 199: Kentucky proposes that suits to which States are parties be tried by Senate, 201; regarding power of Congress to build roads, canals, etc., 205, 206; regarding duellists and defaulters, 210; power of Congress over slavery, 211, 212; limit on the veto power, 213; slavery amendments offered in 1860, 218–220; since the war, 220, 221.

Americanism, native, 88, 89; reason for, 90; is anti-Catholic, 90–92; anti-foreign feeling, 93, 94; rise of Native-American party, 94; principles of, 95; success of, 96; riots, 96; rise of the Know-Nothings, 97, 98; anti-Catholic excitements, 98, 99; Gavazzi, 98, 99; Bedini, 99; riots, 100; success of Know-Nothings, 100, 101; principles of, 102; national Convention of " American Party," 104, 105; split in the party, 105; defeat and decline, 105.

Annapolis, trade Convention at, 110, 111.

Annexation of Texas, 215.
Appointment, the Council of, in New York, 79; struggle for control of, 79-81, 85, 86.
Arbiter, is there a common, for States; Virginia and Kentucky on, 189-191; co-States on, 190, 191; Pennsylvania and Virginia on, in 1810, 193, 194; Ohio on, 201; nullification by South Carolina, 204, 205.
Area of the United States in 1789, 178, 180.

Bank of the United States, debate on constitutionality of its charter, 186, 187; stops loans in the West, 242; attacks on, in Kentucky, 243, 244; in Ohio, 250, 251; outlawed, 251.
Bank of Kentucky, 241; suspends, 242, 244.
Banks, mania for, in the West, 240, 241, 250.
Bedini, Mgr. Gaetano, career of, 99.
Bills of credit, 239.
Blaine, James G., on Monroe Doctrine, 38.
Boundary of the United States in 1789, 178, 179; contest for, 288, 289.
Bourne, Sylvanus, 166.
British, take New York city, 271-273; refugees in, 273, 274; departure of, from New York city, 275-280.
Brune, Marshal, murder of, 6.
Buchanan, James, on Monroe Doctrine applied to Mexico, 33, 34; on coercion and succession, 218.
Bulls, the papal, regarding discovery of America, 281.

Cabinet, origin of the President's, 55, 56.

Canning, proposition to Rush, 14-16.
Carbonari, force Ferdinand to grant a constitution to Naples, 10, 11; liberalism stamped out at Naples, 12, 13.
Cass, Lewis, on Monroe Doctrine and Mexico, 33.
Castlereagh, Lord, opinion of the Holy Alliance, 3, 4; to represent Great Britain at Vienna, 14; death of, 14.
Catholics, feeling against, and cause of it, 90-92; anti-Catholic riots, 93; struggle with native Americans, 95; revival of the feeling against, 97-99; Gavazzi, 98, 99; Bedini, 99, 100; riots, 100.
"Cement for the Union," 156.
Cities, early government of, 317.
Clay, Henry, resolution on the Monroe Doctrine, 23; instructions to Poinsett, 23, 24; on the Panama Congress, 25; on veto power, 213; on one term for President, 214.
Clinton, De Witt, introduces the spoils system into New York, 80, 81.
Clinton, George, contest for office of Governor of New York, 77; frauds connected with, 77, 78; struggle with the Council of Appointment, 79, 80.
Coins, foreign, in circulation 1782, 223; attempt to establish a national coinage, 223, 224; ratio of gold to silver, 224; the mint, 225; first coins, 225; scarcity of, 226, 227, 229; gold coinage act of 1834, 230, 231; "Benton mint-drops," " Jackson yellow-boys," 231; coinage act of 1853, 232; act of 1873, 232, 233; trade dollar, 233, 234; " Sherman Act," 235, 236.
Colonization, Adams on, 19, 20; Monroe Doctrine on, 21.

INDEX. 325

"Colonization" in Maryland, 84.
Common law, efforts to drive out the English, 89.
Compromises of the Constitution: the compromise on representation, 128–130; on slave representation in the House of Representatives, 130–134; on the importation of slaves till 1808, 138–141.
Confederation, the articles of, framed, 107; character of the Government under, 107, 108; powers of, 108; defects of, 108, 109, 154–156; attempts to amend, 109, 110; the Annapolis Convention, 110, 111; the Constitutional Convention called, 111.
Congress, Monroe Doctrine announced to, 21, 22; Clay's resolution, 23; debate on Panama Congress, 27, 28; resolution of the House of Representatives, 29; House of Representatives and Mexico, 36; first, under the Constitution meets at New York, 154; Hamilton and Jefferson on powers of, 186, 187; power of the House over treaties, 189; to build roads and canals, 200; to charter a bank, 200, 201, 205, 206; "gag rule," 209; power over slavery, 210, 211.
Congress, the Continental, character of, 107, 108; powers of, 108; weakness of, 108, 109; calls the Constitutional Convention, 111; fixes date for Constitution to go into force, 150, 151; character and work of, 152–157; expires for want of a quorum, 157; wanderings of, 156; contempt for, 155–157; description of its room at New York city, 164, 165.
Congresses at Aix-la-Chapelle, 8, 9; at Troppau, 11, 12; at Laybach, 13; at Vienna and Verona, 14.

Constitution of the United States, manner of amending, 55; the unwritten, 55, 57–60; amendments regarding the President, 64; Convention called to frame, 111; delegates to, 111–116; Virginia plan, 118–123; New Jersey plan, 123–125; Hamilton's plan, 125, 126; origin of the Senate, 127–130; representation of slaves, 130–134; importation of, 138–141; signing the Constitution, 142–144; sent to Congress, 145, 146; opposition to, 146; ratification, 147; opposition in the States, 147, 148; amendments, 148, 149; Congress fixes the day for it to go into force, 150, 151; inauguration of, 165; objections to, 182; States propose amendments, 183; Virginia urges amendments, 184; ten adopted, 184; strict constructionists and loose constructionists, 184, 185; Hamilton's views, 186; Jefferson's views, 186, 187; attempts to amend, 187, 188; the eleventh amendment, 187, 188; Virginia and Kentucky resolutions, 189–191; attempts to change manner of electing President, 191, 192, 206–208; the twelfth amendment, 192; Pennsylvania proposes a tribunal to try cases to which States are parties, 193, 194; Massachusetts proposes that representation and direct taxes be according to free inhabitants, 194, 195; was the embargo constitutional? 195, 196; amendments offered by Hartford Convention, 198, 199; repealed thirteenth amendment, 199; may Congress charter a bank? 200, 201; may Congress engage in internal improvements? 202; is a protective tariff constitutional? 202, 203; regarding slavery, 211, 212; limit to veto power, 213;

interpretation of the Constitution on party platforms, 214; how may foreign soil be acquired? 215; may slavery be shut out of the Territories? 215–217; may a State secede? 218; may a State be coerced? 218; attempts to amend in 1861, 218–220; the thirteenth amendment of 1861 recalled, 220; amendments and interpretation of, since the war, 220, 221.

Constitutions: that of Sicily overthrown, 5; that of Spain destroyed, 5, 6; promise of one to Germany, 7; of Spain, 9, 10; of Naples, 10–13.

Convention, the Constitutional, at Philadelphia called, 111; delegates to, 111–116; meeting of, 112; popular regard for, 116, 117; feeling against Rhode Island, 117; sources of information regarding, 118; the Virginia plan, 119, 120; Pinckney's plan, 119; parties in, 120, 121; question of the Executive, 120; of representation, 121–123; the New Jersey plan, 123–125; Madison on the New Jersey plan, 125; Hamilton's plan, 125, 126; New Jersey plan rejected, 126; debate on representation, 127, 128; Connecticut compromise, 128–130; rates of representation in House of Representatives, 130, representation of slaves, 130–133; draft of the Constitution, 136, 137; the work of revision, 137, 138; export duty forbidden, 138; tax on slaves, 138–140; compromise regarding, 141; final revision of draft, 142; signing the Constitution, 142–144; sent to Congress and opposed there, 145, 146; sent to the States, 146; ratification of, 147; opposition to, 147, 148; amendments, 148, 149.

Convention, the Constitutional, of 1787: debate on the Executive, 56, 57; on his term of office, 58, 59.

Conyngham, Gustavus, 257, 258.

Court, the Supreme of the United States on the carriage tax, 188; on the right to sue a State, 188; attack on, 187, 192, 193; on removal of justices, 192, 193; Pennsylvania's contest with, 193; Pennsylvania asks for a new tribunal, 193.

Court: "Old Court" and "New Court" in Kentucky, 247–249.

Crapo, resolution of, on Monroe Doctrine, 1880, 38.

Criminals, treatment of, 318.

Cruisers, American, from France, 257, 258.

Currency, kind of, in 1781, 222; disorder of, 222, 223; coins disappear, 224; paper money, 224; United States coins, 224, 229; bank paper, rise of, 228, 229; condition of, in 1816, 229; Gold Coin Act of 1834, 231; coinage act of 1853, 232; of 1873, 232, 233; "trade dollar," 233, 234.

"Cut money," 240.

Dallas, A. J., 74, 75.

Deane, Silas, 255, 257, 258; recalled, 259.

Debate, the Webster-Hayne, 203.

Delaware, religious restrictions in, 72.

Deposit, right of, at New Orleans granted, 294; suspended, 297.

"Dollar, the trade," 233, 234, 235; the United States silver, adopted as the unit, 223; first struck, 225; none struck after 1804, 229, 232, 233; again discontinued, 233.

Douglas, S. A., squatter sovereignty, 217.

Duellists, proposed constitutional amendment regarding, 210.

Electors of President: day for first vote, 152; manner of choosing in New York, 157; contest and failure to elect, 157, 158; contest in New Hampshire, 158; elections elsewhere, 158, 159; election of Washington, 160-162; electoral vote in 1789, 162.

Embargo, the: was it constitutional? 195, 196; excitement in New England over, 196, 197.

Embezzlers, proposed constitutional amendment regarding, 210.

Europe, state of, in 1818, 4; reaction against liberalism, 4; reaction in Italy, 5; in Spain, 5, 6; in France, 6; in Germany, 6, 7; in Russia, 7; in Spain, 9, 10; in Naples, 10, 11; in Portugal, 11.

Evacuation of New York city by the British, 273-280.

Exploration of the United States, Spanish and English, 281-283; French, 283, 284; Marquette, 285, 286; La Salle, 286, 287; Lewis and Clark, 302.

Father Abraham's Address, 253.

Federalists suppress the Pennsylvania Herald, 74, 75.

Ferdinand VII of Spain destroys constitutional government in Spain, 5, 6; rebellion of his American colonies, 8; seeks aid of Holy Allies, 8, 9; attempts to put down rebellion, 9; people force him to restore Constitution, 9, 10; French troops sent to his aid, 14.

Ferdinand, King of Sicily, 5.

"Fifty-four forty," 302, 303.

"Filibustering," instance of, in Pennsylvania Assembly in 1787, 73, 74.

Fish, Hamilton, report on Monroe Doctrine, 37, note.

Florida bought by United States, 301.

"Force Act," the, of 1809, excitement in New England over, 196, 197.

Foreigners, feeling against, 88-90, 92-94; rise of the Native-American party, 94; principles of, 95.

France, purpose of quadruple treaty as to, 4; effect of Waterloo on, 6; liberalism destroyed, 6; sends troops into Spain, 14; meddles in affairs of Mexico in 1860, 33, 34; London newspapers on, 35; United States on the action of France in Mexico, 35-37; France withdraws, 36, 37.

Franchise, restrictions on, 71, 72; 163, 164.

Francis, Emperor of Austria, one of the Holy Allies, 2, 3.

Franklin, Benjamin, urges the signing of the Constitution, 143; remarks on the work of the Constitutional Convention, 144, 145; sent to France, 254, 255; popularity of the American cause in France, 255, 256; American cruisers, 257, 258; Adams joins, 259; business habits, 260; Adams's sketch of, 261, 262; received by France as United States Minister, 262, 263; popularity of, 263-265; abuse of, 265; letter to Strahan, 270; return home, 270.

Frederick William, King of Prussia, one of the Holy Allies, 2, 3; promises constitution to Germany, 7; promise not kept, 7.

Free-soilers, views on slavery, 215, 216.

French: explorations in Canada, 283, 284; discovery of the Mississippi,

285, 286; La Salle, exploration of Mississippi, 286, 287; Louisiana, 287, 288; expelled from America, 287, 288; regain Louisiana, 294–296; sell Louisiana to the United States, 296–300.
Frontier of United States in 1789, 180.

Gadsden purchase, 312.
" Gag-rule," 209.
Gavazzi, Father, career of, 98.
Germany, constitution promised, 7; effect of Wartburg Festival, 7.
" Gerrymander, the," origin of, 81, 82; in New Jersey, 83; in New York, 83; in Maryland, 83.
Grant, U. S., attempt to give a third term to, 67–69.
Great Britain declines to enter Holy Alliance, 4; signs quadruple treaty, 4; persuades Ferdinand to give constitution to Sicily, 5; opposes intervention, 14; Canning's proposition to Rush, 14, 15; views on Monroe Doctrine, 24, 49–54; the Schomburgk line, 39, 40; claims in Venezuela, 40–42; claims to North America, 282, 283; expels the French, 287, 288.

" Hail Columbia," 169.
Hamilton, Alexander, delegate from New York to Constitutional Convention, 115; plan for new government, 125; interpretation of the United States Constitution, 186; his "letters of Pacificus," 189.
Hartford Convention, 198; amendments offered by, 198, 199.
Hayne, R. Y., on Hayti and the Monroe Doctrine, 27.
" Helvidius, letters of," by Madison, 189.

Herald, the Pennsylvania, suppressed by the Federalists, 74, 75.
Holmes, of Maine, on slavery and the Panama Congress, 28.
Holy Alliance, origin of, 2; purpose of, 2, 3; powers invited to join, 3; Metternich on, 3; Lord Castlereagh on, 3, 4; Great Britain declines to enter, 4; Spain appeals to, 8; Congress at Aix-la-Chapelle, 8, 9; at Troppau, 11; circular of Troppau, 11, 12; summon Ferdinand, 12; meeting at Laybach, 12, 13; at Vienna and Verona, 14.
Holy Allies: who they were, 2–4; Great Britain declines to become one, 4; Spain appeals to, 8; Congress at Aix-la-Chapelle, 8, 9; Alexander attempts to meddle in affairs of Spain, 10; the meeting of Troppau, circular from, 11, 12; summon Ferdinand to Laybach, 12; meeting at Laybach, 12; send troops to Naples, 12, 13; Congress at Laybach, 13; Congress at Vienna, 14; at Verona, 14; send a French army into Spain, 14.
" Hoop for the barrel," 156.

Immigration: arrivals of foreigners, 93, 94, 97.
Impeachment of justices of United States Supreme Court, 192, 193.
Inauguration of the Constitution, 165; of John Adams in 1789, 166, 167; of Washington, 173–178.
Internal improvements, Congress to engage in, 200; is this constitutional, 202; constitutional amendments regarding, 205.

Jackson, Major William, 112, 182.
Jay, John, candidate for Governor of New York, 77; defeated by

INDEX. 329

fraud, 77, 78; struggle with Council of Appointment, 80, 81.
Jefferson, Thomas, declines a third term, 60–62; his action approved by the people, 62–64; on the powers of Congress under the Constitution, 186, 187.
Jones, John Paul, 267; his cruise, 267; gets a ship, 267, 268; famous victory, 268.
Judiciary, the United States, attack on, 187; impeachments of Pickering and Chase, 192; on removal of United States judges, 192, 193; Pennsylvania's contest with, 193.

King, fear that the Constitutional Convention was about to establish one, 118.
Kentucky, mania for banks in, 241; Bank of, 241; "the Litter," 242; suspension of banks in, 242, 244; tax on Bank of United States, 243; animosity toward Bank of United States, 243, 244; stay law, 244, 245; replevin law, 245; Bank of the Commonwealth, 245, 246; replevin act not constitutional, 246, 247; "old court" and "new court" parties, 247–249.
Know-Nothings, rise of, 97, 98, 100; success of, 100, 101; principles of, 102; success of, 103; National Convention, 104; platform, 104 105; split in the party, 105; defeat and decline of, 105.

Landais, 267–269.
Labedoyère executed, 6.
Lafayette, his reception in France, 266.
Laybach, Ferdinand summoned to, 12; Holy Allies at, 12, 13; circular of, 12.
Lee, Arthur, 254, 260, 267.

L'Enfant, Major, 165.
Liberalism, reaction against, 4, 5; in Italy, 5; in Spain, 5;· arrest of Liberal leaders, 5; perishes in Spain, 5, 6; in France, 6; in Germany, 6, 7; in Russia, 7; Spanish Constitution restored, 9, 10; the Carbonari in Naples, 10, 11; a Junta established in Portugal, 11; the circular of Troppau, 11, 12; stamped out at Naples, 12, 13; and in Spain, 14.
Lloyd, Thomas, 74, 75.
Louisiana, origin of name, 287; boundary of, 287; occupation of, 287, 288; divided between England and Spain, 287, 288: claims of United States to, 288, 289; part acquired by United States, 289–291; France eager to acquire it again, 294–296; ceded to her by Spain, 296; bought by United States, 296–300; no boundary, 300, 301; treaty of 1819, 301; north boundary, 301, 302.
Louisiana purchase: was it constitutional? 194.

Mace, the, expelled from Pennsylvania Assembly, 89.
Madison, James, delegate to Constitutional Convention, 111; Madison's notes, 118; opposes New Jersey plan, 125; proposes amendments to Constitution, 184; his "letters of Helvidius," 189.
"March, the President's," first played at Trenton, 169, 170; now called "Hail Columbia," 169.
Marquette, discovery of the Mississippi, 285, 286.
Maryland, Senate of, on third term, 63; franchise in, 73; gerrymander in, 83, 84; colonizing, 84.
Massachusetts, restrictions on voters

and office holders, 72; the gerrymander on, 81, 82; delegates to Constitutional Convention, 115; manner of choosing Presidential electors, 158; proposes a constitutional amendment, 194, 195, 212; resists "Force Act," 196, 197; Governor refuses militia to United States in 1812, 197; calls Hartford Convention, 198; threatens nullification, 203; answers South Carolina, 204, 205.

Maximilian in Mexico, 36, 37.

McDuffie, speech of, on Oregon, 309.

Metternich, opinion of the Holy Alliance, 3; character of, 4, 5.

Mexico, Cass and Buchanan on Monroe Doctrine applied to, 33, 34; agreement of the allies as to, 34, note; London newspapers on, 35; Seward on, 35, 36; House of Representatives on, 36; Sheridan on the Rio Grande, 36.

"Mint-drops, Benton," 231.

Mint established, 224; free coinage, 224; coins made, 225; supply of bullion, 225; work of, 226, 227; opposition to, 227.

Mississippi River, discovery and exploration of, 285–287; shut to navigation, 292, 293; right of deposit, 294.

Mississippi Valley occupied by French, 287, 288; divided between Spain and England, 287, 288; acquired by United States, 288–292; part ceded by Spain, 294–296; part sold to United States, 296–300.

Money, Congress given power to coin, 222; a unit chosen, 223; a mint ordered, 224; national coinage established, 224–226; bills of credit, 239; demand for "cheap money," 240, 241; "cut-money," 240; bank paper in Kentucky, 242–249.

Monroe Doctrine, three views regarding, 1; origin of, 1, 2; the Holy Alliance, 2, 3; purpose of Holy Alliance, 3; what the Holy Allies did, 4–14; Canning's offer to Rush, 15; letters sent to Jefferson and Madison, 16; answer of Jefferson, 16, 17; of Madison, 17, 46–48; question of Russian occupation, 17–19; three questions before the Cabinet, 19; Adams on colonization, 19, 20; the doctrine announced, 21, 22; meaning of, 22; reception of, 23; Clay's resolution, 23; Clay's instructions to Poinsett, 23, 24; London newspapers on, 24, 49–54; the doctrine and the South American republics, 27; connection of slavery with, 27, 28; resolution of the House of Representatives, 29; Polk on, in 1826, 30; in 1845, 30–32; and in 1848, 32, 33; Cass and Mexico, 33; Buchanan and Mexico, 33, 34; the case of Mexico, 34–37; report of Secretary Fish, 37, 38, note; resolution offered by Crapo, 38; by Burnside, 38; Blaine's view, 38; Salisbury's view, 42, 44; the doctrine explained, 45, 46.

Monroe, James, announces his doctrine, 1, 2; sends letter of Rush to Jefferson and Madison, 16; answer of Jefferson, 16, 17; of Madison, 17, 46–48; the Russian question, 17, 19; the three questions before his Cabinet, 19.

Morris, Gouverneur, on taxation and representation, 133; proposes form for signing the Constitution, 143, 144.

Naples, kingdom of: the Carbonari, 10; Ferdinand forced to grant a constitution to, 11, 12; Ferdinand

summoned to Laybach, 11, 12; Austrian troops sent to, 12, 13.
Napoleon III, conduct toward Mexico, 33-37.
Napoleon acquires Louisiana, 295, 296; attempts to occupy, 296; sells it to United States, 297, 298.
Neutrality, Washington proclaims, 188; Hamilton and Madison discuss the constitutionality of, 188, 189.
New England opposes purchase of Louisiana, 194, 195; excitement in, over "Force Act" of 1809, 196, 197; Governors refuse to call out militia in 1812, 197, 198; Hartford Convention, 198.
New Hampshire: religious restrictions on office holders, 72; delegates to Constitutional Convention, 111; contest over choice of Presidential electors, 158.
New Jersey, early franchise in, 72; religious restrictions on office holders, 72; Presidential electors stolen, 82; gerrymander in, 83.
New York, condition of franchise in, 72; quarrel over choice of electors and senators in 1789, 75, 76; casts no vote for Washington, 76, 77; the governorship stolen, 1792, 77, 78; the Council of Appointment, 79; struggle for control of it, 79-81; spoils system in, 80, 81; gerrymander in, 83; struggle for the Council of Appointment, 85, 86; delegates to Constitutional Convention, 115; two leave the Convention, 115; city of New York the first capital under the Constitution, 152; casts no Presidential vote in 1789, 161, 162.
New York city, chosen to be the first capital, 152; description of Congress Hall, 152, Congress Hall at,

described, 164, 165; inauguration of the Constitution at, 165; reception of Washington at, 170-172; appearance of the city, 172, 173; inauguration of Washington at, 173-178; taken by the British, 271-273; evacuation of, by British, 273-280.
Ney, Marshal, shot, 6.
"North-Americans," 105.
North Carolina, property qualifications for office holding, 73.
Nullification, resolutions of Virginia and Kentucky in 1798, 189-191; Virginia in 1810 declares the United States Supreme Court a common arbiter, 193, 194; Ohio affirms Virginia and Kentucky resolutions, 201; New York threatens, 201; South Carolina threatens, 201, 202; Webster-Hayne debates, 203; threatened by Massachusetts and Maine, 203, 204; South Carolina nullifies, 204, 205.

Ohio affirms the Virginia and Kentucky resolutions, 201; bank mania, 250; attack on the Bank of the United States, 250; collects tax by force, 250; suit against, 250, 251; affirms Virginia and Kentucky resolutions, 251; outlaws the Bank of the United States, 251.
Oregon, our claim to, 302; joint occupation, 302; dispute with Russia, 302, 303; dispute with England, 303-305; Whitman's mission to, 305-307; Whitman's ride, 307-309; McDuffie on, 309; boundary settled, 309-311.
Oregon country, Russian claims to, 17-19; Adams on, 19, 20.
Orleans Territory Legislature on third term, 63.

"Pacificus, letters of," by Hamilton, 189.
Panama Congress: the invitation, 25; Clay on, 25; Adams's message, 26; opposition to, 26, 27; connection of slavery with, 27, 28; resolution of the House of Representatives, 29.
Paterson, William, delegate to Constitutional Convention from New Jersey, 111; opposes Virginia plan, 121, 122; introduces New Jersey plan, 123.
Pennsylvania: instance of filibustering in 1787, 73, 74; religious restrictions on office holders, 72; debates of Constitutional Convention suppressed, 74, 75; Assembly expels the mace, 89; delegates to Constitutional Convention, 115; choice of Presidential electors, 158, 159; quarrel with United States Supreme Court, 193; wants a constitutional amendment, 193.
Petition, violation of the right of, 209.
Pfyles, composer of the air of "Hail Columbia," 169.
Philadelphia, Congress driven from, 156; reception of Washington at, 168, 169.
Platforms, national party, introduced, 213, 214; National Republican, 213, 214; Democratic, 214; Whig, 214.
Poland, Duchy of Warsaw made Kingdom of, 7.
Polk, James K., on the Monroe Doctrine in 1826, 30; and in 1845, 30–32; and in 1848, 32, 33.
Population of United States in 1789, 178, 181.
Portugal, rise of liberalism in, 11.
President: question of a third term, 55–70; manner of electing, 56, 57; debate on his term of office, 57–59; Washington declines a third term, 60; Jefferson declines, 60–62; action approved, 62–64; attempts to change manner of electing, 64, 65; plans proposed in the Constitutional Convention, 120, 136; name, 137; time for choosing President, 152; Washington elected, 162; attempts to change the constitutional manner of electing, 191, 192; the twelfth amendment, 192; to be chosen by lot, 200; other methods urged, 206–208.
Prevost, J. B., 17.
Progress, industrial and mechanical, since 1692, 318, 319; since 1792, 320, 321.

Quadruple treaty, purpose of, 4, 7, 8.

Ramel, General, treatment of, 6.
Randolph, John, at the inauguration of Adams, 167.
Read, George, circular letter to, from United States Senate, 116, note.
Refugees, the British, in New York city, 273, 274; prepare to leave, 275; begin to go, 275–277; number of, 277.
Replevin, indorsement and replevin law in Kentucky, 245; not constitutional, 246–248; contest over, 248, 249.
Representation in the House, 127, 128; origin of the Senate, 128–130; ratio of, 130; of slaves, 130–134; taxation and representation, 133, 134; ratio changed, 144.
Resolutions, Virginia and Kentucky, of 1798–1799, 189, 190; answer of the States, 190; affirmed by Ohio, 201.
Rhode Island sends no delegates to Constitutional Convention, 111; feeling against, 117.

INDEX. 333

Riots, anti-Catholic, 93; Native-American, 96, 99, 100.
Rush, Richard, Canning's proposition to, 14-16; answer of Rush, 15.
Russia, settlement in California, 17; edict of Emperor Alexander, 18; discussion of, 18, 19; Adams on, 19, 20; claims part of Oregon, 302; "Fifty-four forty," 303.

Salisbury, Lord, effect of his letter on Monroe Doctrine, 1; on the Venezuela claims, 40-42, 44.
San Ildefonso, treaty of, 296.
Schlegel, Frederick, effect of his lectures, 91, 92.
Schomburgk, Robert, sketch of, 39; his famous "line," 39, 40.
Secession, Buchanan on, 218.
Senate of the United States, origin of, 128-130; no quorum on March 4, 1789, 165, 166, note; debate on manner of receiving Washington, 174, 175.
Seward, W. H., on Monroe Doctrine and Mexico, 35, 36.
"Sherman Act," 235, 236.
Slaves, representation of, 130-133; taxation and importation of, 138-141.
Slavery, connection of, with Panama Congress, 27, 28; Hayne on, 27; White on, 27, 28; Holmes on, 28; rise of the abolition movement, 209; violation of right of petition, 209; "gag rule," 209; power of Congress over, 210, 211; constitutional amendment regarding, 211; status of, in the Territories, 215-219; Free-soil view, 215, 216; Democratic, 216, 217; Republican, 217, 218; the question in 1860, 218-220.
South Carolina, restrictions on voters and office holders, 72; defies the United States Supreme Court, 201, 202; on tariff and internal improvements, 202, 203; Webster-Hayne debate, 203; nullifies the tariff, 204, 205.
Spain, Constitution of, destroyed, 5; absolutism restored, 5, 6; revolt of her American colonies, 8; appeals to Holy Allies for help, 8, 9; attempts to collect an army, 9; rebellion in and demand for the Constitution, 9, 10; Alexander attempts to meddle in affairs of, 10; affairs considered at Congress of Verona, 14; French troops sent into, 14; her early claim to America, 281; the Papal Bulls, 281, 282; explorations along the coast, 282; dispute with England, 282, 283; treaty with England, 283; receives part of Louisiana, 288; disputes our claim to Louisiana, 288-292; closes the Mississippi, 292, 293; cedes Louisiana to France, 296; sells Florida to United States, 301.
Spoils system introduced into New York, 79-81.
"Squatter sovereignty," 217.
States, third-term, 1807-1809, 60-62.
Stay law, Kentucky, 244, 245.
Steamboat, effect of the use of, on Western waters in 1816, 240.
Strahan, Franklin's letter to, 270.

Talleyrand eager to acquire Louisiana, 294-296.
Tammany Society of Philadelphia on third term, 63, 64.
Tariffs of 1824 and 1828, excitement over, in the South, 202, 203; nullified by South Carolina, 204, 205.
Term, question of a third, for the President, 55-60; Washington declines a third term, 60; Jefferson

offered a third term, 60, 61; declines, 61; States approve, 62–64; the question in 1823, 64, 65, 207, 208; Jackson on, 66, 208; the question in 1844, 66; in Grant's time, 67–69.

Territories, status of slavery in, 215–217; Free-soil view, 215, 216; Democratic view, 216, 217; Republican, 217, 218.

Texas, acquisition of, 311, 312; annexation of, 215.

Titles of honor, proposed constitutional amendment regarding, 199; once thought adopted, 199.

Thomson, Charles, 166.

Treaties, power of the House of Representatives over, 189.

Trenton, reception of Washington at, 169, 170.

Troppau, meeting of the allies at, 11; circular of, 11, 12.

Tyler, John, his vetoes and quarrel with the Whigs, 212, 213.

United States, area of, in 1789, 178, 180; boundary of, 178, 179; population of, 180, 181; frontier of, 180, 316; Spaniards in, 282, 294, 296, 301; French in, 285–288, 296–300; Oregon, 302, 303; early settlement of, 314, 315; condition of, in 1692, 315–317; life in, 317, 318; progress since 1692, 318–319; state of, in 1792, 319, 320; progress since, 320, 321.

Venezuela, the Schomburgk line, 39, 40; British claims to, 39–42.

Verona, Congress of Holy Allies at, 14.

Veto, attempt to limit, 213.

Vice-President, the twelfth amendment to the Constitution regarding, 192; proposal to abolish office of, 200.

Vienna, Congress of Holy Allies at, 14.

Virginia, delegates to the Constitutional Convention, 111; Virginia plan, 119; contrasted with New Jersey plan, 125; adopted, 126; urges amendments to the Constitution, 183, 184; resolutions of 1798, 189–191; United States Supreme Court a common arbiter, 193.

Voters, qualification of, in old times, 72; in New England, New York, New Jersey, Maryland, South Carolina, 72; colonization of, in Maryland, 84.

Warsaw, Duchy of, made Kingdom of Poland, 7.

Washington, George, declines a third term, 60; chosen President, 162; notified of election, 166; ovations on his way to New York, 167–173; at Alexandria and Baltimore, 167; at Philadelphia, 168, 169; at Trenton, 169, 170; at New York city, 170–173; inauguration of, 173–178; defence of New York city, 271, 272; re-enters New York, 279, 280.

Whigs, constitutional amendments proposed by, 210, 213; first party platform, 214.

White, on slavery and the Monroe Doctrine, 27, 28.

Whitman, Marcus, mission to Oregon, 305–307; his ride to Washington, 307, 308.

Wickes, Lambert, 257.

"Yellow-boys, Jackson," 231.

Yucatan, Polk applies Monroe Doctrine to, 32, 33.

THE END.

D. APPLETON & CO.'S PUBLICATIONS.

JOHN BACH MC MASTER.

HISTORY OF THE PEOPLE OF THE UNITED STATES, from the Revolution to the Civil War. By JOHN BACH MCMASTER. To be completed in six volumes. Vols. I, II, III, and IV now ready. 8vo. Cloth, gilt top, $2.50 each.

". . . Prof. McMaster has told us what no other historians have told. . . . The skill, the animation, the brightness, the force, and the charm with which he arrays the facts before us are such that we can hardly conceive of more interesting reading for an American citizen who cares to know the nature of those causes which have made not only him but his environment and the opportunities life has given him what they are."—*N. Y. Times.*

"Those who can read between the lines may discover in these pages constant evidences of care and skill and faithful labor, of which the old-time superficial essayists, compiling library notes on dates and striking events, had no conception; but to the general reader the fluent narrative gives no hint of the conscientious labors, far-reaching, world-wide, vast and yet microscopically minute, that give the strength and value which are felt rather than seen. This is due to the art of presentation. The author's position as a scientific workman we may accept on the abundant testimony of the experts who know the solid worth of his work; his skill as a literary artist we can all appreciate, the charm of his style being self-evident."—*Philadelphia Telegraph.*

"The third volume contains the brilliantly written and fascinating story of the progress and doings of the people of this country from the era of the Louisiana purchase to the opening scenes of the second war with Great Britain—say a period of ten years. In every page of the book the reader finds that fascinating flow of narrative, that clear and lucid style, and that penetrating power of thought and judgment which distinguished the previous volumes."—*Columbus State Journal.*

"Prof. McMaster has more than fulfilled the promises made in his first volumes, and his work is constantly growing better and more valuable as he brings it nearer to our own time. His style is clear, simple, and idiomatic, and there is just enough of the critical spirit in the narrative to guide the reader."—*Boston Herald.*

"Take it all in all, the History promises to be the ideal American history. Not so much given to dates and battles and great events as in the fact that it is like a great panorama of the people, revealing their inner life and action. It contains, with all its sober facts, the spice of personalities and incidents, which relieves every page from dullness."—*Chicago Inter-Ocean.*

"History written in this picturesque style will tempt the most heedless to read. Prof. McMaster is more than a stylist; he is a student, and his History abounds in evidences of research in quarters not before discovered by the historian."—*Chicago Tribune.*

"A History *sui generis* which has made and will keep its own place in our literature."—*New York Evening Post.*

"His style is vigorous and his treatment candid and impartial."—*New York Tribune.*

New York: D. APPLETON & CO., 72 Fifth Avenue.

D. APPLETON & CO.'S PUBLICATIONS.

A HISTORY OF THE UNITED STATES *NAVY*, from 1775 to 1894. By EDGAR STANTON MACLAY, A. M. With Technical Revision by Lieut. ROY C. SMITH, U. S. N. In two volumes. With numerous Maps, Diagrams, and Illustrations. 8vo. Cloth. $7.00.

"The field is comparatively new, and Mr. Maclay has brought to his task patience, assiduity, and patriotism. . . . Maps and plans, and a great number of illustrations, add value to the book, which is designed to be a permanent and useful contribution to historical literature."—*New York Observer.*

"While the author has had the assistance of Lieut. Roy C. Smith, U. S. N., in preparing those parts of his work which are necessarily technical, he has wisely refrained from confusing the general reader by an undue parade of technicalities. . . . The narrative proceeds in a clear, concise, and vigorous style, which very materially adds to the character of the work." —*New York Journal of Commerce.*

"The author writes as one who has digged deep before he began to write at all. He thus appears as a master of his material. This book inspires immediate confidence as well as interest."—*New York Times.*

"A most conscientious narrative, from which wise statesmen may learn much for their guidance, and it certainly is one of absorbing interest."—*New York Commercial Advertiser.*

"Mr. Maclay is specially qualified for the work he has undertaken. Nine years has he devoted to the task. The result of his labors possesses not only readableness but authority. . . . Mr. Maclay's story may be truthfully characterized as a thrilling romance, which will interest every mind that is fed by tales of heroism, and will be read with patriotic pride by every true American."—*Chicago Evening Post.*

"A more valuable and important work of history than this has not been issued from the press for many a day. It is not only that this book tells a story never before told (for Cooper's works never professed to tell the whole story of our navy, even down to his own day), but that it is told with true historic sense, and with the finest critical acumen."—*New York Evangelist.*

"A work which is destined to fill a noticeable gap in our national annals."—*Philadelphia Bulletin.*

"No better excuse for this important work could be desired than that a navy with such a brilliant career on the whole as has the American navy is without a full and continuous record of its achievement. . . . The author has important new facts to tell, and he tells them in a clear and graceful literary style."—*Hartford Post.*

"Mr. Maclay has deservedly won for himself an enviable place among our American historians. . . . His researches have been exhaustive and his inquiries persistent, and he has used his wealth of material with a proper appreciation of historical value." —*Boston Advertiser.*

"Like the average young American, this author has an enthusiastic appreciation of American valor on the high seas, and he reproduces graphic sketches of battle scenes and incidents in a way to insure for his book a hearty welcome on the part of those who keenly enjoy this sort of literature. . . . The illustrations of the old battle ships and the conflicts at sea, made memorable as long as the history of the American Republic shall live, add much to the attractiveness of this book. . . . Professor Maclay has added a substantial work to historical American literature."—*Philadelphia Telegraph.*

"It fills a place which has almost escaped the attention of historians. Mr. Maclay's work shows on every page the minute care with which he worked up his theme. His style is precise and clear, and without any pretense of rhetorical embellishment."— *New York Tribune.*

New York: D. APPLETON & CO., 72 Fifth Avenue.

D. APPLETON & CO.'S PUBLICATIONS.

THE UNITED STATES OF AMERICA. A Study of the American Commonwealth, its Natural Resources, People, Industries, Manufactures, Commerce, and its Work in Literature, Science, Education, and Self-Government. Edited by NATHANIEL S. SHALER, S. D., Professor of Geology in Harvard University. In two volumes, royal 8vo. With Maps, and 150 full-page Illustrations. Cloth, $10.00.

In this work the publishers offer something which is not furnished by histories or encyclopædias, namely, a succinct but comprehensive expert account of our country at the present day. The very extent of America and American industries renders it difficult to appreciate the true meaning of the United States of America. In this work the American citizen can survey the land upon which he lives, and the industrial, social, political, and other environments of himself and his fellow-citizens. The best knowledge and the best efforts of experts, editor, and publishers have gone to the preparation of a standard book dedicated to the America of the present day; and the publishers believe that these efforts will be appreciated by those who desire to inform themselves regarding the America of the end of the century.

LIST OF CONTRIBUTORS.

HON. WILLIAM L. WILSON, Chairman of the Ways and Means Committee, Fifty-third Congress.
HON. J. R. SOLEY, formerly Assistant Secretary of the Navy.
EDWARD ATKINSON, LL. D, PH. D.
COL. T. A. DODGE, U. S. A.
COL. GEORGE E. WARING, JR.
J. B. McMASTER, Professor of History in the University of Pennsylvania.
CHARLES DUDLEY WARNER, LL. D.
MAJOR J. W. POWELL, Director of the U. S. Geological Survey and the Bureau of Ethnology.
WILLIAM T. HARRIS, LL. D., U. S. Commissioner of Education.
LYMAN ABBOTT, D. D.
H. H. BANCROFT, author of "Native Races of the Pacific Coast."
HARRY PRATT JUDSON, Head Dean of the Colleges, University of Chicago.
JUDGE THOMAS M. COOLEY, formerly Chairman of the Interstate Commerce Commission.
CHARLES FRANCIS ADAMS.
D. A. SARGENT, M. D., Director of the Hemenway Gymnasium, Harvard University.
CHARLES HORTON COOLEY.
A. E. KENNELLY, Assistant to Thomas A. Edison.
D. C. GILMAN, LL. D., President of Johns Hopkins University.
H. G. PROUT, Editor of the Railroad Gazette.
F. D. MILLET, formerly Vice-President of the National Academy of Design.
F. W. TAUSSIG, Professor of Political Economy in Harvard University.
HENRY VAN BRUNT.
H. P. FAIRFIELD.
SAMUEL W. ABBOTT, M. D., Secretary of the State Board of Health, Massachusetts.
N. S. SHALER.

Sold only by subscription. Prospectus, giving detailed chapter-titles and specimen illustrations, mailed free on request.

New York: D. APPLETON & CO., 72 Fifth Avenue.

D. APPLETON & CO.'S PUBLICATIONS.

THE STORY OF THE WEST SERIES.
Edited by Ripley Hitchcock.

"There is a vast extent of territory lying between the Missouri River and the Pacific coast which has barely been skimmed over so far. That the conditions of life therein are undergoing changes little short of marvelous will be understood when one recalls the fact that the first white male child born in Kansas is still living there; and Kansas is by no means one of the newer States. Revolutionary indeed has been the upturning of the old condition of affairs, and little remains thereof, and less will remain as each year goes by, until presently there will be only tradition of the Sioux and Comanches, the cowboy life, the wild horse, and the antelope. Histories, many of them, have been written about the Western country alluded to, but most if not practically all by outsiders who knew not personally that life of kaleidoscopic allurement. But ere it shall have vanished forever we are likely to have truthful, complete, and charming portrayals of it produced by men who actually know the life and have the power to describe it."—*Henry Edward Rood, in The Mail and Express.*

NOW READY.

THE STORY OF THE INDIAN. By George Bird Grinnell, author of "Pawnee Hero Stories," "Blackfoot Lodge Tales," etc. 12mo. Cloth. Illustrated. $1.50.

"A valuable study of Indian life and character. . . . An attractive book, . . . in large part one in which Indians themselves might have written."—*New York Tribune.*

"Among the various books respecting the aborigines of America, Mr. Grinnell's easily takes a leading position. He takes the reader directly to the camp-fire and the council, and shows us the American Indian as he really is. . . . A book which will convey much interesting knowledge respecting a race which is now fast passing away."—*Boston Commercial Bulletin.*

"It must not be supposed that the volume is one only for scholars and libraries of reference. It is far more than that. While it is a true story, yet it is a story none the less abounding in picturesque description and charming anecdote. We regard it as a valuable contribution to American literature."—*N. Y. Mail and Express.*

"A most attractive book, which presents an admirable graphic picture of the actual Indian, whose home life, religious observances, amusements, together with the various phases of his devotion to war and the chase, and finally the effects of encroaching civilization, are delineated with a certainty and an absence of sentimentalism or hostile prejudice that impart a peculiar distinction to this eloquent story of a passing life."—*Buffalo Commercial.*

"No man is better qualified than Mr. Grinnell to introduce this series with the story of the original owner of the West, the North American Indian. Long acquaintance and association with the Indians, and membership in a tribe, combined with a high degree of literary ability and thorough education, has fitted the author to understand the red man and to present him fairly to others."—*New York Observer.*

IN PREPARATION.

The Story of the Mine. By Charles Howard Shinn.
The Story of the Trapper. By Gilbert Parker.
The Story of the Explorer.
The Story of the Cowboy.
The Story of the Soldier.
The Story of the Railroad.

New York: D. APPLETON & CO., 72 Fifth Avenue.

www.ingramcontent.com/pod-product-compliance
Lightning Source LLC
Chambersburg PA
CBHW030315240426
43673CB00040B/1175